THE CLAUSEWITZIAN DICTUM
AND THE FUTURE OF WESTERN MILITARY STRATEGY

NIJHOFF LAW SPECIALS

VOLUME 31

The titles published in this series are listed at the end of this volume.

Netherlands Institute of International Relations 'Clingendael'

The Clausewitzian Dictum and the Future of Western Military Strategy

Edited by

Gert de Nooy

Research Department,
Netherlands Institute of International Relations 'Clingendael'

KLUWER LAW INTERNATIONAL
THE HAGUE / LONDON / BOSTON

A C.I.P. Catalogue record for this book is available from the Library of Congress

ISBN 90-411-0455-0

Published by Kluwer Law International,
P.O. Box 85889, 2508 CN The Hague, The Netherlands.

Sold and distributed in the U.S.A. and Canada
by Kluwer Law International,
675 Massachusetts Avenue, Cambridge, MA 02139, U.S.A.

In all other countries, sold and distributed
by Kluwer Law International, Distribution Centre,
P.O. Box 322, 3300 AH Dordrecht, The Netherlands.

Cover photo: Frits Meyst, Hollandse Hoogte: *Cetniks*

Rebecca Solheim, Linguistic Editing
Kitty l'Ami, Lay-out

Printed on acid-free paper

Printed in the Netherlands

Contents

1 Introduction: The Clausewitzian Dictum and the Future of Western Military Strategy

Gert de Nooy

This publication aims at defining a rationale for the continued use of military armed force(s) by states. Central to the book are the fundamental questions pertaining to the convention of war, as formulated by Martin van Creveld: 'to define just who is allowed to kill whom, for what ends, under what circumstances, and by what means'. Above all, the answers to these questions will have to take into account the developments and trends within the elements of the Clausewitzian trinity supporting the Westphalian nation state: 'The People (or The Society)', 'The Government' and 'The Armed Forces (or The Military)'. The change in the Atlantic-European security environment and the effects this will have on the form and content of national and multilateral security strategies and doctrines (as they are presently defined) form the background of this project. The possible impact of societal changes on West European states, as a consequence of European integration, needs to be discussed. The consequences of 'out-of-area' and police-type functions for armed forces in addition to the classical defence role should be related to the size and composition of future forces.

First, the armed forces of Western states acting as the major instruments of national and multilateral European foreign and security policies will have to be judged on their future relevance, their continued usefulness and the possibilities and risks affecting their interests. Second, the armed forces should be assigned a new rank order, as they are only one of the 'collective goods' for which funding has to be found at a time where uncertainty, the absence of 'an enemy', a new regionalization of security and an increasing lack of financial means are deciding factors. The rationale of separate national military components for each individual state seems to be under increasing pressure.

Moreover, contradicting national security strategies, the internationalization of security problems and the ever-increasing demand for technological advantage are obscuring the road towards an efficient and effective organization of European armed force(s). The dilemma of quality versus quantity where it concerns the material and personnel composition of armed forces has to be tackled: mainly in light of the divergence between the development of very expensive high-tech

G.C. de Nooy (ed.), The Clausewitzian Dictum and the Future of Western Military Strategy, 1-6.
© 1997 *Kluwer Law International. Printed in the Netherlands.*

equipment (well-manned equipment), on the one hand, and the trend towards a rather more low-cost requirement for 'manpower' to conduct present-day peace support operations (well-equipped men); but also in view of the desire of many nation-states to possess their own balanced armed force(s), regardless of the detrimental effects this might have on future multinational cooperation and subsequent integration.

Finally, in addition to these organizational and institutional interests and challenges, current and future common interests for European military forces have to be defined. This also applies to the military threats and risks confronting these interests. This should be done not only in the short to medium term but also from the longer-term perspective. However, before addressing these themes it is necessary to look at the trends and developments affecting the other elements composing Clausewitz's trinity, particularly since societal and political changes will form the driving factors for adapting and altering the deployment and employment of armed force(s) within a changing world.

Clausewitzian Theory and its Continued Applicability

Ideally, the rationale for the continued use of armed forces is embedded in a balanced theory of war and peace. It is therefore paramount to reconsider the Clausewitzian theory of military strategy, in particular his ideas on trinitarian warfare. Moreover, it is necessary to reassess the convention of war in the light of the changing character of present-day conflicts, whether they are inter- or intra-societal or inter- or intra-state. The relevance of the Clausewitzian trinity and the coherence between its elements should be scrutinized. Alternative concepts for a post-Clausewitzian era should be postulated, as biases and omissions are becoming apparent in the discourse on the relevance of Clausewitzian theory and trinitarian concepts of warfare. It appears that new concepts of the convention of war such as non-trinitarian and low-intensity conflict theories do not answer the most relevant questions pertaining to post-modern war and conflict: What are the common features in present-day conflict and how do they impact on the conventions of conflict resolution? Which broad trends affect the relationship between the elements of the trinity? What is the future relevance of nuclear deterrence and its instruments? Is a transformation of war taking place and to what extent?

The Society

Given the multidimensional aspects of security provision (physical, economic, ecological, societal, etc.), the geographical proximity of security risks is again dominating the debate on the protection of societal interests. This in turn affects the specific security tasks that people require of the military, the central question being which role, tasks, missions and required performance lie in store for future (military) security forces. Moreover, present trends in Western societies are underlining an emerging paradox which can be formulated as follows: does 'Security for the People' necessarily imply 'Security by the People'?

Based on the need for individual physical security, it can be argued that the requirement for nearby, local security provisions such as neighbourhood watch and property protection will override the need for collective defence of state territory. Moreover, it seems that the distinction between the application of armed force for internal security purposes (policing, good governance) and external security purposes (defence of sovereign territory and 'peace support' tasks) is blurred by the effects of rapid European political, economic and monetary integration. At the same time, both the militarization of society (arms possession, high-tech communication and control, private security firms, and organized crime) and the civilization of the military (democratic control, 'citizens in uniform', severe restrictions on the use of armed force) is influencing political and governmental decision on future security and warfare concepts.

Another area of concern is the dwindling preparedness of post-modern societies to support and maintain 'armed forces' and concomitant motives preempting the rationale for (a) standing armed force(s) in situations in which society is not prepared to use them. In this respect the formulation of alternative concepts supported by the people is called for (military-in-being, mercenaries, beefed-up police forces, international rapid reaction brigades). The most important questions relating to this topic should be answered: Are people still prepared to offer lives for a 'good cause' and under what circumstances? Will popular support for the future 'military' continue in the case of increasing professionalization of the Western 'military' and how would society keep in touch with military society within the civil society? Would the use of mercenaries or 'dogs of peace' solve the paradox of an increased requirement for action and the growing reluctance to put the traditional soldier at risk?

The Government

When considering the internal erosion of democratic government, the slow decline of Western democracy and its concomitant norms and values might be used as the point of departure. Societal fragmentation and *Politikverdrossenheit* are leading to internal erosion of the national governing powers and the traditional *trias politica*. Increasingly, the originally opposing elements of the legitimate balance between state power and its popular, parliamentary counterweight become intertwined. The societal interaction between the government and the people has been replaced by a free-market relationship. The impact of these trends on the outline for a future political system should be addressed.

One of the main topics under discussion is which new principles and institutions can or should fill the political void now that democracy and the period of enlightenment have reached their nadir. Moreover, it could be argued that the fundamental security issues in the post-political era differ radically from present-day issues. The question should hence be posed of how society could organize itself to minimize the individual and collective damage emanating from the future sources of insecurity and instability. In addition, it is considered doubtful that armed force(s), as we know them now, would find a role in a period that lacks democratic control and a well-defined state monopoly on the employment of armed force.

Another focal issue is the potential demise of the 'Great Powers'. Local and regional conflicts seem to be on the increase. No collective policy or strategy to restore effectively 'law and order' in the affected regions is being developed. Unless the world community is content to live with chronic disorder and widespread violence, a new and perhaps synthetic version of international and collective 'law and order' should be invented. The eroding powers of national and global governing bodies leads to the emergence of alternative and transnational power structures based on common economic, ethnic, financial, and criminal interests. Developing alternatives and minimizing the damage of erosion would constitute a key contribution to filling the global power vacuum, to the advantage of society at large. In this respect two questions need an answer: first, how to create the political will and incentive to use the international 'military' as a convincing instrument of successful intervention in cases where a moral duty to act exists (genocide, mass murder, war atrocities, etc.)?; second, how to organize the restoration of law and order 'on the ground' given the increasing reluctance of national governments and their electorate to provide human capital for these 'high-risk' operations?

The Armed Forces

With respect to the military establishment, the aspects of military strategy in a new era should be investigated. An assessment of the position and role of 'the military' in a world consisting of 'global villages' should be central to this investigation, and it should moreover take into account not only the short- to medium-term interests of armed forces but also deal with the longer-term strategic interests and risks of the military apparatus. Three major issues are at the core of future military strategy. The first concerns the strategic 'threat reduction' (including risks to internal European security) which should be applied to contingencies requiring concerted military action. The second centres on a clear definition of the commonly perceived organizational interests and ambitions shared by the military. Finally, there will be a need to establish the impact of evolving arms control and counter-proliferation initiatives (weapons of mass destruction and conventional weapons) on the future playing field for military strategy.

Although military strategy, especially during the Cold War, focused mainly on the material and equipment side of life, it now seems that the tables have turned in favour of the human being manning the systems. This shift in attention brings with it a whole range of topics, such as the renewed debate on the moral and ethical aspects of European soldiering in the sense of individual and collective readiness to use armed force in order to end political and 'communal' violence. Furthermore, what kind of military personnel is eventually needed is questioned (for instance, the concept of the 'guardian' soldier). It not only implies establishing some kind of optimum profile of the future 'armed force specialist', but also calls for an evaluation of the present concepts of preparation, training, and rapid reaction including the manpower capacity for initial surge, sustainment over prolonged periods (two years or more), and break-off or exit operations. Finally, it might be argued that social-economic and demographic trends have a negative effect on the reconstitution capacity for military personnel and hence on operational readiness and strategic sustainment.

Rapidly developing technologies are the driving factors when looking at the material side of future military strategy and operations. The focus here lies with the required material means for implementing future operational concept and doctrines (peace support or peace-building operations, 'operations other than war', unconventional warfare, tasks of 'good governance', humanitarian support, etc.) and the importance – or lack of it – of the so-called revolution in military affairs (RMA) *vis-à-vis* contingency-specific roles, missions and tasks. Moreover, any military technology assessment should take into account the different environments and settings in which armed forces have to operate and the concomitant requirements for the material involved, including the support and logistic aspects. It is obvious that the rapid advance of information and communication technology on the effective employment of military forces (including real-time media coverage) will not be without a major impact on the way in which military strategy will be executed in future scenarios. In addition, technology will be decisive for establishing the most sensible and efficient composite military element (or building block) when it comes to structuring and integrating Western military forces. More importantly, technology developments are wearing down the rationale for a continuation of functional separation of Western ground, air naval, marine, and military police forces.

Conclusion: Introducing the Project

This introductory chapter forms the background against which this book has been prepared. The questions and issues raised above provide the framework for the contributing chapters, which are written by leading experts in the field of military history and political science. The chapters were discussed during a two-day workshop of experts held at Clingendael Institute on 13 and 14 February 1997.

The subject of this project was chosen for its relevance *vis-à-vis* the outcome of the intergovernmental conference (IGC) of the European Union, which is expected to be completed during mid-1997. The book is the final part of an endeavour about the future of military strategy in general. It was preceded by a similar exercise on the future of naval strategy in October 1995 (published by Kluwer Law International in April 1996), and on the future of ground and air forces in October 1996 (published by Kluwer Law International in May 1997).

The book's contents follow the structure of this introductory chapter. First, in chapters two (Martin van Creveld) and three (Jan Geert Siccama), the Clausewitzian dictum, trinitarian theory, and the – absence of – alternative theories of warfare are discussed. Next, chapters four (Zeev Maoz) and five (Jan van der Meulen) deal with societal changes and trends within Western Society at large which affect the future use of armed forces. Chapters six (Koen Koch) and seven (Jaap de Wilde) concentrate on the future relevance of the nation-state and governing bodies in relation to the ongoing process of European political integration and multilateralization of diplomatic interaction. Chapters eight (Jan Willem Honig), nine (Kees Homan), and ten (Robert Bunker) address how present-day changes and trends affect the armed forces, issues relating respectively to military strategy, personnel, and technology. Finally, chapter eleven (Gert de Nooy and Rienk Terpstra) provides an overview of topical highlights and tentative conclusions emanating from both the chapters and the discussions held during the workshop held in conjunction with this book.[1]

---

1   Chapters were finalized in April 1997. The editor gratefully acknowledges the intellectual contributions of the authors, and of F. van Beuningen, J. Grin, A.E. Pijpers, P.J. Teunissen, B.A.G.M. Tromp, and R. de Wijk who acted as discussants.
    This book was produced under the auspices of the Netherlands Institute of International Relations 'Clingendael', sponsored by the Netherlands Defence Staff and the Netherlands Defence College.

2 What is Wrong with Clausewitz?

Martin van Creveld

The first thing to say is that I do not share the views of those who, like John Keegan, would like to reduce Clausewitz to a mere early nineteenth-century Prussian officer who was frustrated by his lack of advancement and the stultifying regimental atmosphere in which he spent his life.[1] In my view he remains by far the greatest writer on war in the Western intellectual tradition and, apart perhaps from Sun Tzu, the greatest writer on war of all times. As a survey of the leading journals in the field of strategic studies will show,[2] he is the only writer on war who lived over one hundred years ago and who is still regarded as a practical guide to military affairs; from Frontinus to Liddell Hart, he is also the only one who did not content himself with a 'how to', cookbook approach to the problem.[3] Instead he went back to first principles. Next, proceeding by means of a constant juxtaposition of theory and historical reality, he produced a work that is of global historical significance. Alone among his fellow military theorists, Clausewitz has been compared to Goethe, Shakespeare, Machiavelli, Bacon, Hobbes, Marx, and Adam Smith among others;[4] of *On War*, the German military historian Rustow said that it represents a 'work for all times'.[5] A century and a half later this still remains true and is likely to remain true no matter what.

Yet while he transcended time, Clausewitz was also undeniably a Prussian officer of his time. His entire outlook was conditioned by that fact; nor would he himself be inclined to deny it. On the contrary, originally at least, he regarded

---

1   J. Keegan, *A History of Warfare* (New York: Hutchinson, 1993), pp. 15-6, 22.
2   Cf. e.g. *Strategic Studies* and *International Security*. In both of them over the last ten years, no person and no subject over a hundred years old except for Clausewitz has been made the subject of a paper.
3   On this approach see M. van Creveld, 'The Entrant Clausewitz', in M. I. Handel, ed., *Clausewitz and Modern Strategy* (London: Frank Cass, 1986), p. 45.
4   C. von der Goltz, *Das Volk im Waffen* (Berlin: Decker, 1883) p. 1; S. L. Murray, *The Reality of War* (London: Hugh Rees, 1906), p. xiii; B. Brodie, *War and Politics* (New York: Macmillan, 1973), p. 436; and A. Rapoport in his introduction to the Pelican edition of *On War*. For a list of additional quotes see also W. Hahlweg, ed., *Carl von Clausewitz, vom Kriege* (Bonn: Dümmler, 1980), 19th ed., p. 53 ff.
5   W. Rustow, *Feldherrnkunst des Neunzehnten Jahrhundert* (Leipzig: F. Schultheiss, 1967) p. 536.

G.C. de Nooy (ed.), The Clausewitzian Dictum and the Future of Western Military Strategy, 7-23.

himself as a practical officer who put down his thoughts on paper in the hope of instructing other practical officers – an idea that may have originated in the fact that he served as military tutor to the Prussian Crown Prince and his brother.[6] Even later, when his thoughts tended more and more towards abstract realms where he could not expect many others to follow, simply to philosophize was not enough; if anything, it represented a tendency of his for which he was inclined to apologize to his prospective readers.[7] What mattered was to produce a theory which, while not attempting to lay down rules for every case that might arise,[8] would serve as a base for action and make it unnecessary for each person to go back to first principles in each individual instance.[9]

Hence it should come as no surprise that, to endow his theories with a solid foundation in reality, Clausewitz took the circumstances of his time very much for granted. Nowhere in his book did he speculate about a different historical age that might follow his own and which might give rise to a fundamentally different kind of war. Given his wide-ranging studies of history,[10] this was not because he could not conceive of such a thing happening;[11] rather, it represented a limitation which was dictated by the purpose of his work. That purpose was to lay bare the essence of war,[12] not to speculate on what it might one day become if political and social circumstances should undergo some fundamental change. He was producing military theory, not futurology or science fiction.

---

6   Cf. P. Paret, *Clausewitz and the State* (Princeton, NJ: Princeton University Press, 1985), pp. 83-4 for his Clausewitz's early goals in writing.
7   C. von Clausewitz, *On War*, M. Howard and P. Paret, eds (Princeton, NJ: Princeton University Press, 1976), p. 63: 'my nature, which always drives me to develop and systematize, at last asserted itself here as well ... eventually my tendency completely ran away with me... The more I wrote and surrendered to the spirit of analysis, the more I reverted to a systematic approach.'
8   *On War*, p. 140: 'it is simply not possible to construct a model in the art of war that can serve as a scaffolding on which the commander can rely on support at any time'.
9   *On War*, p. 141: 'Theory is meant ... to educate the mind of the future commander, or, more accurately, to guide him in his self-education, not to accompany him on the battlefield'.
10   Cf. Paret, *Clausewitz and the State*, pp. 82-3, for his interest in this subject.
11   *On War*, p. 593: 'Will this always be the case in the future? From now on will every war be waged with the full resources of the state ...? Or shall we again see a gradual separation take part between the government and the people?'
12   *On War*, p. 141: 'Theory will have fulfilled its main task when it is used to analyse the constituent elements of war, to distinguish precisely what at first sight seems fused, to explain in full the properties of the means employed and to show their probable effects, to define clearly the nature of the ends in view, and to illuminate all phases of warfare in a thorough inquiry'.

State versus State

The first factor that Clausewitz took for granted, and which indeed underlies his entire work, is that war is fought by states against each other – and indeed one of the factors that first induced him to write was precisely the sudden and almost total collapse of his own state, Prussia. Nowhere in *On War* does he consider the possibility that it might be waged by other kinds of political organizations, such as (to list but a few out of history's immense treasure bag) decentralized tribes without rulers, more or less centralized chiefdoms, city states with their citizens numbering in the low hundreds or thousands, feudal lords and their vassals, robber barons, religious leagues, secret brotherhoods, etc. Not that he was unaware that, even within Europe, such organizations had once existed (and, in some places, still existed) and waged war against each other; on the contrary, in Book VIII, Chapter 2, Section B, he proceeds to list some of the more important among them. However, to him they were beyond the pale, so to speak. In them, 'the nature of states and societies as they are determined by their times and prevailing conditions'[13] were so different that nothing that could possibly be applied in military practice could be learned from them. Hence, too, his reasoned decision to limit his own selection of historical examples designed to illustrate his theory to the period from the Thirty Years War onwards;[14] the second half of the seventeenth century representing 'that point in history when ... the states of Europe had achieved complete internal unity'.[15]

Not only did Clausewitz take it more or less for granted that the belligerents on both sides should be states rather than other political organizations, but he assumed that they would wage war against each other by means of the regular armies that they possessed. Once again, it was not that he was unaware of the fact that other possibilities existed (for example, with the Tartars, 'people and army had been one'[16]). The composition of armies might also change; was not one of the greatest changes that he himself witnessed, and about which he had a lot to say, the shift from professional armies of the eighteenth century to the *levée en masse* of the nineteenth?[17] Yet at the same time as this shift occurred, he neglected – probably because he took it for granted – to pronounce the most elementary fact of all:

---

13   *On War*, p. 586.
14   *On War*, p. 173: 'examples should be drawn from modern military history, in so far as it is properly known and evaluated ... conditions [were] different in more distant times, with different ways of waging war, so that earlier wars have fewer practical lessons for us'.
15   *On War*, p. 588.
16   *On War*, p. 589.
17   *On War*, pp. 591-2: 'in 1793 a force appeared that beggared all imagination. Suddenly war again became the business of the people ... The people became a participant in war; instead of governments and armies, as heretofore, the full weight of the nation was thrown into the balance'. Note, however, that regular armies remained and that people and army did not become one, as with the Tartars.

namely that, both before and after 1789, the dominant type of military organization in Europe was not the tribal levy, or the classical Greek and Roman host, or the feudal levy, but the regular, state-owned and state-managed army. Forming one element in the 'remarkable trinity' comprising war[18] – if not at all times, then at any rate in his own and the foreseeable future – it was armies of this kind that Clausewitz had in mind when he wrote his book. This was true to the point that, strangely enough, the trinity of government, army and people even permeates the one chapter in his entire work that is devoted to guerrilla warfare.[19]

While seeking to write about the 'universal' attributes of war,[20] Clausewitz thus in practice tended to limit his thought mainly to situations in which it would be waged by states and at the hand of their regular armies 'in the shape familiar to the eighteenth century'.[21] He moreover did so not by accident but by design, for to proceed otherwise would have been to overshoot his goal; which, to repeat, was not to engage in abstract philosophical speculation but to provide instruction for practical soldiers. When combined with the determination to go back to first principles, such an objective is both understandable and ambitious. Yet one cannot overlook the fact – as he himself certainly did not[22] – that other possibilities of both military and political organizations have always existed, still do exist and will exist.

Since 1945 there have been approximately one hundred wars. Out of those, only seventeen were fought by states on both sides,[23] and of those nine took place in

---

18 *On* War, p. 89. The actual quote runs: 'its dominant tendencies always make war a paradoxical trinity – composed of primordial violence, hatred, and enmity ... [ever since 1648] the first of these three aspects mainly concerns the people; the second the commander and his army; the third the government'.

19 *On War*, p. 482: 'a *commander* can more easily *shape and direct* the popular insurrection'; p. 483: 'strategic plans for defence can *provide* for a general insurrection in one of two ways: either as a last resort after a defeat of an a natural auxiliary'; p. 483: 'a *government* must never assume that its country's fate, its whole existence, hangs on the outcome of a single battle ... no matter how small and weak a *state* may be in comparison with its enemy, it must not forego these last efforts'; p. 483: a *government* that after having lost a major battle, is only interested in letting its people go back to sleep'. All emphases are mine; they are intended to illustrate the instrumental character of people's war as conceived by Clausewitz – as something conceived, called forth, and directed and used by a government.

20 *On War*, p. 593. 'War, though conditioned by the particular characteristics of states and their armed forces, must contain some more general – indeed, a universal – element with which every theorist must above all be concerned'.

21 *On War*, p. 588.

22 Of Alexander the Great, for example, he wrote that he was, 'in a sense his own *condottiere*'; *On War*, p. 587.

23 I can think of the First Indo-Pakistan War (1947), the Israeli-Arab War (1947-48), the Korean War (1950-53), the Suez Campaign (1956), The Indo-Chinese War (1962), the Second Indo-Pakistan War (1965), the Six Days' War (1967), the War of Attrition (1969-70), the Third Indo-Pakistan War (1971), the Yom Kippur War (1973), the war between Ethiopia and Somalia (1977-78), the War

just two regions (that is, South Asia on the one hand and the Middle East on the other). Elsewhere in the world inter-state war has become rather rare, and this in spite of the fact that over the last fifty years the number of states has increased by a factor of three to four. Either, as is the case throughout the developed world and also increasingly in such places as South Asia and the Middle East, states are so strong that they either have nuclear weapons or are capable of building them in short order, thus creating a situation whereby they are deterred from fighting each other in earnest; or, as is the case in much of the 'developing' world, they are so weak that they are incapable of setting up regular armed forces at all.

While the occurrence of large-scale inter-state war seems to be receding, there are approximately thirty ongoing wars all over the world. Some of them, as in Afghanistan and the Rwanda-Zaire area, are extremely deadly; others have been going on for years if not decades, flaring up and flickering down but always simmering away and ready to explode. As I predicted in *The Transformation of War*, however, what all thirty have in common is that none of them is waged by states against each other; instead, they are waged either between a state and some other organization or between two such organizations. Nor can there be any question in them of regular armies or a trinitarian division of labour between government, army, and people. Far from fielding armies that are clearly distinct from the people, the organizations in question thrive precisely because their combatants cannot be told apart from the non-combatants by whom they are surrounded. From Algeria to Somalia and from Vietnam to Afghanistan, the almost endless series of defeats suffered by the state-owned, regular armies that are involved in this kind of war speak for themselves. They are largely useless and so, notoriously and for reasons that will be examined more closely later in this chapter, are Clausewitz's theories.

The Law of War

If Clausewitz's theories are powerless in front of non-state, non trinitarian (to use my own term[24]) warfare, another and equally important problem is his failure to take the law of war seriously. To him, war is 'the maximum use of force';[25] 'there is no logical limit to the application of that force',[26] and indeed to dream of conquering without bloodshed was positively dangerous because, everything else being

---

between Tanzania and Uganda (1978), the Chinese invasion of Vietnam (1979), the Falklands War (1982), the Israeli attack on Syria (1982), the Iran-Iraq War (1980-1988), and the Gulf War (1991). Depending on one's definition there may have been more.

24 Cf. M. van Creveld, *The Transformation of War* (New York: Free Press, 1991) pp. 49-57.
25 *On War*, p. 75.
26 *On War*, p. 77.

equal, it merely delivered the side who attempted it into the hands of his more ruthless enemy.[27] If there are 'attached to force ... certain self-imposed, imperceptible limitations ... known as international law' then they are 'hardly worth mentioning';[28] the outcome not of some modification in 'war itself' but in 'the social conditions of the states [sic] that give rise to war'.[29]

Why did Clausewitz, seeking to achieve a comprehensive understanding of war, choose to dismiss the entire vast body of literature that deals with its war in a single sentence? One obvious reason, which he himself gives, is the tendency of the Enlightenment to treat war as if it were merely a game of chess whose violence might be mitigated to the point that might be settled by means of 'algebra'. 'Theorists were already beginning to think along such lines when the recent wars taught them a lesson';[30] part of his own reason for writing was to set the record straight – which means that he was reacting against his predecessors.

That apart, a clue to the answer may perhaps be found in the most famous sentence that he ever wrote, namely, that war is the continuation of policy by other means.[31] As an officer in a regular army, Clausewitz was a servant of the state and sworn to help it realize its aims at the cost of his life, if necessary. By looking at war as 'an instrument of policy'[32] he made it neither good nor bad – much as, for example, the morality of a sword does not depend on its own qualities but on the purpose for which it is used: either carrying out a robbery or defending oneself against attack. Indeed, and given his background as an officer in an absolutist state where policy-making was the prerogative of the king and his ministers, one suspects that one reason why he insisted that 'the political purpose of war has no connection with war itself'[33] was precisely because it delivered him from the need to think of it in moral terms. To put it differently, ignoring the law of war represented one way in which duty could be given exclusive claim. And duty was something of which Clausewitz, like his fellow Prussian officers, was deeply conscious.

Be this as it may, there is no question that Clausewitz's disregard for the law of war does not stand up to criticism – and neither does the modern habit of keeping works about war and law in separate libraries or, at the very least, departments in the same library. However far back one directs one's gaze, war at all time and all places has been subject to certain limitations or rules which surrounded it and lessened its force. Some of these limitations were written down, others not. Some were secular, the majority probably religious by origin – for example, already the

---

27   *On War*, p. 76.
28   *On War*, p. 75.
29   *On War*, p. 76.
30   *On War*, p. 76.
31   *On War*, p. 87.
32   *On War*, p. 605.
33   *On War*, p. 90.

Old Testament contains several chapters that are devoted to the different kinds of war that the Israelites were to wage and the kind of things that were, and were not, permissible in each.[34] Some reflected the prevailing ethos of custom, others formal international law that was hammered out at specially assembled conferences and drawn up and ratified in much the same way that other laws were.

Like any other law, that which pertains to war and seeks to limit it is occasionally – some would say, frequently – broken. The mere fact that the law in question pertains to war, however, does not prove that this happens more often than in other fields, let alone that the law in question does not exist or does not matter. To select just a single extreme example, the Second World War on the Eastern Front came as close to being an 'absolute' conflict as Clausewitz might have wished. Yet even in that conflict, as far as we know, neither Hitler or Stalin tried to assassinate each other (Hitler is said to have rejected the idea when it was proposed to him). Among available weapons, gas was not used; if conquered cities were often looted and their female inhabitants raped, at any rate their (non-Jewish) populations were never killed *en masse* or sold into slavery as used to be standard practice at other times and places. And prisoners of war were certainly treated harshly, often starved or being left to freeze to death, but they were not systematically executed in a variety of more or less exotic ways, as would have been the case at many other times and places.

The purpose of the law of war is not, as Clausewitz seems to think, to assuage the conscience of 'kind hearted people'[35] (to whom he himself, by virtue of his above-mentioned stern adherence to duty, obviously does not belong). Rather, its first and foremost purpose is to protect the armed forces themselves. This is because, as Clausewitz himself emphasizes at considerable length,[36] war is the domain of uncertainty and agony. Nothing is more likely than the terror of war to cause rationality to go by the board, nor is anything more conducive to make even the most even-minded start to behave somewhat strangely. The paradox is that war, the most confused and confusing of all human activities, at the same time is one of the most organized. If armed conflict is to be carried out with any prospect of success, then it must involve the trained cooperation of many men. Men cannot cooperate, nor can organizations even exist, unless they subject themselves to a common code of behaviour. No war can take place unless those who participate in it are given to understand just who they are and are not allowed to kill, by whose orders, for what ends, under what circumstances, and by what means. A body of men that is not clear in its own mind about these things is not an army but a mob.

---

34   *Deuteronomy*, 20; 25, 17-9.
35   *On War*, p. 75.
36   See the excellent discussion in *On War*, Book 1, Chapters 6 and 7.

Besides the need to maintain discipline, a second function of the law of war is to define the difference between war and murder. Killing and shedding blood comprise activities that no society can tolerate unless they are carefully circumscribed by rules: rules whose purpose is to ensure that the killing is carried out only by certain authorized persons, under certain specified circumstances, and in accordance with certain prescribed rules. Although it is true that different societies at different times and places have varied greatly as to the precise way in which they drew the line between war and murder, the line itself is absolutely essential. Where it is not preserved, society will fall to pieces, and war – as distinct from mere indiscriminate violence of everybody against everybody – becomes impossible.

The third and last function of the rules of war is to help determine the outcome by telling the vanquished when to surrender. In a duel – Clausewitz's own metaphor for war[37] – the struggle ceases when one side is dead; not so in war, which is a collective activity involving large numbers of combatants as well as, in one form or another, non-combatants. In practice it seldom if ever happens that every enemy is slaughtered and every enemy's possession destroyed, the reason being that the rules also lay down what, at any time and place, constitutes 'victory'. The nature of 'victory' is usually recognized by both sides; in cases where it is not, war is likely to be exceptionally cruel and barbaric.[38]

Nor is it difficult to see what fate will befall a force that, for one reason or another, fails to observe the rules or, if such a thing were possible, to develop them in the first place. Such an army will most likely turn into a mob, running amok in all directions and inflicting tremendous destruction both on the environment and on itself. So far removed is such uncontrolled violence from war proper, that Greek mythology – always a good source of insight – had two different deities to represent the two. The patroness of orderly, regular warfare was the virgin goddess Pallas Athena. Springing directly from Zeus's row, she was a powerful warrior who is often represented leaning on her spear, lost in thought. The patron of unrestrained violence was Ares, 'mad, fulminating Ares', to quote Homer, an outcast among gods and men. Athena was one of the great gods and had the largest city in Greece named after her as well as the Parthenon built in her honour. Ares, born to the same father in the ordinary way, was a minor deity who had only a few worshippers and fewer temples. *The Iliad* tells how Ares on one occasion met Athena on the battle-field and was soundly defeated by her. Bleeding and trumpeting his pain he ran from the field, ascended to Olympus and complained to Zeus, from whom, however, he received scant sympathy.[39]

---

37   *On War*, p. 75.
38   See the discussion in M. van Creveld, *The Transformation of War*, pp. 90-1.
39   Homer, *The Iliad* (New York: Doubleday, 1974), book 5, line 711 ff.

To sum up, Clausewitz's summary dismissal of the rules of war or the war convention (to call them by their collective name) is one of the most misleading, not to say dangerous, aspects of his theory. At best it misrepresents reality, which from time immemorial has always been greatly influenced, if not governed, by the war convention; at worst it is capable of leading an army to defeat. Nowhere is this more true than in the field of modern non-trinitarian, or Low Intensity, Conflict, which as has been properly remarked really stands for Lawyer-Infested Conflict. Time without number, armies that were engaged in this kind of conflict fell victim to the belief that, since they had might on their side, they could ignore the rules of war by arresting and killing and torturing at will; time after time they found that the price for doing so was collapse. Nor does there seem to be any chance of this situation changing in the future. In a world where the shots are increasingly called by CNN, to say that 'certain self-imposed, imperceptible, limitations ... known as international law and custom ... [are] hardly worth mentioning' is plain nonsense.

The Offence-Defence Relationship

As we saw, the whole of *On War* – including, strangely but significantly, even the one chapter that deals with peoples' war – is written in terms of army-against-army warfare. The distinctions that Clausewitz draws are between strategy and tactics and between wars and campaigns; such concepts as 'theatres of operations', 'bases of operations', 'lines of communication'; 'convergence of attack and divergence of defence'; the 'concentration of forces in space' and 'the unification of forces in time';[40] briefly, 'the essence of the phenomena of war, ... the links between these phenomena, and the nature of their component parts'.[41] None of these would have been comprehensible if he had not taken it for granted that warfare is waged with the aid of large, cohesive organizations; organizations that are coordinated from above and clearly distinct from the people on whose behalf (or, depending on one's point of view, at whose expense) they campaign and fight.

Another consequence of the fact that he thinks in terms of army fighting army is that the time span which Clausewitz had in mind is also relatively brief. There is no question here of either the Hundred Years War or the Thirty Years War, both of which owed their extraordinary length in large part precisely to the fact that they were not waged by regular armies; instead the longest eighteenth century war – the period from which, as we saw, he draws most of his examples – was the War of Spanish Succession which lasted from 1702 to 1714. To Clausewitz, however, even

---

40 Many of these are chapter names in *On War*, whereas the remaining represent some of its principal tools in trade.

41 *On War*, p. 61.

that conflict was already too old to be of much use as a source of practical experience.[42] Instead he preferred to base his theory mainly on the art of war as it had
developed from 1740 to 1815 – a seventy-five year period which, it will have to be
conceded, forms a rather narrow basis for a 'universal' theory of war. Even within
that period, moreover, he preferred to think in terms not of wars but of individual
campaigns: for example, 'Frederick the Great's campaigns of 1742 in Moravia and
1744 in Bohemia, the French campaign of 1743 in Austria and Bohemia, the Duke
of Brunswick's of 1792 in France, and Massena's winter campaign of 1810-11 in
Portugal',[43] and so forth.

The fact that he thought of military operations as being conducted by regular
armies against each other and lasting for weeks and months, not for years or even
decades on end, in turn governed much of Clausewitz's strategic thought. For
example, take the famous discussion concerning the relationship between offence
and defence contained in Chapters three to seven of Book six of *On War*. In
essence, his arguments in favour of the superiority of defence consist of two points.
First, defence is superior because it approaches closer to its lines of communication, while offence, by its very success, gets further and further away.[44] Second,
since the essence of offence consists of getting in a blow whereas that of defence
consists of waiting, whatever does not happen favours the latter[45] – which is merely
another way of saying that it has time on its side. Both arguments, but particularly
the second, are admirable for their sophistication. Yet a little reflection will show
that they take regular armies and a relatively short war for granted.

First, had it been a question not of an army but of an entire people actively
participating in war, then there could have been no question of lines of communication in the first place. Such a people, to quote Clausewitz's own description of 'the
['semi-barbarous'] Tartar hordes', 'searched for new land; [they set] forth as a
nation, with women and children'. They neither depended on their old homeland nor
attempted to supply themselves from it; on the contrary, their whole movement was
little but an exercise in organized robbery and it took them to wherever provisions
were available. Nor, and *pace* Clausewitz, were the 'semi-barbarous' Tartars the
only ones to proceed in this way. Even within Europe, the first tentative attempts to
establish lines of communication in the modern sense were only made by Louvois,
père et fils, during the second half of the seventeenth century. Before that, it was
the 'tyranny of plunder' (as I have called it elsewhere) which prevailed, and which

---

42   *On War*, p. 173.
43   *On War*, p. 478.
44   *On War*, p. 365: 'by initiating the campaign, the attacking army cuts itself off from its own theatre of
     operations, and suffers by having to leave its fortresses and depots behind'.
45   *On War*, p. 357: 'What is the object of defence? Preservation. It is easier to hold ground than to take it.
     It follows that defence is easier than attack, assuming both sides have equal means'.

dictated the directions in which armies could and could not march.[46] Before the modern state, moreover, not only supplies but troops and even entire armies were often recruited from among people who had been traversed or subjugated. Under such circumstances it did not matter much whether an army was operating 'in its own theatre of operations' or hundreds or even thousands of miles away; of which the campaigns of Alexander, Julius Caesar, and Gustavus Adolphus constitute sufficient proof.

Second, time will work against the attacker only if it is limited – if, in other words, we assume that there is a point beyond which military operations must come to a halt, thus leaving the defender secure in his possession. It is possible, however, to imagine a kind of war that lasts for a very long time; and in which, consequently, individual operations and even entire campaigns instead of leading towards some definite outcome merely repeat themselves endlessly. Whatever we may think about the effectiveness of this kind of war, clearly enough of it in time will not work in favour of the defence. In it, moreover, our very concept of linear, Newtonian time, which starts in the past and leads towards the future in a non-repeatable, linear, and uniform manner, may itself not be applicable.[47]

As already mentioned, what is true of the offence-defence relationship is equally true of the remaining terminology that forms the scaffolding of strategy *à la* Clausewitz (and, it must be added, Jomini, Moltke, Schlieffen, Liddell Hart, and co. as well). Once one shifts from trinitarian warfare between states towards non-trinitarian warfare between other organizations, neither 'the unification of forces in time' nor 'the concentration of forces in space'; nor 'convergence of attack and divergence of defence'; nor 'lines of communication'; nor 'bases of operations' nor 'theatres of operations'; nor the distinction between campaigns and wars; nor that between tactics and strategy; make much sense any longer.

More could be said about the fundamental irrelevance of the Clausewitzian framework to inter-state, non-trinitarian war – for example, the fact that it does not naturally tend towards extremes of violence and is not necessarily best understood as a continuation of policy by other means. Not that those studying *On War* in such a context will find a lack of insights; however, they will also find that the philosophical foundations that form Clausewitz's unique strength in relation to other

---

46   Cf. M. van Creveld, *Supplying War: Logistics from Wallenstein to Patton* (Cambridge: University Press, 1978) pp. 5-16; also G. Perjes, 'Army Provisioning, Logistics and Strategy in the Second Half of the Seventeenth Century', *Acta Historica Academiaeu Scientiarium Hungaricae*, No. 16, 1965.

47   I have discussed the relationship between modern strategy and modern, linear, Newtonian time in M. van Creveld, 'The Structure of Strategic Studies', in D. Ball and D. Horner, eds, *Strategic Studies in a Changing World: Global, Regional and Australian Perspectives* (Canberra: Strategic Defence Studies Centre, 1992), p. 67. For the origins of Newtonian time see N. Hampson, *The Enlightenment: An Evaluation of its Assumptions, Attitudes and Values* (London: Penguin, 1982), p. 134 ff; for some alternatives to it, A. J. Gurjewitsch, *Das Weltbild des mittelalterlichen Menschen* (Munich: Beck'sche Sonderausgabe, 1982) p. 28 ff.

theorists have been knocked away. Given that it is itself written in trinitarian lines, this fact even applies to the one chapter that the Prussian writer devotes to people's war. However brilliant its ideas, it is very far from constituting a theory of such a war, let alone of one designed to counter it.

Policy by Other Means

The fourth point on which Clausewitz may be criticized, and which is also linked to his underlying assumption that war is conducted by states, is the famous claim that it constitutes a continuation of policy by other means. In fact it is easy to show that such is not the case; at different times and places war has been regarded as the continuation not of politics but of justice or religion.

For example, during the European Middle Ages – a period of whose 'otherness' Clausewitz himself was well aware – relations between rulers were supposed to be based not on might but on right. Right itself was not understood as man-made[48] but considered as partly divine, partly customary, in origin. Nor did human society comprise a number of sovereign states, each of which was entitled to make law; instead the entire *Respublica Christiana* was seen as a single organism which was itself held together by the law. Law, whether divine of human in origin, was regarded as immanent in the nature of things. The fact that it was often unwritten did not weaken, but rather strengthened, the binding force that it possessed.

With such a view of law as standing above rulers, any decision by one ruler or another to go to war did not so much constitute an act of policy as either an affirmation of justice or a transgression against it. Depending on whether or not they corresponded with certain criteria – the most famous set being the one that was laid down towards the end of the thirteenth century by Saint Thomas Aquinas[49] – a war could be either just or unjust; which in turn did much to determine the way in which it was waged and the kind of treatment meted out to the vanquished. In brief, armed conflict was the court in which members of the upper class – people whose vocation was war and who were accordingly known as *bellatores* (warriors) or *pugnatores* (fighters) or *miles* (soldiers) – settled their differences[50] (for example, who had rights to a castle, an estate, a country, or an heiress).

Another possibility, whose history is even more long and venerable, is to see war as the continuation of religion. To people raised in the Judeo-Christian tra-

---

48   Cf. E. Cohen, *The Crossroads of Justice: Law and Culture in Late Medieval France* (Leiden: Brill, 1993), pp. 4-14, for a short discussion of the medieval concept of justice.

49   F. H. Russell, *The Just War in the Middle Ages* (London: Cambridge University Press, 1975) chapter 7.

50   For the interaction of war and justice during this period, see J. Contamine, *War in the Middle Ages* (Oxford: Basil Blackwell, 1980), p. 280 ff.

dition, such an idea should certainly not come as a surprise; it is already very much in evidence in the Old Testament where wars between different peoples were at the same time conflicts in which the supremacy of their respective gods was proved or disproved.[51] In the book of *Deuteronomy*, a whole series of criteria are spelt out to help the Israelites decide whether this people or that should be subjected to attack and how they should be treated after their defeat; and the same was later true both in (medieval) Christendom and Islam. To anyone familiar with the history of the Crusades, there is scarcely a need to belabour the point. Nor, in our own day, is the concept of Muslim Holy War or *Jihad* exactly unimportant – indeed some would argue that the only people still willing to lay down their lives are those who are inspired by it.

To these reflections it will no doubt be objected that behind both religion and justice it is often possible to find 'practical' political concerns. That such is indeed frequently the case can scarcely be denied; undoubtedly many knights who went on Crusade had their eye on material gain as well as the salvation of their souls. However, the equation can also be turned around. If justice and religion are capable of being 'reduced' to policy, then equally policy is capable of being 'reduced' to underlying ideas concerning religion and justice. At the very least, the claim that it is policy and not justice or religion that have priority and make the world go round cannot be accepted without further proof. In the eyes of some, it is simply cynical.

Furthermore, much depends on what one means by the term 'policy' itself. As one of the participants at the symposium of experts for this book remarked, a case can be made that, since policy presumably seeks to realize those things that the organized community considers good and useful for itself, and since no community goes to war for anything else, any war (or other act) is a continuation of policy.[52] In my view, however, that is probably not what Clausewitz had in mind, or he would scarcely have paid so much attention to the need to make sure that the two are in harmony. Conversely, if he did have it in mind, then it is trite and scarcely deserving of the attention that has been devoted to it since *On War* was published.

Last but not least, all the interpretations hitherto advanced rest on the distinction – which Clausewitz, as a faithful if unprofessed follower of Aristotle, uses as the foundation of his work – between means and ends. It is assumed that war is an instrument whose goals lie outside itself; whether those goals are dictated by policy or justice or religion is, from this point of view, immaterial. And yet Clausewitz[53] to the contrary also found it possible to think of a kind of war in which means and ends

---

51   Cf. the books of *Judges*, 4, 3-17 (capture of the Ark by the Philistines); and *Samuel* A, 17-46-7 (David challenging Goliath to show that 'Israel hath a God').

52   C. Bassford, 'John Keegan and the Grand Old Tradition of Trashing Clausewitz', *War in History*, 1, 1994, pp. 325-6.

53   *On War*, p. 87: 'the political object is the goal, war is the means of reaching it, and means can never be considered in isolation from their purpose'.

are not distinct but merge into one. Such, precisely, is war for existence: the kind of war that is waged not after this objective or that has been chosen by policy, but precisely because policy has broken down, objectives have become irrelevant, and there simply is no other choice.

Such, once the initial moves had been performed, was the First World War and, even more so, the Second World War, which to quote Goebbels was '*ein Ringen um Leben und Todt*' (a life to death struggle). Such, to select an even better example, was the June 1967 Six Days' War. That war was launched by Israel when destruction appeared to look it in the face – precisely at the moment when policy had failed to such an extent that cost-benefit considerations ceased to apply and even the number of prospective casualties no longer mattered. While far from being the only form of war, historically speaking war for existence has been neither unimportant nor particularly rare. And yet it falls entirely outside the instrumental framework that Clausewitz, as its greatest philosopher, creates.

Factors for Fighting

Last but not least, and again precisely because he regards war as a rational act designed to achieve rational ends, Clausewitz never asks what factors drive men to fight. An intellectual framework seeking to create order out of historical chaos may be either etiological or teleological; in other words, it may be driven either by blind causality – as the one created by Karl Marx purports to be – or by men's attempt rationally to adapt actions to ends. Early in *On War*, Clausewitz says that 'the maximum use of force [i.e. war] is in no way incompatible with the simultaneous use of the intellect',[54] and indeed from beginning to end he never ceases to point out the need to adapt 'the scale of the military objective' to 'the effort to be made'.[55] Thus there can be no doubt concerning the framework that he selects, and indeed any other would scarcely result in a practical guide for action.

War, then, is a situation in which the members of one politically organized group set out to attack the members of another, with the aim of carrying out a policy or, to use modern terminology, realize their 'interest'. Yet this formulation already contains a logical contradiction, the reason being that war consists of the willingness to die if necessary (without this willingness there can be no fighting, and it is Clausewitz himself who postulates fighting as the very essence of war[56]) and that people who are facing death have no interests.[57]

---

54   *On War*, p. 75.
55   *On War*, p. 585.
56   *On War*, p. 227: 'Fighting is the central military act: all other activities merely support it ... Engagements mean fighting'.
57   Hence, too, the famous Roman gladiators' cry: *ave Caesar, morituri te salutant.*

As experience shows, men have often been willing – some would argue, all too willing – to put their lives on the line for God, king, country, family, or even all four at once. However, to say that they do so because they have some kind of posthumous 'interest' in the survival even of their nearest and dearest, is to invert the meaning of the term and turn it into a caricature of itself. Considered from this point of view, warfare – the fact that people are prepared to fight and die if necessary – constitutes the great proof that man is not motivated by selfish interest alone; as the original meaning of the term *berserker* (holy fighter) testifies, in some ways it represents the most altruistic of all human activities, akin to the sacred and merging into it.[58] It is precisely the perceived absence of rational goals that explains why society so often confers the highest honours in its possession on those who either brave death or die bravely; even to the point where, like Greek or Norse heroes, they are taken into the pantheon and themselves become gods.

To look at it in another way, the motives that make men risk their lives in the act of fighting are by no means necessarily the same as the ends for which the polity goes to war. The latter are, or at any rate are supposed to be, rational, as policy-makers select this objective or that: the former by definition can never be. In his capacity as an officer who is concerned with the military effectiveness of an army, Clausewitz has a lot to say about the need for the irrational, without, however, ever delving into the question of what the origin of those qualities might be.

And yet, as countless post-1945 armed conflicts in particular have proved, the question of why men are prepared to fight and die makes all the difference in the world. In these conflicts it was almost always a question of 'insurgents' pitting themselves against state-owned, regular, forces; including some of the most powerful, and most ruthless, that the world has ever seen. Initially, at any rate, the insurgents only numbered a mere handful, a few empty-handed men and women with nothing but high courage on their side. Nor, even when the end came and the hour of their victory approached, were they necessarily able to match themselves with their enemies in point of financial resources, organization, training and equipment. Indeed, it could be argued that from Palestine in 1947-49 to Chechnya in 1995-96, much of the military record of the last half century is one long demonstration of where there is a will there is usually a way. And that, on the contrary, where the will is absent, not even the largest numbers, the most abundant and sophisticated weapons, and the most perfect strategy are of much avail.

Since Clausewitz regards war itself as a clash of two wills,[59] in his eyes the true objective of operations must always be to break the enemy's will.[60] Thus the

---

58 See R. Girard, *Violence and the Sacred* (Baltimore, MD: Johns Hopkins University Press, 1977) on the relationship between the two concepts.

59 *On War*, p. 75: 'War is nothing but a duel on a larger scale ... war is thus an act of force to compel our enemy to do our will'.

60 *On War*, p. 75: 'to impose our will on the enemy is its [i.e. war's] object'.

importance which he attributes to the will in war cannot be overestimated. In Book Three, Chapter five, of *On War* he has some excellent things to say about the relationship between military organization and what he calls the military virtues: concerning the deeper origins of those virtues, however, the factors that may strengthen or weaken them, and the way they relate to the political objectives for which the war is fought scarcely a word may be found in all the 562 pages which comprise the standard English-language edition of his great work.

Conclusions

In conclusion, and proceeding backwards the way we have come, *On War* may be criticized – faulted would be too harsh a term for so great an intellectual endeavour – on several counts. First, and for all his emphasis on the role that irrational factors play in war, the very framework that Clausewitz employs prevents him from exploring the origins and nature of those factors, with the result that, time without number over the last half century, armies that on the face of it had might on their side went down to defeat.

Second, and unless one assumes that he has extended the meaning of the term until it becomes virtually meaningless, Clausewitz overestimates the importance of political objectives at the expense of others such as justice or religion. Furthermore, his analysis is based on the harmonization of means and ends. It cannot therefore take account of a situation, known as war for existence, in which the two merge and become one and the same.

Third, when it comes to strategy, *On War* is written entirely in terms of the clashes of one army against another – such questions as how to break the government's will or subjugate the people do not come into consideration at all. Therefore, it cannot provide an adequate framework – indeed it can provide hardly any framework at all – for wars in which this is not the case. At best, what Clausewitz does have to say about these questions only constitute sagacious remarks.

Fourth, in refusing to recognize that rules and limitations on war comprise a cardinal part of war – indeed that without them war is virtually impossible – Clausewitz does violence to historical reality. This is all the more true in modern, low-intensity conflict (or LIC).

Fifth, although he does recognize that other methods of organization are possible, Clausewitz's own analysis of war takes it for granted that war should be based on a trinitarian division of labour between people, army and government and that all three should be united in states. By so doing he forfeits any claim to universality and in effect limits himself to acting as the interpreter *cum* prophet of inter-state, trinitarian war – a much more modest objective, although, to be sure, still one that deserves respect.

Finally, by my reading of *On War*, Clausewitz, unlike some of his modern defenders, was aware of the last-named problem. Did he not write:[61]

> We wanted to show how every age had its own kind of war, its own limiting conditions, and its own peculiar preconceptions. Each period, therefore, would have held to its own theory of war, even if the urge had always and universally existed to work things out on scientific principles. It follows that the events of every age must be judged in the light of its own peculiarities. One cannot, therefore, understand and appreciate the commanders of the past until one has placed oneself in the situation of their times, not so much by a painstaking study of all its details as by an accurate appreciation of its major determining factors ... So the theorist must scrutinize all data with an inquiring, a discriminating, and a classifying eye. He must always bear in mind the wide variety of situations that can lead to war. If he does he will draw the outline of its salient features in such a way that it can accommodate both the dictates of the age and those of the immediate situation.

---

61   *On War*, pp. 593-4.

3 Clausewitz, Van Creveld and the Lack of a Balanced Theory of War

Jan Geert Siccama

What are the roles of 'the people' in the preparation and fighting of wars? In this chapter we will focus on some aspects that seem of the utmost importance for future military strategy, that is, the willingness to provide for military manpower and financial resources and to accept risks, especially in out-of-area operations. First of all, however, it seems necessary to point at some biases and omissions in the discourse on Clausewitzian strategy on this point.

Clausewitz: Three Views on War[1]

In the field of war studies, the name of Clausewitz is indissolubly linked with the political application of force. However, Clausewitz arrived at his instrumental view of war only after two quasi-naturalistic digressions in his thinking: the concept of 'absolute war' and the concept of 'friction'.[2]

THE NATURALISTIC VIEW: ABSOLUTE WAR

The first is 'absolute war', indicating the inevitability of escalation of fighting after war has broken out. Clausewitz's argument regarding total war begins with the following definition:

> ... War is nothing but a duel on a larger scale. ... Each tries through physical force to compel the other to do his will; his *immediate* aim it to *overthrow* his opponent in order to make him incapable of further resistance. *War is thus an act of force to compel our enemy to do our will.* Force ... is thus the *means* of war; to impose our will on the enemy is its *object*. To secure that

---

1 This section is derived from Henk W. Houweling and Jan G. Siccama, *Studies of War* (Dordrecht: 1988), Chapter 2.
2 For quasi-naturalistic detours in the social sciences, see G. Radnitzky, *Contemporary Schools of Metascience* (Gothenburg: 1968); and G. Radnitzky, *Preconceptions in Research: A Study* (London: 1974).

G.C. de Nooy (ed.), The Clausewitzian Dictum and the Future of Western Military Strategy, 25-42.
© 1997 *Kluwer Law International. Printed in the Netherlands.*

object we must render the enemy powerless; and that, in theory, is the true aim of warfare. That aim takes the place of the object, discarding it as something not actually part of war itself.[3]

This definition contains three elements:
- *Force*: the means of conducting warfare (that is, soldiers and their weaponry).
- *Coercion*: the process whereby the opponent is thrown to the ground, rendered incapable of further resistance and disarmed. Clausewitz terms this military goal the *Ziel*, or aim in war.
- The *political objective* of the war: the demands that the victor makes of the defeated upon achieving military victory. Clausewitz calls this political aim the *Zweck* (objective of war).

Clausewitz proceeds to argue that the drive towards unlimited escalation arises from the interaction between the first two elements in the above definition, namely the means of force and coercion. He reasons that in deciding on the scale of military sources to be deployed, each of the parties will act on the assumption that it will lose the struggle unless it throws more resources into the conflict than its adversary: 'If one side uses force without compunction, undeterred by the bloodshed it involves, while the other refrains, the first will get the upper hand.'[4] Each of the parties therefore 'escalates' as quickly as possible in the expectation that his opponent will do the same. Consequently: '... that side will force the other to follow suit; each will drive its opponent to extremes, and the only limiting factors are the counterpoises inherent in war.'[5] This reciprocal compulsion to escalate gives war an ungovernable character, for each side knows that '... I am not in control: he dictates to me as much as I dictate to him.'[6]

Although the cause of unlimited escalation is sought in human conduct, Clausewitz describes the result (absolute war) in terms reminiscent of natural disasters. In his first quasi-naturalistic approach, war appears to follow from 'necessary causes'.[7] War is a blind and ungovernable phenomenon comparable with an explosion of a mine that has been set beforehand.

WAR AS A CHANCE EVENT: FRICTION

The second quasi-naturalistic detour that Clausewitz takes before arriving at his instrumental view is concerned with chance events and probability theory. As it is

3   Carl von Clausewitz, *On War*, edited and translated by Michael Howard and Peter Paret (Princeton, NJ: Princeton University Press, 1976), p. 75 (original emphasis).
4   *On War*, pp. 75-6.
5   *On War*, p. 76.
6   *On War*, p. 77.
7   *On War*, p. 582.

usually fought, war does not escalate instantaneously. It takes time for the war machines to reach top gear. Escalation is also extended in terms of space. Warring parties are sometimes unable or unwilling to concentrate all their forces on one battlefield. All of the factors that restrain escalation and mitigate the competition in military struggles are denoted as friction. Friction is comparable to the faltering performance of a machine as a result of using impure fuel, which creates erratic behaviour. But there is a difference:

> This tremendous friction, which cannot, as in mechanics, be reduced to a few points, is everywhere in contact with chance, and brings about effects that cannot be measured, just because they are largely due to chance. ... It would take volumes to cover all difficulties.[8]

Friction may therefore come from almost any angle:

> Why is it that the theoretical concept (of absolute war) is not fulfilled in practice? The barrier in question is the vast array of factors, forces and conditions in national affairs that are affected by war. No logical sequence could progress through their innumerable twists and turns as though it were a simple thread that linked two deductions. Logic comes to an end in this labyrinth ...[9]

The effect is that the absolute concept of war as developed from the means and military aims explained above should be discarded:

> We must, therefore, be prepared to develop our concept of war as it ought to be fought, not on the basis of its pure definition, but by leaving room for every sort of extraneous matter. We must allow for natural inertia, for all the friction of its parts, for all the inconsistency, imprecision, and timidity of man ...[10]

The new concept of war – that is, when friction has done its work – is as follows:

> War is the realm of chance. No other activity gives it greater scope: no other has such incessant and varied dealings with this intruder. Chance makes everything more uncertain and interferes with the whole course of events.[11]

THE INSTRUMENTALIST VIEW: WAR AS THE CONTINUATION OF POLITICS WITH THE ADMIXTURE OF OTHER MEANS

Clausewitz made a virtue out of necessity by asserting that friction allows policy-makers to intervene in the war process. Contrary to the escalatory interaction between violent means and *Ziel*, the political objective (*Zweck*) exerts a restraining influence on the use of violence.

---

8   *On War*, p. 120.
9   *On War*, p. 579.
10   *On War*, p. 580.
11   *On War*, p. 101.

> Hitherto [war] has been rather overshadowed by the law of extremes, the will to overcome the enemy and make him powerless. But as this law begins to lose force and as this determination wanes, the political aim will reassert itself. If it is all a calculation of probabilities based on given individuals and conditions, the *political object* which was the *original motive*, must become an essential factor in the equation.[12]

Accordingly, political decision-makers cannot leave things to the military after war has broken out. The political objective must:

> permeate all military operations, and in so far as their violent nature will admit, it will have a continuous influence on them ... If we keep in mind that war springs from some political purpose, it is natural that the prime cause of its existence will remain the supreme consideration in conducting it.[13]

Depending on the political objectives, Clausewitz considers that violence may vary from pure threat via deliberate escalation (coercive warfare) to total war. In total or absolute war, each party is fighting for its own existence and its objective is to eliminate the other.

The Paradoxical Trinity

In the conclusion of his treatise on the nature of war, Clausewitz draws some implications for theory:

> War is more than a true chameleon that slightly adapts its characteristics to the given case. As a total phenomenon its dominant tendencies always make war a paradoxical trinity – composed of primordial violence, hatred, and enmity, which are to be regarded as a *blind natural force*; of the play of *chance and probability* within which the creative spirit is free to roam; and of its element of subordination, as an *instrument of policy*, which makes it subject to reason alone.[14]

He then continues by ascribing the core elements of the three different views of war to three social carriers:

> The first of these three aspects mainly concerns the *people*; the second *the commander and his army*; the third the *government*. The passions that are to be kindled in war must already be inherent in the people; the scope which the play of courage and talent will enjoy in the realm of probability and chance depends on the particular character of the commander and the army; but the political aims are the business of government alone.
>
> These three tendencies are like three different codes of law, deep-rooted in their subject and yet variable in their relationship to one another. A theory that ignores any one of them or seeks to fix an arbitrary relationship between them would conflict with reality to such an extent that for

---

12 *On War*, p. 80, original emphasis.
13 *On War*, p. 87.
14 *On War*, p. 89, emphasis added.

this reason alone it would be totally useless. Our task therefore is to develop a theory that maintains a balance between these three tendencies, like an object suspended between three magnets.[15]

Yet, Clausewitz has correctly been accused of not living up in the following chapters of *Vom Kriege* (On War) to the expectation that he would develop a balanced theory. In fact, he devoted most of his attention to military operations during war and his desire that they should be governed by the political goals of state leaders. The people as the third principal component of the paradoxical trinity was almost completely neglected. Most probably, this violation of an even-handed, *realistic* theory can be explained by the *normative* preference to which Clausewitz adhered. Specifically his whole work is characterized by the disgust he felt for the absolute form that violence had acquired during the wars of the French Revolution, which ran counter to the goal of using violence in a limited, controlled way:

Clearly the tremendous effects of the French Revolution were caused not so much by new military methods and concepts as by radical changes in policies and administration, by the new character of government, altered conditions of the French people and the like.[16]

In the same vein, his concluding statement on the issue of 'Absolute versus Real War' ends with a warning about Napoleonic warfare:

We must, therefore, be prepared to develop our concept of war as it ought to be fought, not on the basis of its pure definition, but by leaving room for every sort of extraneous matter. We must allow for natural inertia, for all the friction of its parts, for all the inconsistency, imprecision and timidity of men; and finally we must face the fact that war and its forms result from ideas, emotions, and conditions prevailing at the time – and to be quite honest we must admit that this was the case even when war assumed its absolute state under Bonaparte.[17]

Because normative considerations apparently prevailed upon his original goal to present a complete and balanced view, the people and their passions remained a kind of stepchild on most pages of *On War*. This is even reflected in his chapter on 'The People in Arms':

In the civilized parts of Europe, war by means of popular uprisings is a phenomenon of the nineteenth century. ... a popular uprising should, in general, be considered as an outgrowth of the way in which the conventional barriers have been swept away in our lifetime by the elemental violence of war. It is, in fact, a broadening and intensification of the fermentation process known as war. The system of requisitioning, and the enormous growth of armies resulting from it and from universal conscription, the employment of militia – all of these run in the same direction

---

15   *On War*, p. 89, emphasis added.
16   *On War*, p. 609.
17   *On War*, p. 580.

when viewed from the standpoint of the older, narrower military system, and that also leads to the calling out of the homeguard and arming the people.[18]

In Nazi-ideology, Goebbels' equation of the support of *Das Volk* to total war reinforced the conviction of the Clausewitzians that limited violence should prevail.

'The People' according to Van Creveld

How does Van Creveld fill the gap left behind by Clausewitz, after the latter largely omitted the relationships between society and the political-military authorities? It is at least noteworthy that his radical criticism of Clausewitz does not take recourse to research findings in the field of military sociology (including, among others, the journal *Armed Forces and Society*) which developed after the Second World War. Van Creveld relies very heavily on his own discipline of military history. Consequently, his contribution can be summarized in three main points: (1) in the future (as in the pre-Westphalian system) each man should be considered a potential warrior; (2) aside from other factors, such as reward and coercion, the will to fight originates primarily in the fact that war is enjoyable; (3) war will no longer be fought for the political goals of a state but for 'total' motives (justice; religion; existence).

EVERY MAN IS A POTENTIAL FIGHTER

Van Creveld very strongly resists the tendency to create within a state a division of labour in which the politicians delegate the application of violence to a separate profession, the military:

> It is worth pointing out that tribal societies, which do not have the state, also do not recognize the distinction between army and people. Such societies do not have armies; it would be more accurate to say that they themselves *are* armies, in which respect they are not so different either from the Greek city-state or, to select a contemporary example, the various terrorist organizations at present fighting each other in places such as Lebanon, Sri Lanka or Aberdjan.[19]

In the same vein, he fulminates very strongly against a centrepiece of the laws of war: the distinction between combatants and non-combatants:

> Except when war is waged in a desert, non-combatants, also known as civilians or 'the people', constitute the great majority of these affected. Clausewitz considers them as one leg in his trinity; he explicitly says that a theory that does not take them into account is not worth the paper it is

---

18 *On War*, p. 479.
19 Martin van Creveld, *The Transformation of War: The Most Radical Reinterpretation of Armed Conflict since Clausewitz* (New York: 1991), p. 56, original emphasis.

written on. However, all over the world today, the traditional distinction between peoples and armies is being broken down by new, non-trinitarian forms of war collectively known as Low-Intensity Conflict. Often this is because the line between the two may have been shaky to begin with. Many developing countries in Africa and Asia have never had the time to engage in 'nation-building', let alone to establish proper armed forces on the model of the more developed nations.[20]

A division of labour, leading to differences in experience, is also denied by Van Creveld in explaining the absence of women in warfare. He considers the question of why *men* fight the most important of all:

> To understand the nature of armed conflict, consider the part played – or not played – in it by females of the species. Were war simply a rational instrument for the attainment of rational social ends, then the role of women should have been just as great as that of the men; after all they comprise half of humanity, and by no means its least important half.[21]

The real reasons why women are excluded from fighting are, according to Van Creveld, not military but cultural and social:

> In every human society that has practised it, war has been the field in which sexual differences are most pronounced ... The association between 'man' and 'warrior' is, indeed, so close that in many languages the two terms are interchangeable ... Had men been made to fight side by side with women, or else to confront them as enemies, then for them armed conflict would have lost its meaning and might well come to an end.[22]

WAR IS ENJOYED BY INDIVIDUALS

According to Van Creveld, fighting and the will to fight are the essence of war. The motives for why men are willing to lay down their lives are, however, not related to the goals of society or to national interests:

> At bottom, the reason why fighting can never be a question of interest is – to put it bluntly – that dead men have no interests.[23]

> Just as it makes no sense to ask 'why people eat' or 'what they sleep for', so fighting is not a means but an end. Throughout history, for every person who has expressed his horror of war, there is another who found in it the most marvellous of all the experiences that are vouchsafed to man, even to the point that he later spent a lifetime boring his descendants by recounting his exploits. ... Enjoying themselves, they and their counterparts at all times and places were able to inspire countless followers who, as they went into combat, came to know the meaning of excitement, exhilaration, ecstasy, and delirium.[24]

---

20 *The Transformation of War*, pp. 72-3.
21 *The Transformation of War*, p. 179.
22 *The Transformation of War*, p. 183.
23 *The Transformation of War*, p. 158.
24 *The Transformation of War*, pp. 161-2.

'Danger' is an attractive ingredient of war:

> ... from the point of view of participants and spectators alike, it is among the principal attractions, one would almost say its *raison d'être*. Had war not involved danger, coping with it, and overcoming it, then not only would there have been no point in fighting but the activity itself would have become impossible. Coping with danger calls forth qualities such as boldness, pride, loyalty and determination. ... What makes coping with danger so supremely enjoyable is the unique sense of freedom it is capable of inspiring.[25]

> It is true that other factors – including rewards and coercion – are mixed up with the will to fight, but, since it is the ultimate meeting of men with death that we are speaking of, that is beside the point. ... The joy of fighting consists precisely in that it permits participants and spectators alike to forget themselves and transcend reality, however incompletely and however momentarily.[26]

Van Creveld's reversal of Clausewitz on this theme is summarized perhaps best by his statement that 'In so far as war, before it is anything else, consists of fighting – in other words, a voluntary coping of danger – it is the continuation not of politics but of sport.'[27]

WHY WAR IS FOUGHT

While filling the 'societal' gap in Clausewitz and abdicating from the political element in the explanation of warfare, Van Creveld sticks to the absolute side ('passion') of fighting ascribed to the people by the Prussian strategist. In Chapter V, 'non-political war' is equated with three goals of a rather total nature: 'Justice', 'Religion', and 'Existence'. A controlled use of violence by individuals or the community to which they belong is apparently out of the question. Of these, the first two aims are related to the concept of 'Holy War'. 'Existence', however, can refer as well to the survival of a state as to the well-being of an individual or a sub- or transnational collectivity.

   Van Creveld considers it 'absurd for a person to die for the interest of some- body or something else'. Therefore 'the entire modern "professional" model of armed forces fighting for their "clients" is little better than a description for defeat'.[28]

   It is, however, not fully clear how Van Creveld's future warfare will look:

> In the future, war will not be waged by armies but by groups whom we today call terrorists, guerrillas, bandits, and robbers, but who will undoubtedly hit on more formal titles to describe themselves. Their organizations are likely to be constructed on charismatic lines rather than

---

25   *The Transformation of War*, pp. 164-5.
26   *The Transformation of War*, p. 166.
27   *The Transformation of War*, p. 191.
28   *The Transformation of War*, p. 191.

institutional ones and to be motivated less by 'professionalism' than by fanatical, ideologically-based, loyalties. While clearly subject to some kind of leadership with coercive powers at its disposal, that leadership will be hardly distinguishable from the organization as a whole; ... A warmaking entity of any size will have to be 'in control' of a territorial base of some sort.[29]

Is Van Creveld really sure that the state will die?

The Reversal of Clausewitz by Van Creveld: Some Additional Questions

In his radical critique of 'trinitarian war', Martin van Creveld is correct in two respects. First, inter-state warfare, which was the theme of *Vom Kriege*, has since 1945 increasingly become the exception.[30] The usual types of warfare are of an intra-state nature, encompassing decolonization wars, civil warfare (including anti-regime struggles), secession wars, state terror and other forms of mass killing ('genocides'), terrorism, etc. Owing to the successful application of nuclear deterrence (a new form of total war, this time originating in the absolute character of armaments instead of ideology), collective violence between and among the Eastern and Western blocs could no longer result in a meaningful victory. Consequently, Van Creveld's definition of contemporary armed conflict is almost tautological:

> The principal characteristics of low-intensity conflict (LIC) are as follows: First, they tend to unfold in 'less developed' parts of the world; ... Second, very rarely do they involve regular armies on both sides, though often it is a question of regulars on one side fighting guerrillas, terrorists, and even civilians, including women and children on the other. Third, most LICs do not rely primarily on the high-technology collective weapons that are the pride and joy of any modern armed force. Excluded from them are the aircraft and the tanks, the missiles and the heavy artillery, as well as many other devices so complicated as to be known only by their acronyms.[31]

Since the severity of many of the ongoing struggles can be compared to the Thirty Years War, the term 'low intensity' is perhaps a bit misleading, unless one restricts its meaning to the use of less sophisticated weapons and military units of small size. In this respect, contemporary warfare resembles the clashes between groups of bandits, which was characteristic of Western Europe before the formation of the state system.

Second, Van Creveld's criticism that Clausewitz restricts himself to warfare by states is equally correct. The intra-state character of warfare is demonstrated by the

---

29   *The Transformation of War*, pp. 197-8.
30   See, for instance, J.G. Siccama and A. Oostindiër, *Veranderingen in het conflictpatroon na de Koude Oorlog: misverstanden en feiten* [*Changes in the Pattern of Conflict since the Cold War: Prejudices and Facts*] (The Hague: 1995).
31   *The Transformation of War*, p. 20.

fact that some 30 out of 180-plus states are weakening or even falling apart altogether ('failed states'). Apparently, many states that became independent after colonialism or disintegration of the Soviet empire are lacking legitimacy and the internal capacity to resolve disputes in a peaceful manner. However, this does not necessarily imply that states (and state warfare) have come to an end. Internal conflicts are often fought about the possession of state power or the establishment of new states with the ruling regime on one side. And although some political leaders must be satisfied with the role of roving bandits, stationary warlords still strive for possession of a piece of territory on which they want to establish a weapons and tax monopoly. The crucial distinction between 'democracies', 'stationary warlords' (autocratic or even totalitarian systems) and 'roving bandits' (who have not yet acquired a territorial base) is taken from Olson.[32] According to Tilly, the number of autonomous political units in Europe after the Middle Ages was some 500. This number had been reduced to 25 by the year 1900,[33] to 35 at the end of the Cold War, while it has increased since the disintegration of the Soviet and Yugoslav federations. Apparently the enlargement of scale has been reversed, a process which might also be observed in regions of Africa and Asia. A highly relevant question is therefore *under which conditions intra-state or supra-state collectivities organize themselves to apply violence.* Although all kinds of individual motives (increase in wealth and power) and collective values (shared religion, ethnicity, nationality, etc.) may play a role in this formation, acquiring power over a state territory still seems one of the most important objectives of political entrepreneurs. Unfortunately, Van Creveld does not elucidate much about the interplay between individual motives (joy?) and collective values (justice, religion, existence), which he expects will dominate the future war scene and on which political leaders will rely.

This leads to two other points of discussion in Van Creveld's critique. First, while Clausewitz focused on the execution of instrumental warfare as guided by the policy-makers and neglected to deal with societal aspects, Van Creveld solely indulges in the primacy of 'the people' and forgets about a future relevance of the state (as well as of politicians and the armed forces controlled by them). As a consequence, we are still in need of a balanced and complete theory of war. It is not unlikely that this turn-around of the Clausewitzian trinity is caused by Van Creveld's personal dislike of the state. In an interview with the Dutch bi-monthly *Atlantisch Perspectief*[34] he referred to the holocaust and other forms of state terror, which could only be committed as a result of the monopoly of violence by criminal

---

32 M. Olson, 'Dictatorship, Democracy, and Development', *American Political Science Review*, Vol. 87, No. 3, September 1993, pp. 567-76.

33 'Reflections on the History of European State-Making', in: Charles Tilly, *The Formation of National States in Western European* (Princeton, NJ: Princeton University Press, 1975).

34 Vol. 20, No. 81, 1996, p. 19.

states over a specified territory. For others, such as Dahrendorf,[35] however, only the state has proved to be the institution that is capable in some cases of attaining democracy and safeguarding the protection of human rights. Strangely enough, Van Creveld's hatred of the totalitarian state may resemble Clausewitz's dislike of Napoleonic France, leading Van Creveld to define away the centrally controlled use of war in a similar way to how Clausewitz had defined away the role of 'the people'.

Second, although Van Creveld has undoubtedly read Clausewitz's introduction on absolute war and friction, he deals only with the trinitarian view in which 'society' as an agent is deleted. This reflects, however, as has been shown, solely the political preference of Clausewitz and of most of his contemporary followers. Van Creveld equates 'absolute war' with the ideas in van der Goltz's book *Das Volk in Waffen* (1883), while neglecting Clausewitz's original contribution on three possible metaphysical views on war. This results in the omission of a third important question in *The Transformation of War*: *Under which conditions is it likely that deliberate, limited escalation changes into compulsory, unlimited warfare?* We have already referred to the absolute character of weapons of mass destruction. Some selective nuclear strikes against the territory of an opponent might indeed not be perceived as a small manageable threat, but as a danger to the sheer survival of the attacked country.[36] The highly important possibility of transition from instrumental into existential violence, which cannot be neglected as long as territorial-based political units continue to exist, is completely lacking in Van Creveld's critique of Clausewitz, which is especially surprising because escalation seems most likely as soon as existence (which Van Creveld considers a primary cause of war) is at stake.

An Alternative View[37]

Since warfare is a highly risky activity, from an individual point of view it seems only rational to refuse to participate in military activities. This is even true where the individual concerned believes that warfare or the preparation for warfare is fully justified in the case at hand. The reason for this should be sought in the prisoners' dilemma. If others show up, the presumed benefits of fighting also accrue to those who refuse to participate. If nobody shows up, it would not make sense for any particular individual to participate.

---

35   R. Dahrendorf, *The Modern Social Conflict* (London: Weidenfeld and Nicolson, 1988).

36   Cf. Henk W. Houweling and Jan G. Siccama, 'The Risk of Compulsory Escalation', in *Journal of Peace Research*, Vol. 25, No. 1, 1988, pp. 43-56.

37   This section is based on Henk W. Houweling and Jan G. Siccama, *Studies of War* (Dordrecht: Nijhoff, 1988), chapter 1.

If refusal to fight is the rational response, how is it then possible that so many wars have been fought in the past and probably will be fought in the future? The time difference between recruitment of soldiers and their decision to fight is, in our view, crucial in answering this question. First, governments (or leaders of groups aspiring to acquire governmental status) find it remarkably easy to recruit and mobilize troops. Second, once soldiers are in a fighting situation (either on the battlefield or during guerrilla action), most men fight rather than flee.

RECRUITMENT

Two peculiarities of human learning allow governments to recruit men at relatively low cost.[38] The first is that it is possible to draw individuals into modes of behaviour entailing the probability of serious consequences later on by providing them with rather small, though immediate rewards during the initial stages of the mobilization process. When the delay between rewarded behaviour and the later attendant costs is large, and when these costs are merely probable (not certain), many people find it difficult to avoid such positively loaded traps. This quality of human learning behaviour puts unenthusiastic participation in military activity (for example, because it is rewarded financially) on a par with that of cigarette smokers, drug addicts, or alcoholics. All succumb to the seduction of immediate rewards and accept the risk of serious consequences later on. The second characteristic of human learning behaviour is the desire to avoid immediate and certain costs, even if these are relatively mild, at the price of risking much greater costs later on. This puts participation in military activities on a par with the man who postpones his visit to the dentist repeatedly for fear of the pain he will suffer in the dentist's chair.[39] These characteristics of human learning allow governments to hire professional soldiers for relatively modest salaries and to recruit conscripts while threatening them only with rather modest sanctions. We may conclude that substantial numbers, after undergoing a carefully designed schedule of positive reinforcement, will finally take part in those activities. On the basis of learning theory, we also see that individuals adapt their behaviour to individually divisible benefits and costs.

However, some political philosophers (and Van Creveld follows their example) suggest that individuals pursue collective values, meaning values that can only be produced for a group as a whole, in addition to individual rewards.

---

38   Cf. C.R. Hilgard and G.H. Bower, *Theories of Learning* (Englewood Cliffs, NJ: 1975) (4); R.J. Bandura, *Aggression: A Social Learning Analysis* (Englewood Cliffs, NJ: 1973); V. Vanberg, *Die Zwei Soziologien: Individualismus und Kollektivismus in der Sozialtheorie* (Tübinger: 1975).
39   Cf. J.C. Cross and M.J. Guyer, *Social Traps* (Ann Arbor, MI: 1980); J. Platt, 'Social Traps', *American Psychologist*, 1973, pp. 641-51; C.N. Cofer and M.H. Apply, *Motivation: Theory and Research* (New York: 1964).

The appeal to common bonds and interests may indeed be quite apparent during a recruitment process. Of course, from the perspective of the mobilizing agency, having the 'right' collective values greatly facilitates the recruitment of military personnel by making this process cheaper in terms of real resources. That is why governments invest resources in efforts to influence their subjects' collective system of values.

However, it should be stressed that a military recruitment process that operates exclusively in terms of collective values is unknown, although probably the International Brigade in the Spanish Civil War came close to this. Even during holy wars, however, people joining the crusades to serve their God had the prospect of fringe benefits (remission of earthly debts, forgiveness of sins, booty). And did not the Red Army have to restore military ranks and payment differentials to attract good officers (of the old regime) to fight for the Bolshevik revolution?

In contemporary societies, at least those of the Western world, one can observe systems of recruitment that operate predominantly, if not exclusively, in terms of appeals to individually defined costs and benefits. Western armed services have almost completely dropped references to legitimizing ideologies,[40] and act as just another big firm, offering secure employment, rewarding careers, and good payment.[41] At any event, the apparent impossibility of recruiting military man-power, even if conscripted, at incomes lower than those paid in the private sector, confirms our view that collective values do not propel men to join the armed forces, but are only a helpful factor in legitimizing decisions resulting from individually divisible benefits and costs.

FIGHTING

This leads to the second consideration about the willingness of mobilized forces to fight instead of flee once they have arrived on the battlefield. We will avoid any speculation on the origin of the capacity of people to sacrifice themselves for the benefit of others.

The literature on altruism[42] is of little use for our problem because it seldom deals with the ultimate form of self-sacrifice. Ultimate self-sacrifice is usually observed in the context of close relations in kinship networks. It is interesting to note that it may occur in totally different contexts, such as armed forces. Our first argument, however, is that this characteristic of man makes the world a far more dangerous place than it is in Hobbes's state of nature. Next, we criticize the

---

40   C.C. Moskos, 'From Institution to Occupation: Trends in Military Organization', *Armed Forces and Society* 4(1), 1977, pp. 44-50.

41   See C. Dale and C. Gilroy, 'Determinants of Enlistments: A Macro-Economic Time-Series View', *Armed Forces and Society* 10(2), 1984, pp. 192-210.

42   B. Schwartz, 'The Social Psychology of the Gift', *American Journal of Sociology* 73, 1967, pp. 1-11.

orthodox theory (according to which soldiers are willing to die if they believe that it will benefit their community), arguing that collective values are certainly essential for sustained fighting, but that these values are attached to the fighting group itself and not to the political community to which the soldier belongs.

In Hobbes's model – that is, before the creation of a state – men are essentially equal. Therefore, '(no) one man can thereupon claim to himself any benefit, to which another may not pretend as well as he'.[43] Equality of all men gives rise to equality of hope among them in attaining ends, self-preservation being the most important of these ends. The result of this state of affairs is that: '... if any two men desire the same thing, which nevertheless they cannot both enjoy, they become enemies; and in the way to their End ... endeavour to destroy, or subdue one another.'[44]

In other words, when any two men compete for individually divisible goods, and the preservation of their lives is the most important of these goods, they become enemies. In the ensuing struggle, each individual defines his 'self' in the expression 'self-interest' in such a way as to include only himself. Hobbes's egoists in his model of the state of nature simply lack the capacity to sacrifice themselves. They do not even pursue collective values.

Unattractive as Hobbes's state of nature appears at first sight, on reflection it is not really so bad and dangerous. Of course, there is a state of permanent war: the expectation of violence is never far away and is accompanied by occasional fighting. But the ensuing violence is limited for four reasons.

First, each individual fights alone, for his own benefit and at his own cost and risk. No one is able to form a fighting group or coalition as no one has developed the capacity for self-sacrifice. In Hobbes's state of nature, there simply is no state or civil authority to recruit people, train them, and order them to fight.

Second, each warrior has to fight with home-made tools. No agency specializes in resupplying the warrior after his or her food supply is depleted or after his tools have become useless. There is no state resupplying the front with fresh men when the first wave of fighters has become exhausted – there simply is no front. Only a government can accomplish these tasks: pacify a body of men (to make citizens out of them), use part of the production to feed an army, and supply it with specialized tools of war. The specialized tools of war produced by states have a far greater destructive impact, but generate far less fear than home-made weapons. Home-made tools of destruction are used at close range and have an immediately visible, if limited destructive impact. Since the enemy is visible at close range and the impact of the weapon is clear, there is a sense of danger, stimulating the propensity to flee. On the other hand, the modern soldier's sense of danger and propensity to flee are

---

43   T. Hobbes, *Leviathan* (1651), C.B. MacPherson, ed. (Harmondsworth: 1968).
44   Hobbes, *Leviathan*, p. 184.

probably reduced. Part of the reason for this is technological: weapons have become more destructive as their range has increased. There is also a psychological reason: when combatants who are a source of danger to each other lose sight of each other, they lose sight of the source of danger too. It is easy to understand why an infantry soldier, armed with a bow and arrow, who prepares to fend off an attack by cavalry armed with lances and swords, finds it more difficult to suppress his fear than do soldiers fighting an artillery duel. Engineers launching a ballistic missile are probably even less affected by fear. They can do without a helmet, camouflage or a personal handgun, and can even drink coffee or make love during a lull in the fighting (if they have not yet been destroyed). In comparison with artillery, inter-continental missiles also make flight rather senseless, since there is no better place to go. Like man in Hobbes's state of nature, civilized man is inclined to avoid sources of pain and death that are close. But modern man has the additional problem of developing the ability to imagine danger and visualize destruction in proportion to the destructive capacity of the weapons available to him.

Third, when the preservation of life is the ultimate goal for everyone, fear of death is a major reason for peace in Hobbes's state of nature. There is no state or civil government which promises the soldier that others will benefit from his labours and that legitimizes his effort. There is no mass army, composed of small fighting groups of like-minded men, each one of whose members helps others to overcome his fear of death and promises him symbolic survival in the event of his death; there is no institutional arrangement such as military police for preventing soldiers from fleeing.

Fourth, in Hobbes's state of nature, violence is instrumental at the individual level, flight being an alternative to fighting. The goal is not destruction as such, but to obtain by violence what is required for survival, to make life pleasurable and last longer or to protect these values from being eroded. Fighting will stop only when the desired objects have been acquired or safeguarded or when they prove to be unattainable.

Compared with the contemporary civilized world, in which states and empires have developed means of instantaneous mass destruction, and their strategies testify to their willingness to use these weapons if necessary, the prospects of survival entailed in Hobbes's stateless society are not in fact that bleak. Perhaps the lives of men would not be as 'solitary, nasty, brutish, and short' as Hobbes thought.

In comparison with the individuality of the lonely warrior in Hobbes's state of nature, the civilized soldier, fighting on behalf of a group or state, is group-oriented. Modern soldiers get their job done through disciplined group endeavour. Instilling group discipline in a soldier is not aimed at perfecting the art of killing his enemies, but at his willingness to kill on command in circumstances where fleeing would be more conducive to his own safety and survival than fighting. There is probably no better refutation of the theory of instinctive aggression in man than the efforts invested in preventing the armed forces from fleeing by means of instilling group discipline. Hobbes's fighters do have the option of fleeing without guilt. However, in modern armies, out of any two fighters, one is always in command; Frederick the Great is remembered for stating that discipline is the art of making soldiers fear their officers more than the enemy.

But preventing soldiers from fleeing by means of institutional hierarchy alone does not make for an army that will operate smoothly. The 'shoot or get shot' alternative is simply inadequate for achieving this, although soldiers would be much less dangerous if it worked that way.

Those who have studied battle behaviour have suggested two plausible explanations. The first is that the soldier's loyalty to the small fighting unit (and not his loyalty to his people, his race or his state and its ideology, creed or war goals) is essential for his fighting morale. The following quotation illustrates this:

> Perhaps you will remember that during the last war, i.e., World War II, reports came back from investigators who had asked our soldiers, i.e., American military personnel, what they were fighting for. Everyone was much disturbed by the fact that the consensus was something like this: 'We are fighting to get home and eat some blueberry pie'. Now although I have enormous respect and deep admiration for blueberry pie, what impressed me about this was the answers that were not given. They were not fighting for the shibboleths or slogans or grandiose ideals, they were not fighting for an abstract idea or for somebody's system; and their blueberry pie stood for their distrust of such ideals.[45]

Soldiers are prepared to risk their lives for the unit in which they spend their time and which operates as a small primary group or surrogate family. This is essentially the finding of Shils and Janowitz[46] for Hitler's *Wehrmacht* and of Shirom[47] for the Israeli army. The view that the basic fighting unit is the surrogate family which develops as a response to danger, while ideological beliefs and support for war goals do not predict combat performance, is widely shared in other literature as well as in the two sources quoted.

The disintegration of the American forces during the Vietnam War, however, poses a challenge to this point of view. Some authors fall back on what we called 'the orthodox theory': soldiers are only prepared to die if they believe that the war is necessary or just or on national grounds.

In our view, there is no reason at all for returning to former beliefs. Authors who stress the importance of primary group loyalties to explain the willingness of soldiers to fight and die have never denied that other factors may prevent the formation of these loyalties or destroy them. In the Vietnam War two factors may have had a negative effect on the propensity of primary groups forming among

---

45   N. Goodman, *Problems and Prospects* (New York: 1972), p. 55.
46   E.A. Shils and M. Janowitz, 'Cohesion and Disintegration in the Wehrmacht in World War II', *The Public Opinion Quarterly* 12, 1948, pp. 280-315.
47   A. Shirom, 'On Some Correlates of Combat Performance', *Administrative Science Quarterly* 21, 1976, pp. 419432.

fighting men. The first is the limited nature of the American war effort relative to the total resource base of the United States. Conscripts heading for Vietnam did not have any sense that they were leaving a nation at war; on the contrary, they left a 'business as usual' society and probably none of their relatives and friends was involved in any war-related activity during their office hours. In these circumstances recruitment can be compared with compulsory participation in a lottery with car accidents as prizes. Americans, like any other people, do not stop driving simply because they know that thousands of casualties occur each year on the highways. But imagine that some agency were distributing these accidents deliberately and that some people got the message that next year it would be their turn to become the victim of a possibly fatal automobile accident. These people would certainly stop driving, while other drivers would drive even more recklessly than they did before. Primary groups among future victims would certainly try to destroy the agency responsible; other individuals would try to change the rules by which accidents were distributed. In Vietnam the first mechanism occurred by so-called 'fragging', in which conscripts killed commanding officers. Similarly, the rules of distribution were changed by draft evasion. In so-called 'turn on, turn off' wars of the coercive bargaining type, primary group loyalties among fighting men may well obstruct the war effort.

Another plausible factor for the disintegration of US armed forces during the Vietnam War is the composition of the officer corps. During major wars, for example during both World Wars, the officer corps necessarily comprises a large number of non-professional officers, and the career prospects of these officers are different from those of the professionals. In both World Wars the war effort was so vast that lower-level commanding personnel did not have an opportunity for direct competition with their colleagues. In Vietnam, however, the officer corps consisted mainly of professionals. These professionals were rotated quickly so as to give as many of them as possible an experience of combat; the zone of operations was not that vast and officers were inclined to compete with fellow officers, possibly even risking the lives of conscripts.[48]

The second suggestion of authors investigating battle behaviour is that the surrogate family is a post-enlistment phenomenon, created by the exigencies of battle itself.[49] The phenomenon of mutual support in cases of common danger by members of small groups who know each other intimately is, of course, much older than the state and its armed forces. However, in Hobbes's state of nature there are no such groups. To him men are rather like hedgehogs; they are no great danger to

---

48   J. Balkind, 'A Critique of Military Sociology: Lessons from Vietnam', *Journal of Strategic Studies*, 1978, pp. 235-54.

49   See also J.G. Gray, *The Warriors: Reflections on Men in Battle* (New York: 1970).

others (except mice). But obviously the hedgehog is not a plausible model for human behaviour.

These remarks are of a rather general nature and form at best a framework for spelling out the *necessary* (but not the *sufficient*) causes of fighting as the beginning point of a theory of war. Despite the elementary character of this analysis, it is, however, worthwhile noting that the structural causes point very strongly in the direction of a continuation of some form of state system and of a high degree of political mouldability. Successful political entrepreneurs are apparently capable of mobilizing armed forces and letting them fight for a wide variety of goals they have set for themselves.

Conclusion

Summarizing, we may conclude that Van Creveld has contributed a highly stimulating and even provocative insight to military history – that is, the relative neglect of society by Clausewitz. Unfortunately, Van Creveld himself has to a large extent written off the politico-military (state) sector of warfare, which gives his analysis an equally biased flavour. The way ahead, therefore, seems to require the development of a balanced theory of war, in which attention is paid to all relevant aspects of war, and the interactions between them.

4   Security for the People, Security by the People: The Paradox of Security in Modern Societies

Zeev Maoz

Introduction

This chapter deals with a fundamental paradox concerning the provision of security in modern societies, in general, and in post-modern democracies, in particular. The paradox is this: there is both an objective and subjective decline in the level of strategic threats to modern nations. The reduced gravity of strategic threats is most pronounced in those parts of the globe that are made up of modern, industrialized democracies. Declining threats reduce public willingness to pay the price of maintaining sizeable armed forces. This is often translated into lower defence budgets, smaller armies, and increased sensitivity to human and material costs associated with using these forces in missions. Such constraints reduce both the quality and combat readiness of the armed forces of modern democracies. Concomitantly, reduced threat perceptions raise the reluctance of leaders and the public to use force. This may be exploited by challengers of the current order in ways that the security community in modern democracies may find difficult to meet effectively. The overall cost of dealing with such future challenges may well be considerably higher than the cost of maintaining high-quality professional armed forces.

The major type of military challenge to modern states is that of low-intensity conflict (LIC), and – in a world of increased interdependence – peacekeeping missions. The generally poor performance of armed forces in these settings raises the likelihood of growing challenges to modern states in the future. If and when strategic threats arise again, modern military forces may be at a major disadvantage. The main strategy for coping that is now discussed in modern strategic thinking is technological. Technology is seen as the great leap forward which would provide relatively inexpensive and efficient substitutes for human-intensive armed forces. However, the cult of technology, like other strategic fashions in the past, may be defeated by its own strategic contradiction: primitive warfare.

The aim of this chapter is threefold: First, to document this paradox of modern strategy, by discussing trends in the relations between armed forces and societies in modern democracies, and providing several examples from Europe, the United

G.C. de Nooy (ed.), The Clausewitzian Dictum and the Future of Western Military Strategy, 43-58.

States, and Israel (a supposedly special case). Second, the implications of these relations will be discussed in terms of various scenarios of war and peace in global politics. Third, possible ways out of this paradox will be dealt with, focusing on the traditional people's army concept, the professional army concept, and a mixed approach.

None of these models is satisfactory as a stand-alone strategy. The most effective solution of the problems of modern army and modern security challenges, lies in models of international cooperation rather than on national models of army-society relations.

Declining Threats and Military Policy in Western Democracies

The end of the Cold War was clearly a watershed in threat perceptions in the 'First World'. But the collapse of the Soviet Union was only one aspect of a general trend of reduced threat perceptions all over the world. A number of significant danger spots of a lesser nature outside of Europe were beginning to transform themselves in the late 1980s and early 1990s. In Latin America, long-standing conflicts such as that between Chile and Argentina, and strategic competitions between Argentina and Brazil, reached final settlements. The major conflict in Africa, that in and around South Africa, moved towards resolution. In the Middle East, the Madrid peace process and the subsequent agreements of Oslo, Israel-Jordan, and Is-raeli-Syrian negotiations, along with the continued UN sanctions on Iraq, all served to reduce the immediate risks of large-scale conflagrations around the globe.

These reduced threats were expressed in shrinking defence budgets both of the major powers and of various minor powers. Defence burdens among Western democracies went down by an average of 25 per cent over the last decade. Some Western democracies that had been among the most militarized states in the globe have reduced their defence burdens by a major extent. For example, Israel's defence burden (defined as a proportion of defence expenditures of the GDP) went down from a high of 22 per cent in 1975 to a 9.8 per cent level in 1996. The defence burden of the US went down from 6.6 per cent in 1986 to 3.2 per cent in 1996. In most cases, this reduction in defence burdens was accompanied by shrinking sizes of armed forces. The armed forces of the United States declined by 46 per cent from the mid-1980s. The reduction in the size of the armed forces of other states was more moderate but the trend is crystal clear.

These trends reflect the adjustment of states to a new international environment that is characterized by lower levels of perceived risks. These reduced risks impose lesser security requirements. But they also affect public willingness to bear the – human and material – costs of defence. High defence budgets or large armed forces, as well as a large number of advanced and costly weapon systems, have become more difficult to justify to a public that wants less government spending. Alternatively, public demands for transfer of funds from military affairs to welfare programmes are more difficult to resist given shrinking strategic threats. Thus, both objective needs and public pressure serve to bring about a shrinking of defence spending and smaller-sized armed forces.

SELECTING THE RIGHT KIND OF PEOPLE

These declining threats have also had an important effect on the reduction in the ability of armed forces to recruit the right kind of people for the military profession. First, there is a systematic decline in the prestige and attractiveness of military service in all modern societies. This decline is most pronounced in Western democracies. In the past, military schools have been the choice of some of the most important social elites in such states. This is no longer a fact. The professional officer corps that was made up largely of people trained in military academies is now a changed corps. The armed forces have always been a social mobility instrument for lower classes. These people could rise in the ranks due to their skills and qualities up to a certain point and thus become better integrated into civil society upon retirement. Thus, the attractiveness of military service to both the elites and lower classes served to supply modern military forces with a backbone of commissioned and non-commissioned command and training personnel that could convert a peacetime armed force to a wartime armed force in a relatively short time and a relatively efficient manner.

This capacity to maintain a high-quality permanent personnel at the level of commissioned and non-commissioned command is what enabled rapid expansion of armed forces in wartime situations. But what also helped was the fact that most modern societies were engaged in some kind of warfare or potential warfare throughout the Cold War. Shrinking and declining colonialism had brought with it a series of military challenges that still required active involvement by military forces in combat operations. Most major powers fought some wars throughout the Cold War: the United States in Korea, Vietnam, and the Gulf; the United Kingdom in Korea, Suez, the Falklands, and the Gulf; France in Korea, Indo-China, Suez, Algeria, and the Gulf; the former Soviet Union in Hungary and Afghanistan; and China in Korea, India, and Vietnam.

These war involvements, as well as more limited military operations, have invoked a certain level of patriotism that enabled the various states to sustain a certain level of readiness and proficiency of their armed forces. Although many of these wars have invoked major internal controversies, and have also involved large-scale efforts to evade mandatory draft orders, they have also been responsible for creating active and professional armies with considerable combat experience. Thus, even though the Cold War was mostly cold, the professional armies of most major states kept a relatively effective level of proficiency and readiness, both in terms of human resources and in terms of technology and training.

This applies even more to other states where the level of basic threat remained high throughout their existence. Israel is a good example. The compulsory military service was originally designed to enable a state with a small population to maintain a relatively large standing army. However, over the years, military service became a major social institution. Military service defined a minimum level of social acceptability. Men, but also women who were not drafted, for medical and even more so for non-medical reasons, found it increasingly difficult to get jobs, to become part of social elites, and were openly ridiculed and criticized in public. They were seen as having evaded a fundamental social responsibility. However, social status was affected not only by the question of whether one had served in the IDF, but where and how long one had served. Service in combat units, officer rank, and especially long-term participation in the professional IDF provided entry tickets to the job market, social circles, to businesses, and to respectability in Israeli society.[1]

Under these circumstances, the IDF's main problem has been selecting the best people for its best units, and for professional military careers after three years of compulsory service. The IDF also had more problems of many candidates competing for internal command and staff openings, than in getting the right people to volunteer for such jobs. However, the growing political polarization of Israeli society over basic foreign and security policy issues, the economic development of the state, and the declining level of threat have considerably reduced motivation to join the IDF in the first place, and to continue service in the professional armed forces, in more general terms. Because of a baby boom in the late 1970s, and because of declining defence budgets, the IDF still does not experience acute problems in drafting people, but there are already emerging pockets of volunteer problems, of keeping the right people in the IDF beyond the compulsory service period, and of drafting good people to non-elite combat units.[2]

At present, the IDF drafts less than 80 per cent of eligible males and less than 65 per cent of eligible women. If we consider as problematic those populations that do not finish the entire compulsory service period (those who receive honourable or dishonourable discharge before their time), the numbers are down to 70 per cent for males and 50 per cent for females. Since the structure of the IDF is such that it is based on a sizeable reserve force, these problems are even more pronounced in the turnout of reservists to active duty. The numbers there are unofficial, but in some cases turnout rates are below 50 per cent.

Surveys conducted among high school seniors and among reservists show a fundamental change in norms. Evasion of service is no longer seen as a social

---

1   Edward Luttwak and Dan Horowitz, *The Israeli Army* (London: Allen Lane, 1975).
2   Yoram Yair, 'Security, Human, and Social Challenges for the IDF', in *The IDF, Israeli Society, and the Political Process* (in Hebrew), (Tel-Aviv: Jaffee Center for Strategic Studies, 1995).

taboo. On the contrary, a growing minority views service as an aberration, and volunteering to elite and combat units as not particularly smart or socially desirable. Among reservists, the evasion problem is mostly explained in terms of emulation of what others are or have been doing all the time. Those who show up for reserve service are seen both by themselves and by their peers as 'suckers' and thus feel exploited. From this feeling to actual evasion of service, the road is short.

THE IMPACT OF THE TECHNOLOGICAL REVOLUTION

There is another trend that imposes considerable restrictions on the ability of modern armed forces to cope effectively with the shortage of personnel: the technological revolution. The transformation of modern large-scale warfare from a human-intensive art to a technology-intensive one does not necessarily require large numbers of recruits – in this sense, the technological revolution somewhat relieves the burden of quantitative shortages – but rather the 'right' kind of recruits. Modern armed forces need increasing numbers of technologically proficient and intelligent recruits who would be able to operate sophisticated and extremely expensive equipment. However, these skills are also socially desirable skills. Modern armies must thus compete with modern industries, private organizations, and other social attractions for the same people. Moreover, modern armed forces must not only recruit the right people, they must also keep them. The cost of recruiting and retaining the right people becomes extremely high, and sometimes military commands must make tough choices between developing new equipment, purchasing new weapon systems, and paying personnel to operate old systems. Again, to give an example with which I am more familiar, the salary and compensation bracket in the Israeli defence budget for 1997 is 48 per cent as opposed to 34 per cent in the mid-1980s. The procurement bracket in the IDF budget dropped to 32 per cent from a level of 40 per cent. Considering that modern systems are far more expensive than older versions of the same systems, and given shrinking defence budgets, the problem of maintaining a high-quality military force, both in terms of weapon systems and in terms of personnel, is becoming insurmountable.

As long as the perception of reduced basic threats is commensurate to objective reality, these problems have led most modern armies in the West to a conception of backbone armed forces. Backbone armed forces is a notion that envisions the most important objective of the armed forces in times of peace as being to maintain a certain level of development that would enable them to grow rapidly into large-scale human and material-intensive armies if threats increase. This implies two things. First, in terms of equipment, modernization still has priority. However, since the main trait of the technological revolution is the extremely rapid pace by which it renders obsolete certain weapon and support systems that were considered to be top of the line just few years ago, modernization comes at an increasing cost. Hence, research and development has to a large extent substituted actual mass production of weapon systems. Industries that had produced strictly military equipment are now producing dual-use technologies. Weapon production in the Western world is mostly fed not by internal budgets but by arms sales to developing states. These sales of weapon systems that have become obsolete in the West help pay for research and development of more modern systems in an era where government funds for such purposes are becoming lean. The key effort in terms of technological proficiency is thus to be up to date on research and development, not so much in terms of preparing mass weapon systems that would be available for larger armed forces should they be needed. The assumption here is that the mass production of weapon systems would take place side by side with the quantitative growth of the armed forces if threats change.[3]

Second, in terms of personnel, the existing professional armed forces are seen as the foundation for larger armies. Existing staff will be the superstructure of larger armies, should they be needed. Existing staff will have responsibility for both training and command of the larger armed forces. For that reason, preference is given for lower levels of turnaround inside the armed forces, implying preferences for longer careers than for younger officers. In some sense, we may be going back to a model of professional armed forces of the eighteenth century (and to a lesser extent of the nineteenth century) in terms of development of a model of service careers. The increased cost of human resources reflects this fact quite well.

Maintenance of highly trained professional armed forces, which also serve as a backbone for larger armed forces in times of renewed security threats, has thus become the main challenge of modern democratic societies. The task of developing and maintaining backbone but highly skilled armed forces is facing greater objective obstacles, including declining threat perceptions, lower defence budgets, economic development, and growing competition between military and civilian sectors over similar or identical skills, and declining prestige of and motivation for service in the armed forces. All these objective developments are independent of the changing nature of warfare. They assume, to some extent, that old-style wars which entail large-scale clashes between or among armed forces might return at some point. And armed forces of the present must serve as a backbone for the armed forces that would be needed if good old warfare returns.

There is, however, another challenge to the ability of armed forces to meet future requirements. That challenge involves fundamental changes in the balance and nature of extant missions of the armed forces of democratic states.

---

3   Eric Arnett, 'Military Research and Development', in *SIPRI Yearbook, 1996: Armaments, Disarmament, and International Security* (Oxford and New York: Oxford University Press, 1996), pp. 381-409.

The Social and Strategic Challenges of LIC

Modern democracies face two types of Low-Intensity Conflicts (LIC): guerrilla warfare and terrorism. It is not necessary to discuss these types of LIC in detail here, yet we should describe the kind of problems they impose on the use of force and the social implications of these problems. Five basic characteristics of LIC are important in this context.

First, LIC often eliminate the separation between battlefield and the rear, and between military and non-military victims of combat operations. One could argue that in modern warfare this distinction has also been eliminated in full-fledged wars due to air raids and missile attacks on population and industrial centres. This is true, as long as full-fledged war is viewed as such by everyone, and assuming that there is consensus on the need to fight and win the war, people are willing – up to a point – to pay this price. Since LICs are not regarded as equivalent to High-Intensity Conflicts (HICs), this lack of separation between battlefield and rear, and between military and civilian victims, makes everyone feel vulnerable.

Second, in LIC, the relationship between tactical and strategic victory is not linear. In some cases it may well be an inverse relationship. The uneven sensitivity of the combatants to fatalities may create paradoxical situations of the type experienced by the French in Algeria, by the United States in Vietnam, and by Israel in Lebanon, namely that as the number of tactical victories grew larger, the willingness and ability to bring the war to a favourable military conclusion declined. In fact, all of these states have won all of the battles in these wars. Yet all three states were humiliated by their – weaker – opponents and had to withdraw with their tail between their legs. Over time, the public in states fighting LICs evaluates performance not in terms of the outcome of specific encounters, but rather in terms of the cumulative number of fatalities. At some point this figure becomes unbearable. However, the key to victory in such wars is persistence and willingness to suffer costs. When this balance of resolve and cost-bearing is shifting in favour of the guerrilla or terrorist organizations, the battle was essentially decided.

Third, in LICs, states operate with one of their hands tied behind their back due to legal and moral – internal and external – restrictions on the use of force. States fighting guerrilla and terrorist organizations must do so in ways that could, at least in principle, be defended legally or politically. This imposes considerable constraints on the use of force against opponents. Not only are there obvious legal, moral, and political restrictions on how, when, and where force is used by the armed forces of democratic states, but there is also a question of effectiveness of brute force against a basically hostile population in many of the circumstances where such wars are waged. The use of large-scale brute force typically worked against the democracy using it against civilian populations, while the same type of brute force worked for the guerrillas and terrorists. The reason was that the brute use of force by democracies encountered internal and international opposition due to the seeming violation of legal and moral imperatives, while the same type of use of force by guerrillas and terrorists effectively terrorized populations precisely because it showed the limits of protection by large and cumbersome armed forces.

Fourth, LICs give advantage to parties that are capable of causing considerable damage through the use of primitive technology, rather than to technologically intensive states. As in the case of the relationship between tactical victory and strategic defeat, there is a seemingly inverse relationship between technology and performance in LICs. Sophisticated technology is most vulnerable to primitive technology. If you can shoot down a $10 million attack helicopter with a bazooka that costs a couple of hundred dollars on the black market, technology works against those who own it.

The inability of sophisticated technology to deal with LIC was demonstrated time and again in modern history. However, the Grapes of Wrath Operation in April 1996 demonstrates this extremely well. Over a period of twelve days, the IDF, using smart bombs, attack helicopters, F-15s and F-16 top-of-the-line jets, modern artillery, and unmanned remote-control reconnaissance planes, bombed the hell out of southern Lebanon, bringing about a large-scale evacuation of the area by civilian populations. Yet, during this period, the Hizbollah, through the use of primitive means such as transportation of rockets on donkeys, fired over 56 Katyusha rockets at Israeli villages in the north. The killer of this operation was the blunder bombardment of a civilian shelter in Kafar Kana, where over one hundred women, children, and men were killed by Israeli shelling.

Fifth, LIC changes the balance between ends and means in warfare. Guerrillas use drastic means, from a moral and human perspective, in order to achieve goals that for their targets are limited. Guerrilla operations are eventually successful because they do not threaten basic security goals of the target. What for guerrillas constitutes essential goals, is of limited scope for the targets. This reduces the willingness of the target of LIC to resist this type of warfare. If and when the goals of guerrillas are strategic, or are perceived as such by the target, the balance of forces, rather than the balance of resolve is what determines the eventual outcome of LIC.[4]

These five principles of LIC apply both to guerrilla warfare and to terrorism. Both have succeeded when the balance of stakes favoured the weak party, and both have failed when the target was more powerful and the balance of stakes was even or favoured the target. Yet overall it is generally true that the record of performance of modern armies in LIC is abysmal. And it is also generally true that this record of performance had far-reaching effects on the development and strength of conventional armies, and that this poor performance in LIC imposed great constraints on

---

4   Yehoshafat Harkabi, *War and Strategy* (in Hebrew), (Tel-Aviv: Ma'arachot, 1990).

the use of force by Western democracies in various arenas of limited conflict, especially in the context of peacekeeping operations.

It is equally important to note, however, that the relationship between the success of the weaker, more primitive party in LIC operations is paradoxical in the long term. When guerrilla operations culminated in the realization of the guerrilla movement's goals, chiefly that of national independence, the states that were formed generally emerged as poor, ineffective, even failed states. In many cases, these new states were plagued by internal conflict and civil violence. In many cases, the leadership of the guerrilla organization had an easier time running and winning the military campaign before statehood, than running the state once independence was realized.

Implications: Future Threats to National Security

Several implications follow from the preceding discussion with respect to the kind of security threats that modern, democratic, developed states may face in the future. Not all of these threats are of a military nature, but even so, these threats may have military ramifications.

THE RELATIONSHIP BETWEEN DOMESTIC INSTABILITY AND INTERNATIONAL WAR

It was shown that there is an intimate link between domestic instability and international conflict.[5] States emerging through revolutionary political processes, often involving LIC against colonial states or other types of oppressive political organizations, tend to be involved in a great deal of conflict in the first period of national independence. The same applies to existing states undergoing violent political change. Moreover, violent political change in the strategic environment of stable states often draws them into conflict.

We do not know whether states in the international system are becoming more or less stable domestically, but those states that are threatened by internal violence and internal instability may become the source and target of conflict. As more states

---

5   Steven Walt, *Revolution and War* (Ithaca, NY: Cornell University Press, 1996); Steven Walt, 'Revolution and War', *World Politics*, 44(3), 1992, pp. 321-48; Zeev Maoz, 'Joining the Club of Nations: Political Development and International Conflict', *International Studies Quarterly*, 33(2), 1989, pp. 199-231; and Zeev Maoz, 'The Evolution of the Middle East Military Balance, 1980-1995', in Ephraim Kam and Zeev Eytan, eds, *The Middle East Military Balance, 1994-1995* (Jerusalem and Boulder, CO: Jerusalem Post and Westview Press, 1996), pp. 66-92.

undergo violent political change, the need or urge to use military force against them increases.

ECONOMIC DOWNTURNS AND INTERNATIONAL CONFLICT

Again, recent empirical evidence suggests that economic downturns – that is, negative growth, growing unemployment, inflation, and unpayable foreign debt – are likely to be associated with growing levels of conflict.[6] This is particularly a problem when states that experience economic downturns live side by side with states that experience rapid economic growth. Economic imbalances increase incentives to engage in military conflict.

NATIONALISTIC OR ECONOMIC FRUSTRATIONS MAY BE TRANSFORMED INTO EXPANSIONIST AND AGGRESSIVE IDEOLOGIES

Revisionist ideologies such as Islamic fundamentalism strive on poverty, exploitation, and corruption. They build a popular infrastructure that addresses the needs and hopes of exploited classes in poor states that live under the rule of ineffective and corrupt regimes. Yet the ideologies that these movements produce are not directed at the local government alone, but at the entire regional and international order that tolerates the government, and against neighbours and global powers that are depicted as striving on local misery and poverty. Once in power, these ideologies may either convert into responsible governments that operate under the imperatives of *realpolitik*, yet they may seek to rise to power and maintain it through the use of external scapegoating strategies in which they divert attention from internal difficulties by mobilizing the public against external enemies. Since the targets of such radical ideologies are often to be found in the West, the threat of radicalism constitutes a long-term threat to Western security.

TECHNOLOGY DOES NOT CAUSE WAR, BUT IT AFFECTS THE WAYS IN WHICH IT IS FOUGHT

First, the most sophisticated technologies may be obtained and operated by radical movements and factors and used to blackmail and terrorize modern states. The use of chemical terrorism is no longer in the realm of fiction since Tokyo's subway attack. The potential to acquire fissile material and to produce a bomb or to get hold of a nuclear weapon has increased dramatically since the collapse of the Soviet

---

6   Zeev Maoz and Bruce Russett, 'Normative and Structural Causes of Democratic Peace, 1946-1986', *American Political Science Review*, 87(3), 1993, pp. 620-38; and John Oneal, Frances Oneal, Zeev Maoz and Bruce Russett, 'The Liberal Peace: Interdependence, Democracy, and International Conflict, 1950-1985', *Journal of Peace Research*, Vol. 33, No. 1 (February 1996), pp. 11-28.

Union. On the other hand, sophisticated technology may define uncrossable limits that are so clear that they limit escalation by nuclear states against non-nuclear threats. It is no mere chance that while nuclear states did not fight each other, they did fight non-nuclear states. Not only did their success rate in these wars leave something to be desired, but they failed to use or threaten the use of nuclear weapons in any effective manner.

Moreover, LIC-related threats may turn into HIC-related threats at more advanced stages of warfare, and as guerrillas feel increasingly confident and approach the stage of statehood. By that point, the resolve of the opponent is exhausted, and thus even if the opponent is strategically superior, it cannot or will not convert this superiority into a final victory on the battlefield.

WARS ARE FOUGHT OVER A FAIRLY NARROW RANGE OF ISSUES

The issues underlying traditional war have not disappeared. There is no structural reason why states would not continue to pursue their objectives through the large-scale use of force.

Some of the principal issues over which war was fought consist of the following:[7] territory, ideas, people and resources. The world in which we live has yet to find solutions to most of these problems. In addition, some of these problems have now assumed compound proportions (for example, lots of people have few resources, while few people enjoy an increasingly large share of the world's resources. This imbalance is the stuff upon which radical ideologies and radical movements develop and thrive).

REDUCED WILLINGNESS TO FIGHT AND TO BEAR THE BURDEN OF WARFARE

The reduced willingness to fight and to bear the human and material burden of warfare may expose modern developed states to increased challenges of a direct and indirect nature in the future. The more reluctant that these states appear to be at present, the more likely such threats are to materialize in the future. Saddam Hussein's decision to invade Kuwait was probably influenced by his belief that the United States would not react militarily to this invasion. It was also influenced quite probably by his perception that the Arab League would not join the bandwagon. Finally, his crisis management technique during the period between August 1990 and January 1991 was based on the notion that, when push comes to shove, the West would try to avoid high-casualty warfare and would back down at the last minute. He was not too wide off the mark, considering the vote in the US Congress.

---

7   John A. Vasquez, *The War Puzzle* (Cambridge: Cambridge University Press, 1993).

The Cult of Technology: Western Strategic Thought and the Response to the Security Paradox

Strategy progresses in paradoxical cycles, because it is essentially a duel of minds in which each side it trying to outsmart the opponent, thus taking him out of balance.[8] For that reason, as long as the opponent is powerful, technologically advanced, socially homogenous and politically unified, LIC constitutes the more effective means of warfare. Yet LIC has important limitations. First, LIC does not, in and of itself, produce the infrastructure for the guerrilla organization to function as a government. As soon as it realizes its goals, which are – by and large – national independence, most successful guerrilla organizations make poor governments in failed states. Very often the groups that bring states to independence tend to fail as governments. Unless new groups or coalitions come to power which can better function as civil governments, many governments that were successful in defeating powerful colonial opponents become the worst enemies of the new states. If we look at some of the most glorious victories of guerrilla operations against powerful states some years after independence or liberty, we see Algeria crumbling in civil war, Vietnam beginning to develop only twenty years after liberation, Afghanistan replacing war of liberation with civil war that rips that country apart, Kenya still searching for its path to development, and Yemen and Aden still one of the poorest, least stable and underdeveloped states on this planet.

Likewise, those powerful states that have failed abysmally in their LIC experience are the most effective, prosperous, stable states, and have become increasingly so after abandoning their colonial experience. States such as the United Kingdom and France may have lost their empires, but on balance they may be better off without their colonies than with them.

However, as the ability of modern industrialized democracies to sustain large-scale, effective armed forces diminishes, and as democracies are increasingly perceived as vulnerable to risky military operations which entail major loss of life, the temptation to pose political and military challenges to democracies – especially of an indirect nature – may actually increase. This is the problem that constitutes the principal nightmare of strategic planners in modern industrialized democracies.

Under these circumstances, several key principles characterize the response of modern strategic doctrines and force building and deployment practices of Western democracies.

---

8   Zeev Maoz, *Paradoxes of War: On the Art of National Self-Entrapment* (Boston, MA: Unwin Hyman, 1990).

MAINTENANCE AND OPERATION OF BACKBONE ARMED FORCES

These are small, professional armed forces, with a rapid deployment capacity that serves as a foundation for larger armies. The idea here is that if the fundamental threats change again, the professional army will constitute the first rapid deployment contingent of initial warfare, mostly through high-tech air and sea power as well as through special force operations. Moreover, the personnel of these armed forces will serve as the nucleus of training and command of general conscript armed forces which would have to be mobilized.

TOP-OF-THE-LINE TECHNOLOGY, DESIGNED TO SOLVE PROBLEMS AND SUBSTITUTE FOR LACK OF PERSONNEL

Increasing resources will go to establishing technological superiority, thus resulting in qualitative arms races that are in some respects more expensive than quantitative arms races. States would try to establish deterrence through qualitative edge and technological superiority. Because both politicians and generals are incapable of finding effective solutions to the deterioration of the military profession's prestige and the quality of personnel, they will try to deal with the problem by throwing money at it. The military solution will be to create narrow specializations, thus somehow enabling the gap between declining manpower quality and military effectiveness to narrow. We see the implications of this trend in the Middle East, with the Egyptian and Saudi (and recently the Jordanian) armed forces undergoing technological revolutions. In the Egyptian and Jordanian case, there is enough high-quality manpower to support the technological revolution. However in the Saudi case this is throwing good money after bad, because Saudi society lacks the basic skills to sustain high-tech armed forces. The only use of these weapons systems are as pre-positioned systems in the case of threat to be met by American troops.

THE CULT OF TECHNOLOGY

Star Wars-like military doctrines are seen as an ultimate escape from the paradox of security: where people are not willing to bear the human costs of warfare (or as Martin van Creveld put it, they lost the will or the reason to be willing to die), technology is seen as providing a substitute. There are several problems with these solutions.

First, these solutions are susceptible to LIC. No technological innovation can overcome the primitive and brutal nature of LIC, especially in terms of its terrorist version. In fact, as armed forces become increasingly dependent on technology, the gap between potential and actual performance is wider and causes greater psychological and political problems. Second, in the final analysis, it is labour-intensive warfare that determines decision in war. Old-fashioned occupation of territory through the use of land engagements, command of the air and the seas cannot be substituted by precision guided munitions (PGM) warfare.

Many future threats to peace are of a non-military nature, and many solutions to these problems are collective solutions, of both a military and non-military nature. The problems of modern armies are not only about how to fight and win wars, but how to prevent them from breaking out. War prevention must deal with the underlying causes of the war, because technology may not be useful in deterring immediate causes once these are expressed.

Every technology can be exploited. Consider nuclear weapons, and the performance of nuclear powers in LICs. The Roman Empire was not defeated by an opposing power of its own size and sophistication. Nor did the British, French, Russian, and even the American empires collapse because they lost the arms race or were washed away by technological breakthroughs. Rather, these empires collapsed in the face of rather primitive opposition from a strategic perspective, where technology could not be applied to solve the problems.

Models of Army-Society Relations

Three major models define relations between armed forces and society. The first is the comprehensive draft model, which relies on compulsory service for males in a certain age group (and in a state such as Israel includes women). In this model, the armed forces and society are one and the same, and in some cases this unity is preserved even after compulsory service because of reserve duty. This model can survive as long as security threats are considered significant or because of long-term convention (such as in some European states like Switzerland), but only when service period is relatively brief. On the whole, declining threats make this model inapplicable, and over time there is an erosion in the comprehensiveness of the service, even when threats are considered relatively high.

The second model is the professional armed force: an all-volunteer armed force in which people serve for an extended period and develop long-term military careers. This is the prevalent model in most Western democracies, and some of its problems were discussed above. It can work well as long as there is a nucleus of high-quality professional officer corps that can develop and sustain a highly professional military force, and as long as the level of recruits is sufficiently high to permit a backbone armed force that serves both as a rapid deployment force in short-term emergency situations and as a skeleton for a comprehensive drafted armed force if things become really bad for a longer period.

The combined model consists of a skeleton of a professional armed force, which constitutes an almost exclusively professional set of services (for example, the air force and navy), and a mixed professional-general recruitment armed force in the army. Since the air force and navy are more technology intensive and technical than the army, they are less dependent on large quantities of personnel at a lower level. What they require is people with specific skills and long experience. Hence it makes more sense to base them on a professional career personnel. On the other hand, non-commissioned personnel in the army can operate best if drafted for a limited period, and some gradually advanced in rank. Since not everybody can be advanced, it makes more sense to base lower rank personnel on people drafted for a limited period.

This model may overcome some of the previous problems, but it also suffers from the same difficulties as the two previous models. Over time, the objective factors that work against a high-quality professional armed force are bound to affect the professional branches of the air force and navy. The problem of army recruitment is bound to be the same as in the general draft model, and – because this model is based on selective draft – is more serious in the long run.

Conclusion

The factors mentioned herein suggest constant erosion in the quality of armed forces in modern developed democracies. As long as the threats facing such democracies remain low, this may not be a major problem. Modern states prosper in their non-military functions. They become welfare-providing agents more than security-providing ones. And in this capacity, modern democracies are doing quite well. Yet security threats may not diminish, rather they may become even more pronounced because of the perceived deterioration in the capacity of modern democracies to meet challenges by force. These trends, then, threaten the long-term revival of effective armed forces.

Is there a solution to the paradox that states governed by the people may be ill-equipped to provide long-term security for the people? Since the future problems facing modern democracies are not necessarily of the 'good guys' 'bad guys' type, the answer seems to lie in strategic cooperation, burden-sharing, and division of labour among Western democracies. Given that democracies do not fight each other because of shared norms of compromise and cooperation,[9] the challenges come from outside the democratic network or from non-democratic forces within those networks.

Despite significant problems, NATO is still one of the most successful models of collective security and strategic cooperation in modern history. NATO expansion must be done not in terms of who is in and who is out, but in terms of strict definition of common values and common stakes. Everyone sharing and exercising

---

9   Zeev Maoz and Bruce Russett, 'The Liberal Peace' (see note 6).

these values, most importantly the effective practice of democracy, should be made part of the Alliance. Strategic cooperation may enable each state to keep a small but high-quality standing armed force. The reason is that challenges and threats are not presented to the public in strict national terms, but rather in a collective one. The missions for such armed forces go beyond the national, but the security of the state is ensured by a relatively small investment. In such cases, it is the collective armed forces of the security community that provide a deterrent in the case of larger threats, and the level of readiness and proficiency at a collective level can compensate for some of the problems of professional armed forces at the national level.

5 Post-modern Societies and Future Support for Military Missions

Jan van der Meulen

Introduction: Towards a Constabulary Force

Almost forty years ago, in the midst of the Cold War, Morris Janowitz, dean of military sociology, formulated a visionary rationale for the armed forces: 'The military establishment becomes a constabulary force when it is continuously prepared to act, committed to the minimum use of force, and seeks viable international relations, rather than victory, because it has incorporated a protective military posture. The constabulary outlook is grounded in, and extends, pragmatic doctrine. The constabulary force concept encompasses the entire range of military power and organization. At the upper end are the weapons of mass destruction; those of flexible and specialized capacity are at the lower end, including the specialists in military aid programmes, in para-military operations, in guerilla and counter-guerilla warfare.'[1] Understandably, in recent years this rationale is again frequently being called upon and paraphrased.[2] Its main terms – 'continuously prepared to act', 'minimum use of violence', 'viable international relations', 'protective posture', 'pragmatic doctrine' – all these elegantly fit post-Cold War conceptions about intervention and crisis management. It has been argued that because of the connotation with the unarmed British constable – 'keeping peace through civility, morality and his whistle' – the choice of words is unfortunate.[3]

---

1 Morris Janowitz, *The Professional Soldier: A Social and Political Portrait* (New York: The Free Press, 1960), p. 418.

2 See, especially, James Burk, ed., *The Military in New Times: Adapting Armed Forces to a Turbulent World* (Boulder, CO: Westview Press, 1994) in chapters by Burk (p. 16), Dandeker (p. 121), Segal and Waldman (pp. 163-4). See also G. Teitler, *Grensbeveiliging en Grensverlegging* (Breda: Koninklijke Militaire Academie, 1993), p. 11; Wilfried von Bredow, *Turbulente Welt-Ordnung: Internationale Politik am Ende des 20. Jahrhunderts* (Stuttgart: Kohlhammer, 1994),p. 108; and Bernard Boëne, 'Minimum Force, Third Party Action and Humanitarian Assistance', *Conference Paper* (Bielefeld: ISA World Congress, RC01, 1994), pp. 6-8.

3 David Segal, *Recruiting for Uncle Sam: Citizenship and Military Manpower Policy* (Wichita, KS: University Press of Kansas, 1989), p. 131.

59

G.C. de Nooy (ed.), The Clausewitzian Dictum and the Future of Western Military Strategy, 59-74.
© 1997 *Kluwer Law International. Printed in the Netherlands.*

Admittedly, the temptation is real to overlook the proviso of the constabulary concept: 'encompasses the entire range of military power', to wit, all the way from nuclear weapons to humanitarian aid. In fact Janowitz himself occasionally preferred to focus on the lower end of the spectrum, for instance, when contrasting his views with those of military professionals. The latter, preoccupied with the upper end of the application of force, just as he had expected, did not like the word 'constabulary', but Janowitz stressed: 'I like the symbolism of international policing and peacekeeping'.[4]

In a way, however, this temptation (momentarily) to forget about the upper end of military means, along with the more violent options at the lower end ('contra-guerilla'!), makes the constabulary concept all the more suited to present-day circumstances, because the identification of evolving soldierly tasks and skills with 'peacekeeping' can be looked upon as the very challenge that 'the people', 'the government' and 'the military' are wrestling with. Each player in the trinity has its owns reasons, methods and moments for either emphasizing or downplaying the centrality of peacekeeping, with or without whistle.

In this chapter, the perspective of 'the people' and the ways in which its relationships with the military, with soldiers and with the application of force are changing will be focused upon. At its most concise this comes down to interpreting public support for (new) missions; at its broadest our focus implies an analysis of civil-military relations, of armed forces within post-modern societies. By now the latter adjective and its connotations – turbulence and fragmentation, uncertainty and relativism – have become fairly common in the paradigm of military sociology. Characteristic for the overall development of society, post-modernity is looked upon as including current and future conflict but also military organization itself.[5] Admittedly, with the vanishing of the Cold War and the phasing out of the mass army, some 'big stories' (*'grosse Erzählungen'*) have reached the end of their line. Again, the vision of a constabulary force seems to fill the gap nicely, as (long as) it is tailored to the numerous 'niches'[6] that crisis management on the international security market offers.

The issues at hand will be tackled as follows. First, through exposing major developments in civil-military relations ('trends: demilitarization and civilian-

---

4   Morris Janowitz, 'Civic Consciousness and Military Performance', in Morris Janowitz and Stephen D. Wesbrook, eds, *The Political Education of Soldiers* (Beverly Hills, CA: Sage Publications, 1983), p. 76.
5   For instance, Jim Seaton, 'Shedding our Skin: Approaching Post-modern Conflict', *Conference Paper* (Baltimore, MD: Inter-University Seminar on Armed Forces and Society [IUS], 1993); Von Bredow, *Turbulente Weltordnung;* Charles C. Moskos and James Burk, 'The Post-modern Military', in Burk, *The Military in New Times*, pp. 141-63; Jürgen Kuhlmann and Ekkehard Lippert, 'About the Decline of Conscription in Post-modern Germany', *Conference Paper* (Baltimore, MD: IUS, 1995).
6   'Niche-warfare' is an expression used by A. Toffler and H. Toffler, *De nieuwe krijgselite - Strategie, tactiek en de derde golf* (Amsterdam: 1994).

ization'), we will further pin down the framework and the focus of this chapter. Then in subsequent sections, we will close the net around public support in two steps: the end of conscription ('zero-draft: causes and consequences') and the tolerance for casualties ('zero-dead: the meaning of risks'). In the concluding section ('no mandate for all seasons'), we will briefly, and a little polemically, summarize the thrust of the argument.

Two final preliminary remarks: first, two main perspectives are traditionally used in the literature on civil-military relations. On the one hand, as in this chapter, a general sociological perspective entailing 'society' and 'public'; on the other hand a more narrow one, fitting in with political science, focusing on the dynamics of political control of the military versus professional autonomy. Of course, at certain points and moments the two perspectives intersect, but basically the latter one will not be our business here. The second remark: the scope of this chapter is the West, but this will not in any way entail a systematic comparison of say sixteen countries, (former) neutrals and Anzacs to be added. Instead, the presupposition is that, notwithstanding noteworthy peculiarities, the major trends apply to most, if not all, Western countries. This legitimizes hopping from one country to another and shopping through a diversity of data, but of course it results in a somewhat haphazard, or shall we say, post-modern picture?

Trends: Demilitarization and Civilianization

When public opinion is asked in a survey to give priority to policy goals, one can almost be certain that 'defence' ranks low in comparison to education, health-care, fighting crime, creating jobs, environmental care and other things directly related to daily life and daily discourse.[7] Granted we can expect some fluctuations, in time and between countries, but this looks like an almost 'natural' ranking for defence, unless of course an immanent threat to national security is at hand and/or unless we are dealing with a garrison-state type of society. In years to come, in the Western societies to which we are referring, these other priorities – social and economic – will definitely go on to be felt as even more pressing than military defence against diffuse threats, or even military intervention for the sake of humanitarian causes. In itself this should not be interpreted as a pertinent sign of public indifference or apathy towards the military. And as we shall see later, it does not preclude support for intervention. It does tell us something, however, about the 'place' of armed

---

7   An example of such a priority list in the UK is quoted by Christopher Dandeker, 'The Military in Democratic Societies: New Times and New Patterns of Civil-Military Relations', *Conference Paper* (Marshall Center: Garmisch Partenkirchen, 1996).

forces in society, and this is an observation to be kept in mind when trying to assess major trends *vis-à-vis* the military.

POST-MILITARY SOCIETY

We are witnessing a 'demilitarization' of society in the West.[8] Allegedly, the process is not without ambiguities and it does not imply the impending vanishing of military organizations. Society can be looked upon as becoming 'post-military',[9] in the same vein as it is labelled post-industrial or indeed post-modern. Neither industry nor modernity have disappeared. With yet another comparison: secularization will not bring about the end of the church, let alone of religion. There is no denying, however, that over time its role in Western society has changed, dare we say diminished, dramatically. All three examples testify to transformations that tend to be defined as fundamental, as making a 'historical' difference, structurally and culturally, institutionally and professionally.

As for the military, the understanding is that the end of the Cold War has accelerated and made visible developments which were well under way for decades, perhaps from the Second World War onwards, or even further back, depending to what exactly one is referring. To be sure, it is not particularly easy to discriminate between 'normal' post-1989 demobilization effects and long-term demilitarization. Apart from that, these developments seem to bring about a 'decline' of armed forces, in terms of purpose, priority and presence, or with other catchwords, in terms of meaning, money and manpower. The word 'decline', used often, makes sense, because the overall direction of the development seems to point to 'less' of everything: less men and less money, but also less central (purpose), less relevant (priority), less visible (presence), less clear (meaning). Yet 'decline' also sounds a bit plaintive, sometimes conveying a somewhat conservative or institutional bias, a preoccupation with what has been lost while turning a blind eye to what may have been won. 'Marginalization' might be a slightly more neutral term to suggest what is happening to the armed forces in the West, although it will probably not become popular with the military establishment either.[10]

As an overall trend, 'demilitarization' is plausible and can be accepted as a fruitful perspective. In doing so, it should be remembered the 'place in society' that military defence almost naturally has. Moreover, one can think of different time-spans and analytical frameworks as well as numerous indicators to prove or

---

8 Karl Haltiner, *Milizarmee: Bürgerleitbild oder angeschlagenes Ideal?* (Frauenfeld: Verlag Huber, 1985). This is one of the most thorough empirical studies about value change and 'demilitarization'.

9 Martin Shaw, *Post-Military Society: Militarism, Demilitarization and War at the End of the Twentieth Century* (Cambridge: Polity, 1990).

10 'Marginalization' is a central concept in G. Teitler and B. Timmer, 'De toekomst van Defensie: Taakverschraling en marginalisering', *Bestuurskunde*, 1995, 7, pp. 296-304.

disprove the overall thesis. Given my Dutch nationality, it is tempting to choose as a point of departure the 'Hollandization' of the world, a theoretical notion which hypothesizes the psychological 'retreat from Doomsday', eventually making war 'subrationally unthinkable'.[11] The latter process could be looked upon as the ultimate 'demilitarization' of society. I will refrain from adopting this particular framework, if only because it covers some two centuries (along the way overlooking the fact, so it seems, that in the Dutch East Indies 'Hollandization' has some very violent connotations).

The indicator to be scrutinized in this chapter, while not unrelated to this framework, will be a little more straightforward and simple. It stands for something which used to be called 'the will to fight'. A more timely expression is: 'the readiness to apply force'. Two related questions will be asked and answered: what does the disappearance of conscription convey; and what is the meaning of the evolving tolerance for casualties? Both questions will be projected against the notion of demilitarization, that is, as a sensitizing concept, not as a conceptual strait-jacket.

Before unravelling this twofold indicator of post-military society, however, I will complicate things a little more by looking at the 'civilianization' of the armed forces. Put simply, this is about the same trend: demilitarization. In an organizational context, however, the process tends to be confronted with different viewpoints and interests, generating consequences which may or may not coincide with the preferences of 'stakeholders' on the outside – the public included. Some of the 'arrangements' which are the outcome of this kind of civil-military interaction will be touched upon briefly. These 'arrangements' are not always directly or visibly related to the 'readiness to use force', our central indicator. The criss-crossing of professional identity and public image, however, very much belongs to civil-military relations and more or less bears upon our central issues.

CIVIL-MILITARY ARRANGEMENTS (I)

'Civilianization' or 'convergence' is a long-standing organizational process, during which the military became less 'isolated' and less 'unique'.[12] Part of this process can be looked upon as a kind of 'silent civilianization', deriving from professional logic and technological necessity. If anything, the influx of information and communication technology (ICT) will even further 'civilianize' the military profession. Caveat: to the degree to which the military applications of ICT

---

11   John Mueller, *Retreat from Doomsday: The Obsolescence of Major War* (New York: Basic Books, 1989).
12   For a detailed overview of the literature, see B. Boëne, 'How Unique should the Military Be?', *European Journal of Sociology*, 1990, pp. 3-59.

become available to some 'non-governmental organizations', not all of them in good legal standing, one might speak of a (re)militarization of society![13]

Like technology, and partly as an effect of it, management styles and practices will civilianize as well, adding a new chapter to a long history in which the military has been just as often a model as an imitation of 'how to organize'. Now, however, the pressure to apply new management is not just a matter of professional judgement and of making a fit with ICT. It very much derives from a choice that replaces the classical rhetoric of 'guns or butter'. Now it has become 'money or management', and as the amount of the former will probably go on to decline, the military will be hard pressed to exploit the latter. That is, to make a radical leap in efficiency, to become really cost-effective and to use any managerial tool which has proved itself elsewhere, privatization of some of its branches should not be excluded.[14]

Evidently, there are huge differences in the way that processes like these make themselves felt throughout the organization. It does make sense, or so it seems, to look upon the military as 'segmented' or 'pluralistic'.[15] It may even become useful to conceptualize (and manage!) it as an organizational 'archipelago', which probably will not coincide with traditional ways in which the military has subdivided itself. Nor would it be evident which branch, if any, of this plural military can serve as a (cultural) touchstone for the rest.

The military did and will (have to) respond to these forms of civilianization, sometimes initiating and sometimes resisting them. In the meantime, it will probably not let go of its claim to be different, of its right to isolation and its need for uniqueness, at least to some degree. The limits of civilianization have never ceased to be under debate, especially *vis-à-vis* personnel policies. On the one hand, armed forces have had no choice other than to cope with changes in professional motivation and the occupational outlook of its members. As a consequence the military has become less of a 'total institution': less greedy and less generous.[16] On the other hand, however, most military organizations in the West still see themselves as incompatible with some of the outcomes of the 'citizenship revolution'.

---

13 Toffler and Toffler, *De nieuwe krijgselite.*
14 About 'efficiency leaps' and other managerial catching up, see J. Soeters, *Verschuivende en vergruizende grenzen: Over de doordringbaarheid van organisaties (met toepassing op de krijgsmacht)* (Breda: KMA, 1995).
15 The observation about the 'segmented', 'pluralistic' military was made by Charles C. Moskos. For a recent evaluation, see David R. Segal, 'Organizational Designs for the Future Army', *Special Report 20* (Army Research Institute, 1993).
16 Charles C. Moskos and Frank R. Wood, eds, *The Military: More than just a Job?* (Washington, DC: Pergamon-Brassey's, 1988).

The refusal to admit unions is a case in point.[17] The issue of whether armed forces can accommodate homosexual men and women in their midst is another typical example of ongoing debates about whether and why the military should be exceptional. Until now, different answers are being given in different countries and different 'arrangements' have been worked out regarding the presence of gays and lesbians. To some degree these differences will persist, although it can be expected that sooner or later more and more militaries will 'give in', whether or not under the temporary pretext of 'don't ask, don't tell'. It fits in with the pattern of accommodation that other minorities have gone through, as well as with civilianization in general.[18]

Generally speaking, civilianization of the military, in its silent as well as in its noisy variants, goes on to constitute a major trend. It encompasses more countries as well as more variables, so it seems, ranging from management to minorities. The 'blurring of civil-military boundaries',[19] while not an original metaphor, seems more topical than ever. On the other hand, however, one would expect some evidence of counter-trends. Pluralistic armed forces on their way to becoming an organizational archipelago should show a degree of re-emphasizing or reinstalling 'classical' military culture. If only theoretically, an enhanced sense of uniqueness and a concomitant need for isolation could be predicted, for certain periods, for certain units, for certain operations. In short, remilitarization as a counter-trend would make sense and, in fact, this is what is happening in practice. In the next section this counter-trend will be touched upon, because while the switch to all-volunteer forces on the one hand only favours civilianization, it also provokes some remilitarization.

Zero-Draft: Causes and Consequences

Conscription has been very much part of modernity and of the nation-state which it helped to create. It has figured as a proud symbol of citizenship, but along the way it has been as effective a means of recruitment for democracies as for totalitarian regimes. It has been heralded by the political right and by the political left for quite different reasons. It has been all too good at making total war possible; it proved a

---

17 About the 'citizenship revolution', as well as the 'threat of military unionization' (p. 198), see David R. Segal, 'US Civil-Military Relations in the Twenty-first Century', in Don M. Snider and Miranda A. Carlton-Carew, eds, *US Civil-Military Relations: In Crisis or Transition?* (Washington, DC: Center for Strategic and International Studies, 1995), pp. 185-200.

18 Wilbur J. Scott and Sandra Carson Stanley, eds, *Gays and Lesbians in the Military: Issues, Concerns and Contrasts* (New York: Aldine de Gruyter, 1994).

19 Soeters, *Verschuivende en vergruizende grenzen*.

poor instrument for fighting limited ones. The latter 'shortcoming' now appears to be fatal to its continuance, but this is hardly the only explanation for its demise.

This section will take a close look at what it stood for, as well as at why it is being phased out and with what consequences, bearing in mind the major trends and, of course, our main dependent variable: (public) readiness to apply force.

END OF MASS ARMY

Since the end of the 1950s, the decline of the 'mass army' has stood among the central observations of military sociology. Gradually but inevitably, technological sophistication and occupational specialization seemed to make a labour-intensive military obsolete. The phasing out of conscription could be looked upon as a logical outcome of this process. In the Anglo-American world, the draft was brought to its conclusion, although this probably fitted a return to traditional models of recruitment for nations without land borders as much as the end of the mass army *per se*. In the United States, growing division over the war in Vietnam eventually did much to enhance the political expediency of an all-volunteer force.

While in continental Europe the draft did not escape debate and change, it survived until the early 1990s. Roughly speaking, it maintained its legitimacy and its effectiveness in making soldiers out of not-so-eager citizens. The willingness of young men to allow themselves to be conscripted had been declining – an observation which became very much part of end-of-the-mass-army theory. A change of values and lifestyles (individualistic, hedonistic, post-deferential) suggested growing incompatibility between the new generation coming of age and military organization, which stressed obedience and austerity, especially at its sharp ends.

No doubt the 'revolution of the 1960s' contributed to a climate that was critical of armed force(s), which to some degree also touched upon the draft. There has been no lack of compromise between the demands of the military and the preferences of the draftees. Almost everywhere the term of service was shortened at regular intervals; monetary and 'cultural' compensation were offered in some countries (Denmark, the Netherlands); a virtual free choice between military and civic service came to exist in others (Germany). In some countries, however (France, Italy), the typical draftee did not receive much compensation, nor did he get many free choices, before or during his time in the army, which makes it all the more remarkable that the draft could be kept intact until the end of the Cold War. As a particular 'settlement between state and society',[20] it did not break down because of value change, nor, for that matter, for strictly organizational reasons. The impact of both variables, however, could be all the more thorough now that a new strategic landscape has made the mass army obsolete at last.

---

20   Burk, 'Decline of Mass Armed Forces'.

It is being predicted that ten years from now, all-volunteer forces will have become the rule in Europe. An extrapolation of quantitative and qualitative indicators suggests that Finland, Switzerland, Greece and Turkey are the most likely candidates to be exceptions, still implementing the draft.[21] The examples of Belgium, the Netherlands, and especially of France, inventor of the *levée en masse*, doing away with the draft, are bound to be followed by more and more countries. The same structural forces can be detected everywhere: the long-term decline of the mass army is accelerated by the logic of much smaller militaries made fit for crisis-management operations. This logic creates two virtually unsolvable dilemmas: first, the equation between those who serve and those who do not reaches a point which can no longer be either legitimized or handled in semi-official ways; second, the vast majorities of politicians and publics alike principally disapprove of sending draftees out of area, unless they explicitly volunteer. What could be done in the context of colonial warfare (Dutch East Indies, Algeria), as well as at Cold War frontlines (Korea, Vietnam), proves to be no longer a viable option within the parameters of the current international system. More or less literally, conscription has come home.

This second dilemma bears directly upon the central issues of this chapter. On the one hand, the decision to skip the draft conveys an enhanced readiness to apply force. In fact, the latter is a direct inducement to this particular development, although again, not at all its only reason. On the other hand, while professional forces in principle make a better fit with new out-of-area-missions, they can hardly be deployed unconditionally. In fact, doubts have risen – if not a general (public) reluctance – about undertaking risky missions, seriously hampering the use of any military force, even if recruitment is all-volunteer. Of course the latter point very much touches the heart of civil-military relations, indeed of public support for new missions. It brings up the question of what it really means to decide in favour of a zero-draft? Certainly the logic to do so is strong, but how clear are the consequences?

Before trying to answer this particular question with immediate regard to 'readiness to use force', a slight digression will be made towards the kind of broader 'civil-military arrangements' that develop once a zero-draft has its way. In doing so an argument developed in the last section will be picked up, that is, about the civilianization of the armed forces as a major trend and remilitarization as a (possible) counter-trend.

---

21   Karl Haltiner, 'The Definite End of the Mass Army?' *Conference Paper* (Zürich: European Research Group on Armed Forces and Society, 1996).

CIVIL-MILITARY ARRANGEMENTS (II)

The end of conscription clearly strongly contributes to the 'demilitarization' of society, in terms of presence, of collective awareness and memory. It might even be looked upon as the best single indicator of this trend, especially in countries which have no all-volunteer tradition in the modern period. The number of people who have first-hand, real-life experience with the armed forces dramatically declines. Young- and old-boy networks, generated by the draft, will disappear and military service will be absent in the average curriculum vitae. In due time a generation of decision-makers will have no insider knowledge whatsoever on defence matters.[22] This trend is slightly counterbalanced when, as in the United States where reservists form a substantial element of virtually all operations, situations other than war are included. It has been pointed out that a total force concept makes the deployment of an all-volunteer force more difficult, especially for high-risk missions.[23]

While society demilitarizes because of the zero-draft, all-volunteer forces themselves can be expected to favour 'civilianization', at least in some respects. Recruiting members on the labour market, the military has to use competing incentives, monetary and otherwise. If not as a matter of organizational responsibility then certainly as an extra incentive, armed forces will also offer their short-term soldiers direct and indirect schooling, as well as bonuses to enhance post-military career prospects. On top of that, it seems to make sense for living conditions and perhaps even relations on the work-floor to be brought to a more equal footing with the outside world. Remembering the evolving pluralistic military, however, no doubt the latter tendency would be more conspicuous at some places and moments than at others.

As a counter-trend, in some parts of the organizational archipelago the temptation will be real to enforce more strict disciplinary codes and cultivate a more soldierly image. Working with youngsters who volunteer and who are presumably positively motivated to the point of being really eager, gives a professional opportunity for re-emphasizing classical military virtues, indeed for the remaking of soldiers. A high amount of remilitarization probably comes as naturally to (new!) all-volunteer forces as a strong dose of civilianization, which is to underscore that a heterogeneous kind of civil-military arrangement is in the making.

One main issue stands out in balancing this arrangement, whether looked upon from the organizational or from the public perspective: the composition and quality of the new labour-market-recruited soldiers. They will no doubt be less 'representative' than draftees used to be, constituting a cross-section of male youth. On

---

22   Mark J. Eitelberg and Roger D. Little, 'Influential Elites and the American Military after the Cold War', in Snider, *et al.*, *US Civil-Military Relations*, pp. 34-68.
23   Harvey M. Sapolsky and Jeremy Shapiro, 'Casualties, Technology and America's Future Wars', *Parameters*, summer 1996, p. 124.

average their educational level will be lower, technically better matched with functional levels, but possibly making a worse fit with the additional roles ascribed to soldiers, especially during peacekeeping missions. Constabulary tasks do not automatically suit the typical 'squaddy' or 'mud-soldier',[24] not even (or perhaps especially not?) their brothers in arms from elite units. While fears about recruiting 'scum of the earth'[25] do sound pathetic and outmoded, the quality and mentality of the new soldiers will demand much attention and scrutiny. It also calls for critical thinking about 'remilitarization'. Logical and legitimate to some degree (at certain moments for certain units), it might narrow the appeal of (part of the) the military to an overly homogeneous group of gung-ho youngsters. While the military cannot do without a number of the latter, it can hardly afford to let them function as informal 'gatekeepers', blocking diversity, not only in a demographic sense (gender, ethnicity), but also in terms of lifestyles, attitudes and values. In fact, such a development could be detrimental in a threefold way: to recruitment; to performance; and to image. The interaction and impact of these three variables should not be taken lightly in a post-conscription, demilitarized society, in which public support for (new) missions is vital.

Zero-Dead: The Meaning of Risks

The frequency of military deployments since the end of the Cold War, ranging from the Gulf War to a heterogeneous mix of major and minor peacekeeping missions, has drawn (renewed) attention to the risks of life and limb that soldiers are running. Historically, those risks could hardly come as a surprise. For most armed forces in the West, however, during the days of deterrence they had been theoretical rather than real, give and take a number of British and French engagements overseas, respectively *outre mer*. For the one military establishment that recently did suffer a substantial number of casualties (most of them draftees!) during a relatively lengthy period – the American forces in Vietnam – this very memory has become a source of the utmost risk awareness, if not the main drive towards risk avoidance. 'We [Americans] have grown ever more sensitive about casualties – our own military casualties, opponent and neutral civilian casualties, and even enemy military casualties – and we seek to avoid them.'[26] The conventional wisdom has

---

24   John Hockey, *Squaddies: Portrait of a Subculture* (University of Exeter: 1986); George C. Wilson, *Mud Soldiers: Life Inside the New American Army* (New York: Charles Scribner's Sons, 1989).
25   A phrase which has gained some prominence in the Netherlands during the transition to an all-volunteer force.
26   Sapolsky and Shapiro, 'Casualties', *Parameters*, p. 119.

taken root that generally in the West tolerance for casualties – in ugly jargon: for 'body bags' – has become low, almost calling for a 'zero-dead doctrine'.[27]

Explanations for this state of affairs range from the macro-level of the global system ('declining willingness to invest lives in hegemonic power'[28]) to the micro-level of family size (in small families the emotional meaning of losing a child is unbearable[29]). The latter explanation can be upgraded by placing it in the context of culture-shift and value-change (see the former section). The scope of the former explanation can be broadened by rephrasing it as a perceived lack of vital threats to national security. When all of these variables are taken together, quite a case can be built, which, besides its general plausibility, has its own *causes célèbres*: the American retreat from Somalia and European reluctance to intervene in Bosnia. Risk avoidance is mostly referred to as something to worry about, because it seems to hamper the pursuance of a, if necessary, forceful security policy. Hence the stern admonition that 'the people in the West have to accept that sometimes their armies have to go into battle and that young people will be maimed and killed'.[30] Could it be that this sort of patronizing tone no longer suits today's (young) people?

PUBLIC OPINION

Clearly, this whole framework of notions and hunches strongly conveys an image of demilitarized societies. At the same time it invites systematic theorizing and empirical testing to a degree that has not been realized until now. In fact, it is probably true that we lack 'systematic evidence of changes in mass or elite attitudes towards war'.[31] What we do have, however, are plenty of public opinion surveys that document people's attitudes towards post-Cold War military missions, in general as well as in specific cases, *causes célèbres* included.

If one looks at these data, either from Spain, from France, from the Netherlands or from the United States among other countries, they all suggest a substantial level of public support for new missions.[32] Whether these are phrased as humanitarian missions, as peacekeeping, as crisis-management or even as intervention, majori-

27 Boëne, 'Minimum Force, Third Party Action and Humanitarian Assistance', p. 13.
28 Immanuel Wallerstein, 'Peace, Stability and Legitimacy, 1990-2025/2050', in Immanuel Wallerstein, *After Liberalism* (New York: The New Press, 1995), p. 28.
29 E. Luttwak, 'De grote mogendheden blijven liever thuis bij de kinderen', *De Volkskrant*, 20 August 1994.
30 *Economist/HP de Tijd*, 13 January 1995.
31 William R. Thompson, 'The Future of Transitional Warfare', in Burk, *The Military in New Times*, p. 90.
32 Philippe Manigart, ed., *Future Roles, Missions and Structures of Armed Forces in the New World Order: The Public View* (Nova Science Publishers, 1996); David R. Segal and Bradford Booth, 'Public Opinion on American Soldiers' Participation in Multinational Peacekeeping Operations', *Conference Paper* (Siena: 1996).

ties are in principle backing them up. Before any further qualification, it seems reasonable to look upon this public mood as remarkable, perhaps even historically remarkable. The fact that post-national goals are ascribed to armed forces throughout the West, cannot fail to attract attention, even if this generally would be done in addition to rather than as a replacement for traditional defence. Typically, in some countries, in particular the United States, public opinion makes the multinational character of missions a condition *sine qua non* for its support.[33] Again, this is something to ponder upon.

Even more telling is the conclusion that has been drawn from scrutinizing public-opinion polls in different countries with regard to a number of specific military engagements, Bosnia and Somalia among them. The insight reached in one of these analyses appears to apply to other cases as well: 'No doubt, public approval and willingness to sustain peacekeeping operations is conditional. But it is not conditioned by a knee-jerk reaction to casualties ... it is conditioned rather by the demand that casualties be incurred for some clear and worthy purpose'.[34] To be sure, the latter observation does not prove that public opinion in the West would easily sustain any number of casualties, no matter how clear and worthy the purpose at stake. It does suggest, however, that the acceptance of risk is related to the meaning of missions, politically and militarily; this sounds like a truism, but one that often seems to be forgotten amid fashionable notions and hunches about 'body-bags'.

In general, while weighing public opinion, it should also be remembered that the public's attitudes towards defence and security policy over the years have been characteristically stable and consistent, conveying the impression of a 'rational public'.[35] There seems no reason to assume that with regard to new military missions, people have suddenly become irrational and volatile, saddling decision-makers with impossible mandates. Rather, the public's mandate seems to give room to political and military elites to take responsibility and, if necessary, to take risks.

---

33 David R. Segal and Bradford Booth, 'Public Opinion on American Soldiers' Participation in Multinational Peacekeeping Operations'; and Philippe Manigart, 'Public Opinion and Security in Europe in 1995', *Conference Paper* (Breda: ERGOMAS, 1996).

34 James Burk, 'Public Support for Peacekeeping in Lebanon and Somalia', *Conference Paper* (Baltimore, MD: IUS, 1995), pp. 26, 27; P.P. Everts, 'Het maatschappelijk draagvlak voor militaire vredesoperaties: de slachtofferhypothese nader bekeken', *Transaktie*, 1996, 1, pp. 44-69.

35 David Capitanchik and Richard C. Eichenberg, *Defence and Public Opinion* (London: Routledge and Kegan Paul, 1983); Benjamin I. Page and Robert Y. Shapiro, *The Rational Public: Fifty Years of Trends in Americans' Policy Preferences* (Chicago, IL: University of Chicago Press, 1992), see especially chapters 5 and 6.

ELITES AND OTHER STAKEHOLDERS

Decision-makers have been criticized, especially in the case of former Yugoslavia, for underestimating the sustainability of public opinion. Allegedly the latter's 'lack of stomach' served as an alibi for non-intervention policies, to a degree setting off a self-fulfilling prophecy.[36] It is beyond the scope of this chapter to assess the dynamics of decision-making in specific cases or in general, but a few tentative observations have to be made.

Are we witnessing, to paraphrase Christopher Lasch, a 'revolt' of security elites, categorically lacking courage and vision? They definitely do wrestle with the rationale for the use of force, with conditions and criteria, very much including the attitudes of their constituencies.[37] Part of this seems 'normal', characteristic for a period of fundamental transformation (structurally and culturally, institutionally and professionally!). Perhaps it is naive to assume that such a process can be mastered and managed within a couple of years – although of course this does not offer much consolation to the people who might have profited from a more sturdy, straightforward and consensual intervention policy. Part of the elite's wrestle, however, might also derive from typical post-modern turbulence: stretching from the chaotic spectre of threats and conflicts, which defies clear-cut doctrines and criteria, to the ways in which 'distant violence' is being 'represented' in the West.[38] Society is involved in the latter, not just through 'public opinion', especially not in its more scientifically and clinically assessed manifestations. Quite a range of 'stakeholders' raise their voice: internal ones (soldiers and their families) as well as external ones, with non-governmental organizations and mass media prominent among them. In the heat of stakeholders' debates, and because of the pressure on decision-making, public opinion tends to become instrumental: 'poll taking is not a simple matter of record keeping: it is also an exercise of power'.[39]

Of course the media has won the reputation of being a powerful player, influencing public opinion and elites alike. For the elites, management has become an important objective: while classical censorship has not vanished, the nature of conflict theatres together with media-technics and -tactics allegedly induce military

---

36   'I shall always believe that the governments concerned underestimated the steadfastness of their own electorates, and that the excessive timidity was unnecessary'; Anthony Parsons, *From Cold War to Hot Peace: UN Interventions 1947-1994* (London: Michael Joseph, 1995), pp. 242-3. For a similar critique, see Bart Tromp, *Verraad op de Balkan: Een kroniek* (Uitgeverij Aspekt, 1996), p. 18.

37   Charles A. Stevenson, 'The Evolving Clinton Doctrine on the Use of Force', *Armed Forces and Society*, summer 1996, pp. 511-35.

38   Martin Shaw, *Civil Society and Media in Global Crises: Representing Distant Violence* (London: Pinter, 1996).

39   Murray Goot, 'The Polls', in Murray Goot and Rodney Tiffen, eds, *Australia's Gulf War* (Melbourne: Melbourne University Press, 1992), p. 181.

establishments to the 'courting' of journalists.[40] The power of mass media in framing problems, staging the suffering and, last but not least, the surveillance of risks can hardly be underestimated. They have supposedly contributed to what has been called 'mass spectator sport militarism'.[41] Together with the impact of violence-prone entertainment culture, this might induce the public with a twisted image of how and when military force can be applied to what results. Public opinion might get hooked on technological fixes, which are relatively bloodless, at least from a distance. In fact, this is a set of notions and hunches in itself, which deserves rigorous theorizing and testing. It must be admitted though that the way in which the Gulf War was televised seems to give an extra dimension to the interaction between media, public, politicians and military professionals. The Gulf War also contributed to the impression that tolerance for 'wasting' lives has declined(!), including soldiers and civilians on the other side.[42] This does put governments as well as military establishments under extra pressure to avoid 'collateral damage'. If casualties are unavoidable they had better be meaningful. Should this be considered a token of 'declining' public readiness to apply force? In terms of what was said in the second section of this chapter, it can also be looked upon as if something, instead of having been lost, has been won.

Conclusion: No Mandate for All Seasons[43]

If our most general conclusion proposed that there is definitely a public mandate for new military missions, including a readiness to apply force in such a context, a simple objection might be: yes, but what about 'old' missions? How would the public react, a typical rhetorical question goes, 'if the armed forces were ever to suffer losses on a scale remotely comparable to that which was taken for granted during the Second World War?'.[44] We have no real way of knowing, of course, although evidently this is not the scenario now being planned in the West. Not in the public mind and certainly not in terms of manpower, conscripted mass armies fighting a total war are on the way out and their reinstallment, while not impossible to envisage, is very remote indeed. It does not seem very enlightening or relevant, however, to project hugh numbers of casualties without depicting any meaningful political and military context. Thus, no mandate for all seasons – let us first see if

---

40 C.C. Moskos and T.E. Ricks, *Reporting War When there is No War* (Chicago, IL: Robert R. McCormick Tribune Foundation, 1996).

41 Michael Mann, quoted by Shaw, *Post-military Society*.

42 John Mueller, *Policy and Opinion in the Gulf War* (Chicago, IL: University of Chicago Press, 1994).

43 'The armed forces are moving into the direction of an "agency for all seasons"'; Wilfried von Bredow, 'The Profession of Arms as Social Work?', *Conference Paper* (Baltimore, MD: IUS, 1993), p. 14.

44 Michael Howard, 'The Armed Forces and the Community', *RUSI Journal*, August 1996, p. 11.

the decision-makers can handle the season at hand! It might be argued that the degree to which they do effectively use the whole spectre of new military missions makes the necessity of any return to old missions – to wit, major war – even more remote and obsolete.

The introduction to this chapter recalled Morris Janowitz's rationale for a constabulary force, committed to the minimum use of force and seeking viable international relations rather than victory. This rationale is surely still visionary to a considerable degree, projecting notions of world citizens in uniform, keeping and enforcing peace within a regime of collective security. The cycles of the global system, the clashes of civilizations, not to speak of the obstacles towards integrated European security policy, all of these do not immediately or visibly favour effective international policing – unless a whistle suffices. Clearly, the constabulary concept, too good to be true, needs a strong dose of wishful thinking. Yet it does offer an opening to evolving trends, also in terms of public attitudes and institution-building, which is at least as useful as models of days gone by, whether derived from the Second World War, from colonial warfare or from such extremes as mercenary forces and Spanish brigades. Commitment to the minimum use of (meaningful) force suits the mood of the public and fits civil-military relations, centring around professional militaries. The importance of the latter can hardly be overestimated and an ongoing awareness of the difference that a zero-draft makes – politically, socially and organizationally – is vital. Much of this is about demilitarization, but, if necessary, it does not preclude some remilitarization.

All this is not to idealize public opinion, neither to turn a blind eye to its darker sides nor to overlook its chances of being caught up in the turmoil of stakeholders' power games. While the sustainability of the public has almost certainly been underestimated, often in an unduly patronizing way, it should not be overestimated either. Up until now, it has hardly been tested to the utmost, and it is a conditional mandate that the public gives to political decision-makers and military professionals. The impression is warranted, however, that both, in a mutually reinforcing way, have a difficult time in assessing the parameters and using the room of this mandate.

It is argued that 'national cultures' 'supply meagre symbolic resources to enable the soldiers and sailors who act as peacekeepers, their family and friends, or even the population at large to state and justify the significance of what they are doing'. Because of this, we are witnessing the workings of a 'cultural lag': 'world structures currently favour increased reliance on multinational peacekeeping forces'.[45] Basically, this is an elegant and convincing way of putting things in the perspective of fundamental long-term transformation. It must be remembered, however, that probably the most conspicuous 'lag' is not on the side of the public.

---

45   James Burk, 'Thinking Through the End of the Cold War', in Burk, *The Military in New Times*, p. 21.

6 State, Security and Armed Forces at the Turn of the Millennium

Koen Koch

Approaching the End of the Millennium

The specific *fin de siècle* mood, reinforced by the end of the Cold War and the demise of the Soviet Union, seems to inspire many authors to declare the end of almost everything. We have Fukuyama's 'end of history', Guéhenno's 'end of democracy' and Tromp's 'end of politics'. As a consequence of the process of European integration, we witness the revival of the old debate about the end of the state, which had already started in the nineteenth century when authors such as Karl Marx and Saint Simon, for different reasons by the way, prophesied the withering away of the state.[1] At that time, this withering away was considered as a positive development. Nowadays, apart from optimists like Fukuyama, others emphasize the possible negative aspects of the 'end of the state'. Robert D. Kaplan describes the horrible situation in West Africa where states have almost ceased to exist for all practical reasons. He considers disease, overpopulation, unprovoked massive crime and refugee migration as '*the* symbol of world-wide demographic, environmental and societal stress, in which criminal anarchy emerges as the real "strategic" danger.' Kaplan's argument is that 'West Africa's future, eventually, will also be that of most of the rest of the world'.[2]

We do not have to accept the far-reaching claims of this male Cassandra to admit that his thoughts reflect fundamental developments and changes in and of such essentially important phenomena as the state, democracy and politics, or for

---

1   Francis Fukuyama, 'The End of History', *The National Interest*, 16, summer 1989; J.M. Guéhenno, *La fin de la démocratie*, 1994; B. Tromp, *Het einde van de politiek?*; Stanley Hoffmann, 'Obstinate or Obsolete? The Fate of the Nation-State and the Case of Western Europe', *Daedalus*, Vol. 95, No. 3, 1966, pp. 862-915; Alan S. Milward, *The European Rescue of the Nation-State* (London: Routledge, 1992); William Wallace, 'Rescue or Retreat? The Nation State in Western Europe, 1945-93', in John Dunn, ed., *Contemporary Crisis of the Nation-State?* (Oxford: Blackwell, 1995), pp. 52-77.

2   Robert D. Kaplan, 'The Coming Anarchy', *The Atlantic Monthly*, February 1994, pp. 46-8.

G.C. de Nooy (ed.), The Clausewitzian Dictum and the Future of Western Military Strategy, 75-91.

that matter, security, war and the role and even the *raison d'être* of the armed forces.

The developments to which the authors of 'endism' refer are very serious indeed. When we accept, for instance, the claims about the end of the state, we have to answer many disturbing questions. At the least we have to rethink and reconsider our traditional concepts and conceptions, theories and doctrines about the relationships between state and war, between state, security and the armed forces and between state and democracy.

If these relationships are analysed from the perspective of the withering away of the state, we have to start with a clear idea of what is withering away. Here the traditional Weberian concept will be used of the state as the organization that exercises the monopoly of the legitimate use of violence, rule-making and taxation for a specific territory. In such a state the role and function of the armed forces (police and regular army taken together) is rather clear-cut. On the one hand, their function is to provide internal order and the ultimate sanction on the basis of which the monopoly of rule-making and taxation is exercised. On the other hand, the armed forces protect the territorial integrity of the state in question, giving meaning to the idea that the state is the organization that claims the monopoly of rule-making and taxation for a 'specific territory'.

In the recent literature about the end of the state, two strands of reasoning about the withering away of the state can be distinguished. The first approach concentrates on the disappearance of monopoly violence *per se* as the direct cause of the state's demise; the second approach emphasizes the loss of territoriality as the cause of the state's demise. In the former instance, the armed forces of the state, and with them its monopoly of violence, have ceased to exist; in the latter instance the armed forces (and the monopoly of violence) are still in place, but to put it bluntly there are no longer any borders to defend.

Kaplan, of course, provides a telling example of the first approach. His interpretation of the withering away of the state is focused on the disappearance of the state monopoly of violence. State-controlled armed forces, providing internal order and external security, no longer exist. Smaller and larger armed bands will roam the cities and the countryside, more or less like the armies in the Thirty Years War, 'like locusts living off the country' by pillaging and stealing everything that they meet on their way. The issues at stake here are what the causes of the disappearance of the monopoly of violence are, to what extent this development is really global and inevitable, what possibilities there are to restore that vital monopoly, and what specific role the armed forces of the still existing states that want to come to the rescue of 'failed states' can possibly play in restoring that monopoly.

Examples of the second approach are provided by analysts of the consequences of the processes of European integration and of internalization. They are concerned with the diminishing importance of territoriality, that is, with the diminishing autonomy of state in the fields of rule-making and taxation for a specific territory.

Among others, William Wallace emphasizes that 'states in Western Europe no longer control their national economies'.[3] Richard Rosecrance developed the concept of the 'trading state', the state that shifts its efforts from controlling territory by military means to augmenting its share of world trade.[4] In both cases, the monopoly of violence as such is not at issue and is more or less in place. The primary role and function of the armed forces, however, is defence of the realm. When borders are becoming less and less important and territoriality is loosing significance, this role will probably be undermined. In the long run, becoming superfluous, or at least considered so by a growing part of the population, the armed forces will lose their legitimacy and perhaps even their *raison d'être*. In a paradoxical way, this can jeopardize the monopoly of violence in the end, making Kaplan's prophecy for the twenty-first century also true for the now rather peaceful and opulent countries of the West. The intriguing issue here then is about the possibility of maintaining the monopoly of violence when the state has lost its territoriality.

Even when we take the continued existence of the armed forces and the monopoly of violence represented by them for granted, the withering away of the state poses another important problem. Many writers claim that democracy cannot survive without the protective shell of the nation-state. When this is true, we have to worry about the possibilities for democratic control of the armed forces when the nation-state has withered away. Will these forces become more or less 'autonomous', self-regulating and self-interested entities because the structures for democratic control and legitimation of the armed forces have disappeared with the state as such? Will these armed forces behave in a decent way as if nation-states and democratic control still existed? Or will they become modern versions of the medieval robber barons or *condottieri*, rendering their services when the right price is paid? Again, Kaplan's scenario becomes at least plausible. Indeed, the end of the state can be the beginning of an era of endemic violence, epitomized by the current situation in West Africa, which reminds us of the period of European violence before 1648. This brings home the point that in a period of fundamental transformations, summarized in the literature of 'endism', we really need to rethink the relationships between state, war and security.

This will be done later in this chapter. It will become clear that the firm existence of the state will not solve all security problems, but is a security risk in itself, and that only under very specific conditions will state and security go together. A stateless system as well as the state system are characterized by their own specific forms of violence, calling for specific security policies. When the world is charac-

---

3   William Wallace, 'Rescue or Retreat?', p. 67.
4   Richard Rosecrance, 'The Rise of the Trading State: Commerce and Conquest in the Modern World' (New York: Basic Books, 1986); see also Richard Rosecrance, 'The Rise of the Virtual State', *Foreign Affairs*, Vol. 75, No. 4, July/August 1996, pp. 45-61.

terized by a strange combination of stateless and state systems, things are still more complicated.

In the third section, the claims of the theorists of 'endism' will be analysed. Are states withering away, or all states withering away, and are they withering away in the same way or not? It will become clear that there is no such thing as one single, uniform global development towards the end of the state. Instead, a threefold regional differentiation can be distinguished. In some parts of the world we see a trend towards failed states, in other regions the consolidation of the nation-state can be distinguished, and in Western Europe we have of course the very specific process of European integration. These diverging trends produce for each region qualitatively different security issues. As a consequence, we have to conclude that there no longer exists such a thing as a global security problem that is the same for all the states concerned. This was the case during the Cold War when the global security issue was the prevention of all-out (nuclear) war between the two super-powers and their allies. Policies and armies of all states were in that sense similar. Now, however, governments in different regions are confronted with different security issues, will develop different policies and will organize and train their armed forces for different emergencies. In the long run, this will probably hamper the possibilities for international and world-wide cooperation in the security field.

Finally, the specific situation of West European states such as the Netherlands will be analysed. Are these states withering away as a consequence of the European integration process? What are their specific security problems? What will be the future role of the armed forces?

State and Security: An Uneasy Partnership

It is only appropriate to start the discussion of the relationship between state, war and security with the Clausewitzian concept of war as the continuation of state politics with the admixture of other means. However, when security is conceived of as the absence of threat of massive organized violence, it will become clear that this Clausewitzian concept of the relationship between state, war and security is rather limited. Apart from war, the inter-state, or international aspect of security, at least three other types of violence have to be distinguished: endemic violence, civil war and state-organized violence (genocides, politicides, etc.). A security policy should address all four aspects, and the role of the armed forces should be specified in this policy framework.

ENDEMIC VIOLENCE

We have to admit that when war is conceived of as inter-state violence, the end of the state will mean almost by definition the end of war. But will this also mean the end of massive organized violence and the inception of Kant's *Ewige Frieden*, or a more secure world at least? Unfortunately, this will be highly improbable.

Security is more than the absence of inter-state war. In the very first instance, it has to do with more or less pacified, non-violent relationships in society, the necessary basis for social, economic and cultural development.

It has recently been seen that the sudden breakdown of states as organized entities will be accompanied by massive violence and numerous atrocities, as is exemplified by what has happened in many parts of Africa and in the Balkans. These occurrences bring home the old wisdom that a necessary condition for a more or less peaceful society is a monopoly of the means of violence, organized in a centralized entity called the 'state'. This monopoly seems to be an indispensable instrument to deter, prevent or suppress massive organized violence.

It is only reasonable that many argue that without this monopoly, residing in the controlling and restraining framework of states, it is to be expected, as Robert Kaplan for instance argues, that we have to witness on a world scale a period of endemic massive violence, such as Europe experienced in the fifteenth and six-teenth centuries. In a world without states, the Hobbesian condition of war of all against all, where life is short and nasty, is looming around the corner.

Fearing the possible violent implications of a world without states, many tend to prefer the certainty and security of the system of states. On normative grounds, they defend the state and the state system as the guarantor of peace and security, and they are in deep trouble indeed when on empirical grounds we have to accept the claims of 'the end of the state' authors. Their way out is their reassuring claim that in the long run some kind of monopoly of violence, and, for that matter, some sort of state will be re-established. However, as Keynes's quip noted so appropriately, in the long run we are all dead, and taking the European experience as our example, it took many centuries before these monopolies were firmly established, and this will mean that many people will fall victim to this kind of violence until in the long run everything is fine again. Policy is about what we can do in the mean-time.

Precisely because the instances of breakdown of order and of the disappearance of the monopoly of violence are rather recent, there is no standard policy repertoire for saving or reinstating failed states. Well-intentioned efforts in this field, in Somalia for instance, became a gloomy disaster. The European experience has taught us that the establishment of a monopoly of violence is a long process of mostly violent elimination of all armed individuals and groups, except one, the eventual 'state'. Our armed forces are trained for fighting similar armed forces, not for a process such as 'disarming' armed individuals and groups in a social, political and geographical context that is completely strange for them. Reading Clausewitz will not be very helpful here. Moreover, for outsiders restoring a monopoly of violence, it is very difficult to decide which of the contending groups and factions must be eventually endowed with the newly established monopoly of violence.

These two factors – the political uncertainty about which party to support and the lack of adequate instruments to establish a monopoly of violence – will inhibit other states to come to the rescue of failed or failing states. But perhaps the most important factor preventing other states from intervening, is that their own security interests are not directly at stake when people in other regions fall victim to armed bands and common criminals, the more so when these failed states are situated in other continents, thousands of miles away. Precisely for this reason, the horrible situation of endemic violence in a stateless world can drag on for many years.

INTER-STATE WAR

As a stateless world has its type of violence, a world of states also has its specific types of massive violence, calling for specific security policies. In other words, the Hobbesian solution for the security problem is not as perfect as it may seem at first sight, and the state's claim to be the guarantor of peace is rather unwarranted. When security – the absence of the threat of massive violence – is the fundamental issue at stake, we have to admit that the state and the system of states is a solution as well as a problem.

The necessary condition for a peaceful society and the remedy for the Hobbesian condition – the monopoly of the means of violence – also provides a necessary condition for inter-state violence. Armed forces guarantee 'internally' peace and quiet, but provide 'externally' the necessary wherewithal that states need to fight their wars. Internal pacification is bought at the price of the possibility of inter-state war.

The prevention of inter-state war is the primary topic of traditional security policy, of debates about the balance of power, multipolarity or bipolarity, about military doctrines, about the best mix of conventional and nuclear weapons, about the desirability of disarmament or arms control, about the possibility of collective security or the necessity of collective defence. The way in which our armed forces are organized, equipped and trained, reflects the result of these debates. Their traditional predominant function and role is to defend the territorial integrity of the state and to prevent war at the same time, a rather impossible task as European history has demonstrated so abundantly. It is here that Clausewitz's dictum is still alive and kicking.

CIVIL WAR

In a world of states, the amassed power in the state apparatus, produced by the monopoly of the means of violence, is a very enticing bounty for every individual or group that wants to use the power of the state to further its own interests. The existence of states implies a permanent struggle about the control of state apparatus. This struggle is fought not only in a peaceful and democratic but also in a violent way, ranging from *coups d'état* to all-out civil war. Security, then, is also concerned with the possibility of democratic control of the state, with peaceful change of leadership and, for that matter, with democratic control of the armed forces. Again, the relationship between politicians and the military is rather strained, as European history has shown. The clear subordination of the military to the civilian leadership, one of the key elements of Clausewitz's doctrine, is, unfortunately, not self-evident. In this sense, Clausewitz should indeed be read by every new generation of military men.

GENOCIDES AND POLITICIDES

Sadly enough, we have to acknowledge that the power of the state can be used in a very violent way against its own population, as the many instances of genocide and politicide have proven during the twentieth century. In retrospect, I am inclined to consider this kind of violence as the most important security problem with which our era has had to cope. Irving Louis Horowitz reminds us of the fact that during this century governments have been directly responsible for the deaths of roughly 120 million people, while war (both international and civil) accounts for 35 million deaths. Over three-and-a-half times as many people have been killed by their own governments as by opposing states.[5]

The problem is all the more serious because other states are very reluctant to intervene, and in the last analysis the offending state can be forced to stop its murderous actions only by military intervention by other states. But by their intervention to put an end to the large-scale violation of fundamental human rights, these states risk an inter-state conflict – war – with the offending state. This they would like to avoid at almost any price. The result will be that the probability of an effective outside intervention in these cases will not be very great, and will be the smaller the more powerful the offending state is. This conclusion is borne out by the rather disturbing fact that from 1945 until the 1980s, the number of victims in inter-state wars (3.35 million) and of victims of civil wars (3.13 million) is so much smaller than the number of victims of genocides and politicides (between 6.8 and 16.3 million).[6]

5   Irving Louis Horowitz, *Taking Lives: Genocide and State Power* (London: Transaction Publishers, 1996), p. 28; see also R.J. Rummel, 'Deadlier than War', *Institute of Public Affairs Review*, 41, No. 2, spring 1985, pp. 24-30.
6   Barbara Harff and Ted Robert Gurr, 'Toward Empirical Theory of Genocides and Politicides: Identification and Measurement of Cases since 1945', *International Studies Quarterly*, Vol. 32, No. 3, 1988, p. 370.

'NEW' AND 'OLD' SECURITY ISSUES

In any case, as the above makes clear, a comprehensive security policy should address the four aspects of security described above at the same time: the monopoly of violence within the state to secure a peaceful society must be upheld; the risks of inter-state violence must be limited; the armed forces of the state must be controlled and contained in a democratic manner; the chances of genocide or politicide by the state must be eliminated.

Success on all four counts at the same time is difficult to achieve. When the state is our level of analysis, we see that for instance European states with pacified societies and civilian-controlled armed forces have lived for centuries with the risk of inter-state violence. The history of European states is correctly called the history of European wars. This explains why emphasis in Europe is laid on traditional security policy with its doctrines of balance of power, alliances and collective defence, on armaments, arms control and disarmament, and on strategies and tactics for the armed forces, however outdated these concepts, and Clausewitzian doctrine for that matter, may be at this time.

When the international system is our level of analysis, we see how difficult it is to develop security policies that provide for stable states with an adequate monopoly of violence, for a reliable system of collective security, for democratically controlled armed forces and for an efficient and effective system of humanitarian intervention. Instead, we see the chaos and violence in so-called 'failed states' such as Somalia, Sudan and Albania, the (threat of the) occurrence of inter-state war in some parts of the world (the Middle East, Asia), and civil wars and genocides, or 'ethnic cleansing' as it is called euphemistically nowadays.

Recent international endeavours to alleviate these problems, with all their good intentions, unfortunately show poor results in most cases. Concepts and strategies for saving failed states, for intervention in civil wars (or wars of secession), and for humanitarian interventions are lacking; and the armed forces, geared to their traditional security tasks, seem inadequately organized, trained and equipped for these 'new' security tasks. There is a glaring discrepancy between available security hard- and soft-ware, amassed in the countries of the West, and the real security needs of many millions in Africa and elsewhere.

SECURITY AND THE 'END OF THE STATE'

It is only fair to emphasize that this discrepancy will not be solved, but will be augmented when we broaden our analysis by taking the claims of the 'end of the state' theorists into account.

Some will rejoice because with the disappearance of the state the possibility of inter-state violence and of state-perpetrated genocides will also disappear. But most will be haunted by the spectre of a situation without the monopoly of the means of violence residing in the state: a Hobbesian situation aggravated by the abundance of the most awful weapons of mass destruction.

This is the one fundamental question that all the theorists of 'endism' have dodged answering: will a monopoly of violence be possible without the existence of the state and the system of states? In the global market in which the system of states will be transformed, the provision of security will cease to be a collective good, and security will become a market commodity such as food, housing, education and health care. But can we imagine security as something other than a collective good? And if we cannot, what kind of institution could provide such a collective good, in absence of the state? And if we can imagine security as a market commodity, how will this commodity be produced? Will there be the growth of private security corporations, managed by fashionable businessman who provide security at a fair price on a free and competitive market, as is already the case in some rich parts of the industrialized world? Or will the future 'stateless' period develop modern versions of the medieval robber barons or *condottieri*, forcefully exacting high levies from the population in exchange for so-called 'protection'? Or in the future will we experience the imagined state of nature that Thomas Hobbes wrote about? Indeed, speculating about some of the aspects of what is called the post-political era, is a rather horrifying experience. Of course, we do not have to take the claims of the ideologues of 'endism' at face value, with a resignation approaching fatalism and preparing for the worst. On the other hand, dismissing out of hand the arguments brought to the fore just because we 'need' the state, democracy and responsible and responsive armed forces for a well-ordered, non-violent society, is a sign of unscientific teleological thinking and boils down to whistling in the dark.

We have to steer a middle course between the Scylla of resignation and the Charybdis of denial, by analysing the actual processes of formation of states, their growth, demise and eventual withering away. This will be done in the next section.

The 'End of the State' Thesis Reconsidered

DIVERSIFYING, NOT DISAPPEARING[7]

A discussion of the probability of the 'end of the state' thesis has to start with the simple remark that it is not very helpful to make statements about 'the' state in the singular, for instance about the enduring strength or existence, or for that matter, the demise or withering away of the state. As Inis Claude wrote: '... one is tempted to pontificate that any statement that begins with "All states are ..." or "All states

---

7   Michael Mann, 'Nation-states in Europe and Other Continents: Diversifying, Developing, Not Dying', *Daedalus*, Vol. 122, No. 3, summer 1993, pp. 115-40.

act ..." is certain to end in either a truism or a falsehood; to be true it must be trivial'.[8]

States differ, as J.P. Nettl noted, in 'stateness', the extent to which they in actual fact exercise the monopoly of the legitimate use of violence, rule-making and taxation for a specific territory, the hallmark of the traditional Weberian conception of the state that is used here.[9] The specific configuration of external and internal conditions (geopolitical, military, economic, political, etc.) with which a given state has to cope, and the adroitness of the political elite to build and maintain the threefold state monopoly, determine the 'stateness' of a given state, the extent to which a state possesses the monopoly of violence, rule-making and taxation.

Actual states do not only differ in their respective 'stateness', but can develop at the same time in different directions, some losing and some augmenting their 'stateness'. 'Strong' states coexist with so-called 'quasi-states', or even 'failed states', and of course states that pool their sovereignty lose some of their stateness, as is the case in the process of European integration.[10]

In this sense, it is impossible to speak about a universal and unilinear trend towards the withering away of the state, or, for that matter, for the undisturbed existence of the state. In other words, we reject a determinist view of the process of state-making. On the one hand, there is no reason to believe in the inevitability of the withering away of the state as such. On the other hand, we reject the idea that the state will be the ever-lasting form of political organization. As a very specific form of political organization, the state as we know it is the peculiar outcome of very specific historical circumstances and processes. The origins of the state lie in the fifteenth and sixteenth century north-western part of Europe, and very slowly the state became the dominant form of political organization. Only in the second half of the twentieth century as a result of the process of decolonization, has the state nominally become the universal form of political organization.

Political development will not stop at the start of the third millennium and its outcome is open-ended. All we can tell is that we now see a process of diversifica-

---

8   Inis L. Claude Jr, 'Myths about the State', *Review of International Studies*, Vol. 12, No. 2, 1986, pp. 1-2.

9   J.P. Nettl, 'The State as a Conceptual Variable', *World Politics*, Vol. 20, No. 4, July 1968, pp. 559-92.

10   Robert H. Jackson, *Quasi-states: Sovereignty, International Relations and the Third World* (Cambridge: Cambridge University Press, 1990); Robert H. Jackson and Carl G. Rosberg, 'Why Africa's Weak States Persist: The Empirical and Juridical in Statehood', *World Politics*, Vol. 35, No. 1, October 1982, pp. 1-24; Gerald B. Helman and Steven R. Ratner, 'Saving Failed States', *Foreign Policy*, No. 89, winter 1992-93, pp. 3-20; Robert O. Keohane and Stanley Hoffmann, 'Institutional Change in Europe in the 1980s', in Robert O. Keohane and Stanley Hoffmann, eds, *The New European Community: Decision-making and Institutional Change* (Boulder, CO: Westview, 1990), pp. 1-39.

tion, as Michael Mann remarked, and not a unilinear trend towards the end of the state, or towards a universal consolidation of the state in its Weberian form.[11]

This process of diversification seems to show a regional pattern and this will have important security consequences. For instance, in Western Europe we see the process of integration: by 'pooling' their sovereignty, the member states of the European Union lose some of their 'stateness'. In many parts of Africa, we see a growing number of quasi-states or failed states that are not capable of upholding the monopoly of violence. In Asia, we see the consolidation of rather efficient nation-states.

REGIONALIZATION OF SECURITY OR THE 'DECOUPLING' OF SECURITY ZONES

It is important to note that this regional pattern of state formation is considerably matched by the regional pattern of occurrence of war and other types of violence. Since 1945 most conflicts have been in the 'Third World', and these conflicts were either primarily intra-state in character or possessed a substantial intra-state dimension even if they appear to the outside observer to be inter-state conflicts, as Mohammed Ayoob noted.[12] From the data that Kalevi Holsti provides, one can conclude that Asia and the Middle East are the regions where inter-state war is still predominant, and Africa is the region of predominantly intra-state war.[13] Apart from a zone of peace stretching from the North American continent to Western Europe, there are at least two other security zones to take into account. A zone where inter-state war is a serious possibility stretches from the Middle East towards Asia; and the continent of Africa seems to be a zone of chaos and endemic violence.

The rejection of the general 'end of the state' thesis in favour of the 'diversifying' thesis complicates our analysis of security problems. The security problems in a system of more or less similar states that are characterized by the same extent of 'stateness' are rather clear-cut. States confronted with the same security problems will develop similar strategies and doctrines, and they will organize their armed forces in a similar way. In the classical Westphalian system of sovereign states, all states entertained more or less the same perception of security, the same policies of balance of power, alliance formation, armament and arms control, and their armed forces are organized in the same way in order to perform the same tasks.

---

11   Michael Mann, 'Nation-states in Europe and Other Continents'.

12   Mohammed Ayoob, 'State-Making, State-Breaking and State Failure: Explaining the Roots of "Third World Insecurity"', in L. van Goor, Kumar Rupesinghe and Paul Sciarone, eds, *Between Development and Destruction: An Enquiry into the Causes of Conflict in Post-Colonial States* (London: Macmillan, 1996), p. 67.

13   Kalevi J. Holsti, *Peace and War: Armed Conflicts and International Order, 1648-1989* (Cambridge: Cambridge University Press, 1991), pp. 274-8.

The Clausewitzian dictum is in full force. In these circumstances it is rather easy –
in principle but not of course in practice – to develop an international security
policy, for instance to organize a system of collective security or a system of
collective defence. The leaders of the armed forces are in a comfortable position:
they know for which kind of conflict they have to prepare and train their troops. But
in a diversifying system of states with different security zones the security problems of and between dissimilar states and groups of states are no longer as clear-
cut. States in different regions are confronted with different security problems.

In regions that resemble the classical Westphalian system, states have to cope
with different security problems than West European states, which with their
pacified societies and their pacified inter-state relationships form a security
community where the threat of armed conflict is highly improbable. In the first
case, role and function of the armed forces are defined by the traditional – for
instance Clausewitzian – doctrines and strategies; in the last case, the *raison d'être*
itself of the armed forces is at stake. Why maintain armed forces when the probability of war is dwindling down to zero? The security problems in the region of failed
states are from a completely different order than in the regions mentioned above.
Here the problem is to organize a workable monopoly of violence.

In a system of diversifying states, security problems also diversify. The consequences of this development are far-reaching. Goldgeier and McFaul introduce the
idea of 'decoupling' of the different security regions. Precisely because security
problems of failed states are not directly related to security in other regions, states
in the zone of peace or the zone of traditional war may lose interest in the problems
of these failed states: '... the great powers will neither intervene to preserve the
security of peripheral states nor constrain the peripheral states from belligerent
actions 'unless' core economic interests are threatened'.[14]

Even when there is some humanitarian urge to intervene, the 'decoupling' of
security regions will have serious consequences. Strategies and formats of armed
forces of specific states reflect, of course, the security needs of these states. They
will be trained and equipped to meet security threats that are specific to their 'own'
region. When these forces have to operate in other regions with other security
needs, they are faced with great difficulties. An army built around Clausewitzian
principles is not very well suited to organize an effective monopoly of violence, in
other words to build a state, in far-away regions, or to intervene in a civil war.
Precisely this operational incapability, exemplified for instance by the Somalian
disaster, may induce states to refrain from these kinds of interventions, indeed
emphasizing the 'decoupling' of security regions.

---

14   James M. Goldgeier and Michael McFaul, 'A Tale of Two Worlds: Core and Periphery in the Post-
     Cold War Era', *International Organization*, Vol. 46, No. 2, spring 1992, pp. 486-7.

Western Europe: Some Security Problems of a Zone of Peace

Karl Deutsch coined the phrase 'security community', a situation in which the actors consider the probability of war among each other extremely low.[15] Such a security community seems to exist in Western Europe. The probability of war between West European states is considered nil, the chances of war with our neighbouring superpower, Russia, are extremely low. It is not necessary here to analyse the causes of this happy situation, but in passing I would like to mention the pacifying aspects of the process of European integration on the one hand, and the nuclear revolution on the other, which put an end to the illusion of Clausewitzian war between nuclear powers and which led to the stand-off in Europe between the two alliances, headed by the United States and the former Soviet Union.

It should be emphasized that the future security problems and policies of the West European zone of peace are from three different perspectives, all related however to the relationships between state and security described above. The first has to do with the consequences of peace for the future of the state and its monopoly of violence; the second with the consequences of the above-described 'decoupling' of security zones; and the third with the specific character of the European integration process.

IF WAR MADE STATES, WILL PEACE UNMAKE THEM?

As Charles Tilly formulated provocatively: War makes the state, states make war.[16] With all due reservation, this thesis reveals an important perspective on European history. It is still more stimulating, however, to think about the corollary of this thesis: when war has become very improbable for whatever reason (technological, political, economical), this must have consequences for the process of state-making, more specifically for the chances of states to maintain their threefold monopoly, and for the enduring existence of the armed forces, or at least for public willingness to maintain such forces.

Commenting on the unintended consequences of nuclear deterrence and the ensuing nuclear peace, Michael Howard remarked in 1979:

> ... the State *apparat* is likely to become isolated from the rest of the body politic, a severed head conducting its intercourse with other severed heads according to its own laws. War, in short, has

---

15   Karl W. Deutsch, *et al, Political Community and the North Atlantic Area: International Organization in the Light of Historical Experience* (Princeton, NJ: Princeton University Press, 1957).

16   Charles Tilly, 'War-Making and State-Making as Organized Crime', in P.B. Evans, D. Rueschemeyer and T. Skocpol, eds, *Bringing the State Back In* (New York: Cambridge University Press, 1985), pp. 169-91.

once more been *denationalized* ... The identification of the community with the State, brought to its highest point in the era of the two World Wars, can no longer be assumed as natural or, military speaking, necessary ... The disintegration of the Nation-state as a consequence of the erosion of the loyalties built up during the era of the World Wars has been regressive. As a result, it is increasingly difficult for the State to fulfil those functions, not simply of defence, but also of the maintenance of acceptable order, the administration of communally agreed justice, and the management of economic resources, that are its *raison d'être*.[17]

The arguments of Tilly and Howard taken together seem to lead to a rather disturbing thesis: the more improbable that inter-state war will be, the less probable it will be that states can provide internal security on the basis of a robustly upheld monopoly of violence.

The experience in Western Europe and the United States lends support to this thesis. Paradoxically enough, states that do not have to worry about their external security, by sheer lack of enemies or by their overawing military power, seem to lose their internal monopoly of violence to a considerable degree, as is exemplified by the growth in the United States and also in Western Europe of so-called *no-go areas* on the one hand and the growth of walled and fortified hamlets, sometimes resembling medieval castles, of the well-to-do on the other. In all of these countries we see the growth of legal, and illegal, private organizations providing 'protection' for citizens. The possibility that security ceases to be a collective good provided by the state, and becomes a marketable commodity provided by businessmen in a competitive market, is becoming a reality. In the United States, the money spent on private security corporations begins to equal the budget of the ministry of defence. In the long run, of course, this development will undermine the legitimacy and prestige of the 'official' security forces. A radical redirection of the armed forces towards the provision of internal security could stop this unhappy development, but will be very difficult to organize and implement. In any case, developments in the United States in particular show how internal security can be produced without a firm state monopoly of violence, although this image of the future is in my opinion not very attractive.

'DECOUPLING' OF SECURITY ZONES

In the last section, the concepts of diversifying security zones and of 'decoupling' security zones were analysed. The conclusion was that for all kinds of reasons – political, strategic, and technical – the more that these security zones diversify, the less that governments and public opinion in one zone will be interested in the security problems of other zones, or for that matter be prepared to intervene. For Europe, this boils down to the thesis that the more that Western Europe becomes a

---

17   Michael Howard, 'War and the Nation-state', *Daedalus*, No. 108, 1979, pp. 106-8.

zone of peace, the more inept, the less prepared and the less willing that Europe – the EU – will be to intervene in zones of war or of endemic violence and chaos.

This sounds like cynicism, true, but it also reflects reality. After what may be called the interventionist euphoria of the first years after the fall of the Berlin Wall, we can now observe a definite intervention weariness. In the so-called *Toetsingskader Notitie* (July 1995), the Dutch government describes the criteria that must be used in the decision-making process about Dutch participation in peacekeeping or peace-enforcing operations. When these criteria are taken seriously, it is highly improbable that the Netherlands will participate in any major peacekeeping operation outside Europe. In the long run, this will have grave consequences for the *raison d'être* of the Dutch armed forces, especially reorganized after 1989 to participate in these kind of operations. After 1989, the traditional defence task and the peacekeeping function of the armed forces were brought on equal footing. When, however, this peacekeeping task will not be fulfilled, the legitimacy and prestige of the armed forces will be questioned by the general public. The future existence, then, of the Dutch armed forces will rest partly on the relative strength of the strange but very holy alliance of interventionist humanitarians and military people: the former claiming that in a case of humanitarian emergency, something must be done; and the latter assuring that something worthwhile could be done by military personnel.

EUROPEAN INTEGRATION, THE STATE AND SECURITY

The process of European integration will only complicate our analysis of the relationship between state and security in one of three situations. When the integration process leads to a fully blown United States of Europe, the security problems of this new state can be analysed as those of every other consolidated state. When the integration process is not more than a form of intergovernmental cooperation, the participating member states will retain the essential character of states, with their traditional security problems. Only when the integration process does not lead to the United States of Europe, but nevertheless affects the character of the members as states in a fundamental way, will a new complicated situation develop.

In my opinion, this third possibility will be the most plausible for the foreseeable future. The debate about the character of the process of West European integration is too easily reduced to taking sides in the controversy between the federalist/functionalist position, which entails the vision of 'ever closer union', and the Hoffmann/Milward thesis which holds that integration has come to the 'rescue of the nation-state'.[18] In this controversy, I reject the federalist vision as well as the thesis of the strengthened and unchanged state. As a mostly unintended conse-

---

18   Alan S. Milward, *The European Rescue of the Nation-State*.

quence of their 'intergovernmental' cooperation, the participating states, the smaller more than the more powerful, have to a considerable degree lost their 'stateness', without the growth of the 'stateness' on a European level. Autonomy has disappeared in many respects, as Wallace noted, but is not transferred to the European level.[19]

The process is best described by Hedley Bull's concept of neo-medievalism: '... a structure of overlapping authorities and criss-crossing loyalties ... From a situation of protracted uncertainty about the locus of sovereignty, it might be a small step to the situation of a "new medievalism", in which the concept of sovereignty is recognized to be irrelevant.'[20] The successive rounds of future enlargement of the EU, the urge for 'flexibility', the inevitable trend towards a Europe of more speeds and Europe *à la carte* will only strengthen this development towards this 'new medievalism'. In this context, territoriality, and for that matter the defence of national, internal borders, will lose much of its significance. The national armies will to a considerable extent lose their primary task and function.

Of course, the defence of the EU's external borders will remain on the agenda. However, again we have to think of the reversal of Tilly's state-warmaking proposition. The more improbable that war will be in Europe, the less the process of European integration will lead to the formation of a European (super)state, and the more difficult the hammering out of a common European security and defence identity will be. Governments will be inclined to pursue their traditional security policies, favouring NATO for instance instead of European solutions, or preferring to keep to their own traditional policies of neutrality or idiosyncrasy.

IN LIEU OF A CONCLUSION

Looking from the perspective of the 'end of the state' theorists to future security issues and to future tasks and functions of the armed forces has provided a few interesting insights. At the level of the international system, the emergence of a number of rather new security issues has been noted: upholding the state monopoly of violence, the rescue of 'failed states', intervention in civil wars and wars of secession, and intervention to put an end to gross violations of human rights. These new security issues call for multifunctional armed forces that must abandon their preoccupation with their traditional task of defending the territorial integrity of their respective states.

However, the concept of diversifying security zones and its corollary of 'decoupling' security interests was also developed. This 'decoupling' will hamper

---

19   William Wallace, 'Rescue or Retreat?'.
20   Hedley Bull, *Anarchical Society: A Study of Order in World Politics* (London: Macmillan, 1977), pp. 255, 266.

the development of these multifunctional armed forces because governments and electorates will see no compelling reason to prepare for solving security problems that are absolutely not their own. This brings us to the conclusion that the existence of such a multi-functional armed force will depend on the holy alliance of humanitarian interventionists and military professionals.

Countries in Western Europe face a difficult problem. Precisely because of the low probability of inter-state war in Europe, the necessary condition for the continuation of this situation (an adequate defence force in the framework of the Atlantic Alliance) will be in jeopardy. Why spend money for such a superfluous instrument as an army when there is no enemy around? The paradox here, of course, is that the low probability of war, one way or the other, has to do with the existence of reliable armed forces, however small they (owing to happy circumstances) may be. The longer that European peace endures, the more difficult it will become to explain this paradox to the electorates. Peacekeeping disasters such as the Dutch experiences in Srebrenica will not contribute to this necessary exercise in public education.

7 Friction Rules (States Win): The Power Politics of Institutional Cooperation

Jaap de Wilde

The paradox of international organization is that the very structures that help to improve the functioning of states in the international system undermine its essence, the principle of state sovereignty. Therefore, the attempts to organize anarchy at the international level may well stimulate the growth of anarchy at the substate level. The ability of governments to rule hangs in the balance: internationally, institutionalization in various forms helps to improve the ability to rule – there is more information exchange on a structured basis, there is more institutionalized negotiation, there is more regime formation, international law and even an increased tendency to intervene in state behaviour in the interest of the 'international community' of states, embodied by the United Nations. Policy-oriented studies such as Boutros-Ghali's *An Agenda for Peace* and scholarly developments such as the neo-liberal institutionalist approach in the study of International Relations (IR) give voice to these new opportunities for governments to fulfil one of their basic tasks, to provide external security.[1]

At the same time, the disability of states to perform other basic tasks 'at home' – especially to disarm their subjects successfully and to guarantee law and order – hits the headlines time and again. Martin van Creveld's analysis, especially in its popularized form as presented by Robert Kaplan, sketches a world of not just high-tech terrorists and merciless gang-wars in the 'no-go areas' of many megalopolises, but also of armed private security firms and re-armed commercial ships (against piracy) who fill the vacuum left by governments.[2] The dilemma is that states are caught in the turbulence between the success of institutionalization at the macro

---

1   Boutros Boutros-Ghali, *An Agenda for Peace: Preventive Diplomacy, Peacemaking and Peacekeeping* (New York: United Nations, 1992); Robert O. Keohane, *International Institutions and State Power: Essays in International Relations Theory* (Boulder, CO: Westview Press, 1989).
2   Martin van Creveld, *The Transformation of War* (New York: Free Press, 1991); Robert D. Kaplan, 'The Coming Anarchy: How Scarcity, Crime, Overpopulation, Tribalism, and Disease are Rapidly Destroying the Social Fabric of our Planet', *The Atlantic Monthly*, February 1994, pp. 44-76.

93

G.C. de Nooy (ed.), The Clausewitzian Dictum and the Future of Western Military Strategy, 93-107.
© 1997 *Kluwer Law International. Printed in the Netherlands.*

level of politics and the negative aspects of fragmentation at the micro level of politics.[3]

The heart of the matter is that integration and disintegration feed upon each other and that state formation processes are determined by the friction between the two.[4] This is friction in the Clausewitzian meaning of the term. Integration has its own logic *in abstracto*; a world society headed by a sovereign world government is its extreme. *In abstracto* integration creates an absolute hierarchical order. The logic of disintegration, however, leads to the image of a fragmented world of sovereign individuals, living in an extreme form of anarchy. Both extremes can be found in the work of Hobbes:[5] his 'state of nature' and his Leviathan provide good images of the theoretical extremes of anarchy and hierarchy, and the measure of fragmentation/integration associated with them. Hobbes presents them not as a dialectical pair, but as alternatives, and this is how most scholars think about integration and disintegration. The ideal types are, however, closely related, and dialectical in the sense that each of them bears the seeds of the other.

An integrated society is a prerequisite for specialization and hence for individual development.[6] Specialization and the accompanying social processes of group or class formation, however, are forms of fragmentation, feeding disintegration. Vertical and horizontal struggles for power ensue. In these struggles friction is unavoidable: the borders of states are not drawn by functionalist logic alone (the integrationist line, in which the collective interests dominate individual ones), nor by liberal logic (the disintegrationist line, in which individual interests dominate collective ones), but by their historic collisions, and, Clausewitz could add, the ability of the genius to exploit the circumstances.

The friction between integration and disintegration makes it hard to predict at what level – compared to the present state level – the new Leviathans will emerge. Are these located at the substate level, the present state level once again, or the regional and global levels? At present, states seem to be captured in the turbulence between globalization and individualization. Some scholars argue that the state will lose out in this process, either because fragmentation will 'win' – Kaplan's coming anarchy – or because integration will 'win' and create new political units at a regional and global level. Given the yin-yang nature of (dis)integration, both processes may be expected to coexist in future.

---

3 James N. Rosenau, *Turbulence in World Politics: A Theory of Change and Continuity* (New York: Harvester Wheatsheaf, 1990).

4 J.H. de Wilde, 'The Continuous (Dis)Integration of Europe: A Historical Interpretation of Europe's Future', in J.H. de Wilde and Håkan Wiberg, eds, *Organized Anarchy in Europe: The Role of States and Intergovernmental Organizations* (London: I.B. Tauris, 1996), pp. 85-106.

5 Thomas Hobbes, *Leviathan: Or the Matter, Forme and Power of a Commonwealth Ecclesiasticall and Civil*, edited by Michael Oakeshott (Oxford: Basil Blackwell, 1946 (first published in 1651)).

6 K.N. Waltz, *Theory of International Politics* (Reading, MA: Addison-Wesley, 1979).

The question, addressed in this volume, is how this affects the role of armed forces in the security policies of national states. Any answer has to begin by assessing these states and their security policies. One of the conclusions in *The Transformation of War* is that the state 'may be on its way to oblivion'.[7] Two World Wars (the 'thirty years war of 1914-1945', as Van Creveld calls them) and the birth of the nuclear age have put an end to the military struggle for power among national states, just like the devastation of the first Thirty Years War (1618-1648) put an end to the era of religious wars. Subsequently, the main actors have to leave the stage, which they indeed did in the seventeenth century. National states, however, are still the organizing principle of politics, and this chapter argues that, in contrast to the era of religious wars, their struggles for power have not disappeared, but merely have lost their direct military dimension – at least in various parts of the globe. The transformation of war at the substate level is but one trend in contemporary history; the transformation of the interstate struggle for power another. A theoretical starting point for this hypothesis can be found in Clausewitz's theory of war; part of concrete indications can be found in contemporary Europe.[8]

The Distance between Objective and Means

Clausewitz's theory of war can very well be interpreted as a theory of interdependence. The essence of the laws of warfare, which he discovered in his mental laboratory, is the idea of reciprocity: what is true and reasonable for me, must also be true and reasonable for my opponent, hence he prescribes the laws for me, which I prescribe for him. The security dilemma is one of the most studied outcomes of this form of interdependence, but the thesis that in anarchical structures the units will be functionally alike[9] can also be defended on this ground: enemies come to look like one another because enmity prescribes the same rules of the game to all the participants in it. Waltz, in contrast to Van Creveld, argues that anarchy rather than enmity is responsible for functionally undifferentiated actors: the lack of law and order forces them to mistrust one another, which of course easily finds an expression in enmity.

Both aspects are present in the frequent attempts to escape this logic. The answers are sought either in attempts to replace enmity by amity or in attempts to reduce the uncertainty inherent in anarchical structures, for example by creating hegemonic orders or by institutionalizing cooperation. The problem of these alternatives is that they require a change of parameters, and say little about this

---

7   Van Creveld, *The Transformation of War*, p. 193.
8   Carl von Clausewitz, *Over de oorlog* (Bussum: Wereldvenster, 1982), translation of *Vom Kriege* books I, II and III, first published in 1832, 1833 en 1834.
9   Waltz, *Theory of International Politics*; M. van Creveld, *The Transformation of War*, p. 195.

process of change. While the theory of Waltz is altogether unable to explain structural change in the international system, it is illustrative that, for example, Morgenthau ends his analysis of power politics with the hopes (hope rather than a conclusion) that the UN system will in the end overcome all the uncertainty and insecurity of the anarchical relations among states.[10] In *Vom Kriege* this 'Utopian' trap is absent. It should be realized that Clausewitz was not writing about ways to prevent war. Up until the First World War, warfare in the European tradition was perceived by many as the crown on diplomacy, and by even more people as unavoidable. The only good reason to avoid war was uncertainty about the ability to win. Only after the Great War and the Second World War was warfare widely perceived as the failure of diplomacy. It is illustrative that the memorials of both World Wars and the wars thereafter are devoted to their victims rather than their generals.

The overtures of this development can be found in peace treaties that concluded periods of devastating warfare, such as the Peace of Westphalia (1648) and the Congress of Vienna (1815), as well as The Hague Peace Conferences of the late nineteenth century. In the twentieth century the League of Nations and, even more so, the United Nations codified that the intrinsic logic of war should be tamed rather than exploited. The value of Clausewitz in this respect is that he reasoned the other way around. He would never accept the possibility that a moral principle could rule out war. His dominant question, therefore, was not how to avoid the logical extremes of war (that is, how to avoid an ultimate concentration of destructive power in time and place), but why the extremes did not occur in practice. What kept warfare from its logical extremes? These modifications had to be present in the 'real' world. Owing to this reverse sequence, he unwillingly developed a Realistic peace theory – or in less provocative words: a theory about the factors that make total war unlikely. Not all of these 'modifying factors' are equally important any more. Particularly his arguments about immobile fortresses that physically obstruct the ability to concentrate military means in time and place are outdated in the era of nuclear weapons and ICBMs. His central argument, however, still stands. War serves *political objectives* and is embedded in a *wider context* of relations between the antagonists. These objectives and their wider context determine the instrumental value of means of violence.

To preview some of the conclusions: terrorists, gangs, crime syndicates, ethnic groups, etc., tend to have a limited number of (often far-reaching) objectives which legitimate the use of all means and allow for a high price, whereas states in their mutual relations tend to have a wide variety of (often limited) objectives which put a bonus on continuous weighing of appropriate means at lowest costs.

---

10   Hans J. Morgenthau, *Politics Among Nations: The Struggle for Power and Peace* (New York: Alfred Knopf, 1948).

I am not interested here in the modifying factor of the 'wider context'. Let me merely mention that this can be linked to modern interdependence theories, especially to the hypothesis by Robert Keohane and Joseph Nye that in situations characterized by complex interdependence, warfare, as an instrument of rational politics, loses all meaning.[11] Clausewitz's argument that war is kept from its extreme because it is not an isolated event, supports this hypothesis: the more that military antagonism can dominate relations between actors, the more likely it is that the wars between them will be total wars (compare Cold War scenarios, and, nowadays, the Huntington scenario of a clash of civilizations).[12] It makes a difference whether warfare is the only expression of the struggle for power between actors, or whether this 'test' is embedded in all kinds of other expressions of this struggle. The presumed causality between wider context and total war is, however, too linear and too simple; all major wars have been fought within a wider context of complex interdependence;[13] and high levels of interdependence do not rule out enmity patterns that make actors filter all objectives through an ingroup/outgroup lens, in which case the density of an issue and its complexity merely feed extremist solutions.[14] But Clausewitz does point out that it makes a difference whether the wider context provides a rich arsenal of objectives and instruments for power politics or merely the threat of war.[15]

More important here is the modifying influence of the political objective. At stake is the extent to which the direct effect of military action coincides with the government's ultimate objective. If the physical destruction of an enemy is the political objective, armed force can be quite effective and no warnings are necessary. Genocides, ethnic cleansing, etc., are the sad expressions of such political objectives that coincide with the direct ends that can be achieved by military and police means.[16] If conquest of territory is the objective, again the military provides a suitable instrument. If robbery is the objective, armed forces play first of all a psychological role: the threat is more important than the bullet, and the victim has to weigh the risk of being shot against the price of losing property. The difference is that between the objective and the instrument a third element arises: the victim's perception of threat. Deterrence is an example of such an intermediate goal. The ultimate objective of deterrence is to be left alone. But as soon as more complicated

---

11   Robert O. Keohane and Joseph S. Nye, *Power and Interdependence: World Politics in Transition* (Boston, MA: Little Brown, 1977).

12   Samuel P. Huntington, 'The Clash of Civilizations?', *Foreign Affairs*, 1993, pp. 22-49.

13   Waltz, *Theory of International Politics*.

14   About the cognitive dimension of interdependence, see J.H. de Wilde, *Saved from Oblivion: Interdependence Theory in the First Half of the Twentieth Century* (Aldershot: Dartmouth, 1991).

15   Clausewitz, *Over de Oorlog*, pp. 38-9.

16   Albert J. Jongman, ed., *Contemporary Genocides: Causes, Cases, Consequences* (Leiden: PIOOM, 1996).

favours are demanded, the relationship between military means and political objectives becomes blurred. Modern societies are based on these more complicated service structures. To put it simply, an enemy state can destroy a high-tech state like Japan, but it cannot conquer its wealth or take over its firms by military means.

It is clear that if state formation is not a spontaneous process, armed forces and coercive means are necessary to enforce compliance. This process resulted in Leviathans and balances of power between them. The success of the Leviathans, however, slowly stimulated the marginalization of armed force in domestic affairs.[17] The point is that in most societies the link between political objectives and coercive instruments gets complicated over time. The hierarchical structure allows for specialization, and, as a consequence, the services required by the authorities become more complicated and skilled. The importance of willing compliance increases and replaces the options for enforced compliance.[18] Democracy – in which the government serves the public rather than the other way around, and in which the military stick to their barracks – is one of the culminations of this process; it is a polity that can exploit the power of willing compliance relatively successfully (but not by military means).

The price of specialization, however, is fragmentation. Substate actors develop their own transnational networks of contacts and interactions; they globalize and individualize; others fall back to small-scale historical ties (ethnocentrism) to escape the complexity of modern society. New types of law and order emerge within and across national borders, and anarchy increases. This weakens the state, but is enabled by the initial law and order that it created. (Weak and strong states are defined by Barry Buzan; in strong states the internal pacification has been success-ful, whereas the principal distinguishing feature of weak states 'is their high level of concern with domestically generated threats to the security of the govern-ment'.)[19] In other words, disintegration at the substate level is more than just a control problem of globalization's side-effects, it is also a spin-off of successful state formation. There seems to exist a circular relationship: if the state system is undermined by the effects of globalization, ultimately globalization itself will be undermined. This adds to the paradox that the very structures that help to improve the functioning of states in the international system undermine its foundation, the principle of state sovereignty.

---

17 Charles Tilly, *Coercion, Capital, and European States, AD 990-1990* (Oxford/Cambridge, MA: Basil Blackwell, 1990); Charles Tilly, 'War-Making and State-Making as Organized Crime', in John A. Hall, *The State: Critical Concepts* (London: Routledge, 1994), pp. 508-29 (originally in P.B. Evans, *et al., Bringing the State Back In*, 1985, pp. 169-91).

18 De Wilde, *Saved from Oblivion*, ch. 4.

19 Barry Buzan, *People, States and Fear: An Agenda for International Security Studies in the Post-Cold War Era* (New York: Harvester Wheatsheaf, 1983), p. 99.

This circle also provides a clue to the paradoxical role of warfare at the various levels of the international system: that is, the concurrence of relatively peaceful interstate relations and increasingly explosive intra-state relations. The two dominant lines in intra-state violence are organized crime and civil war. The political objectives of gangs and crime syndicates are of a 'rob-thy-neighbour' nature, and this is what they do. The political objectives of actors involved in civil strife are to eliminate the power ambitions of one another. Physical destruction directly contributes to that end. The effectiveness of small arms, moreover, reduces the minimum group size necessary to make an impact. Especially in 'failed states' and the inner cities of megalopolises, Tilly's analysis of state formation forces appears to be quite topical.

Uncertainty Avoidance

Why, however, did these dynamics disappear from the interstate scene? Within the limits of the argument above, the reason must be that apparently the distance between political objectives and the effects of military instruments has widened to the extent that warfare as the 'ultimo ratio' in international politics has moved beyond the immediate horizon as far as its instrumental value is concerned. How can this be explained? Three hypotheses come to mind. The first is the assumption that US-Soviet bipolarity and, presently, US military hegemony provide sufficient order in the anarchical international system to frustrate the translation of political objectives into military ones. In Clausewitzian terms this would not mean that objectives and means are incompatible, but that time is not ripe. Emerging great powers can challenge the order and eventually this is what they will do. This argument is in line with the literature on hegemonic cycles and long waves.

The second hypothesis is that nuclear weapons have disrupted the usefulness of armed forces for hegemonic ambitions. Emerging great powers have to resort to other means to challenge the position of older ones. This would mean that technological developments in the arms industry do not just influence but determine politics. In a more subtle variant, the emphasis is put on the role of perceptions: in the context of the Cold War both superpowers seemed to rule out the option of total war after the Cuban missile crisis. The image of total destruction and moral condemnation of it, rather than the destructive technologies as such, should be held responsible.

The third hypothesis, and of most interest to this chapter, is a rebuttal of the axiom that the maximization of power is the ultimate objective in politics. Peter Haas has pointed out that governments can be analysed as being driven by the desire to reduce uncertainty.[20] To maximize one's power is a very attractive strategy to achieve this end: it requires unilateral decision-making only, and, if successful, it allows control of other actors' behaviour in specific areas, hence reducing existential uncertainties (risks, insecurity, threat perceptions, etc.). In this sense, 'uncertainty avoidance' could turn out to be the deeper motive behind 'struggle for power'. The third hypothesis says that 'uncertainty avoidance' is the ultimate bottom line for units in political systems.

Centuries long, the struggle for power has been the dominant expression of this ultimate objective. It has resulted in hierarchical political structures (states and empires in varying forms) and balances of power and other types of order in anarchical political structures – ultimately tested by war. The first hypothesis claims that this practice is still in place, and I do not want to test or challenge it here. The second hypothesis claims that technological discoveries, their applications and perceived values have made this practice so irrational that the traditional struggle for power is over. The third hypothesis claims that other forms have replaced the traditional, military-based, struggles for power. New structures, different from both hierarchy and anarchy, are emerging, in which the costs and benefits of independence and freedom (plus the accompanying risks of random behaviour) versus dependence and subordination (meaning an optimal predictability of behaviour, but at the risk of killing initiative and creativity) are better balanced. This does not imply an end to power politics, but a transformation of power politics to new areas, and hence a transformation of the political role of the military in international relations.

New Battlefields in Europe

The dominant theatre for power politics has always been territorial. The ability to control land, sea and, in the twentieth century, air forms the starting point of traditional power politics. Territorial borders symbolize the limits of governmental power. They also symbolize the distribution of power among states. These functions of territory obviously highlight the role of military power throughout history: the ability to occupy land or to destruct the living conditions on the lands of others, and the ability to protect one's own possessions against intrusions. Up until the Second World War, the possession of Alsace-Lorraine, for instance, symbolized the balance in the German-French struggle for power in Europe. Poland, similarly, has been a battlefield for centuries in European history, with Germany (Prussia,

---

20   Peter M. Haas, 'Introduction: Epistemic Communities and International Policy Coordination', *International Organization*, Special issue on 'Knowledge, Power, and International Policy Coordination', Vol. 46, No. 1, 1992, pp. 1-35.

Austria), Russia and Sweden fighting for dominance. Border conflicts in general are a dominant theme in the history of European power politics. Up to and including the Cold War, political power was literally fenced off by flags and barbed wire. This practice still exists, for instance in former Yugoslavia, but for a proper understanding of contemporary power politics and security in Europe other battlefields have become more important.

In face of the hegemony thesis, it is possible that we are dealing with a temporary shift (which has already existed since 1990), but post-modern power politics is about international organizations (IOs) rather than territory. 'Membership' of exclusive international organizations tells us as much about the distribution of power among states as sovereign control over home lands and colonies did in the past. Even membership of inclusive international organizations, such as the United Nations, is a stake in the struggle for power: would-be states need membership as proof of their recognition by the outside world. As soon as membership is acquired, the distribution of power within the organizations, and the underlying struggle for power, dominate politics. This is a new theatre for power politics, which has re-articulated the role of the military.

What are the symptoms? First of all there are the bids for integration by Central and East European states and the power politics related to them. Second, there is the experience over a longer period among the Western states, including at times Japan. Since 1989 the main theme in European politics is the question of when and how the Central and East European countries are allowed to enter Western international organizations. All the former Eastern bloc states, often including the Russian Federation, try to improve their international position by joining typically Western organizations, whether it is the Council of Europe, the European Union, NATO, the WTO or the OECD.

The Russian Federation is obviously in a special position: achieving recognition as a member of the G-7 has higher priority and is more realistic than gaining NATO or EU membership. This global orientation is partly due to lack of power on the European institutional battlefield, because of West and Central European unwillingness to cooperate fully with the Federation. If the ultimate political objective of Western and Central Europe had been a pan-European and transatlantic security order, it would have been more rational to mobilize the OSCE for this purpose, given its wider membership.

The unwillingness to turn the OSCE into Europe's main organization shows two things: first, that IOs are indeed a manifestation of power politics – their purpose goes beyond cooperation as such; second, it shows the limits of the enlargement processes of the EU and NATO – apparently, it is not the intention to reach OSCE proportions, because in that case a more direct route could have been chosen.[21] As a consequence, the new 'Polands' and 'Alsace-Lorraines' will be at the borders of NATO and EU membership.

The tactical moves for enlargement show from a number of symbolic initiatives – and all of them refer to international organizations: the Association Treaties, the North Atlantic Cooperation Council (NACC), Partnership for Peace (PfP), the Balladur Plan (or Stability Pact) and also the EBRD. Together they form an institutionalized waiting room for EU and NATO membership. Moreover, these specific outcomes reflect the various moves on the chess board of international organizations. In the IO theatre, there is friction, space for genius and concurrence of circumstances. Although it may be doubted whether all players have similar strategic goals, one of the most plausible policy objectives that show from the battlefields is how to create a 'Europe-without-Russia', without falling back into the traditional struggle for power, known from the Cold War, in which the risks are so much higher.

The Russian Federation still tries to avoid such a peripheral role by full participation in the present institutional battles. The 'European House' is the main trump card that they have to support their option of a 'Europe-including-Russia', and they play it time and again. In this struggle for power between the Russian Federation (and, symbolically, the CIS) and EU/NATO, the military sector can play no active role. Still, the outcome is crucial for the distribution of power in Europe. The main function of the military, and the military potential of each state, is to keep the memory of the traditional battlefields alive. A territorial struggle for power can easily re-emerge, as the Balkans, the Caucasus and the tension between Greece and Turkey help to remind us.

Abrupt membership for the former non-Soviet Warsaw Pact countries to NATO, the WEU or the CFSP of the EU could create a self-fulfilling prophecy, and force Russia back in its old familiar role of the enemy state that has no interest in post-modern and post-sovereign power politics. As long as the OSCE option is Utopian, it could be of strategic value to postpone EU and NATO enlargement as long as possible – without, however, frustrating Central European hopes too much. This seems to be the Western policy objective for the time being. New steps in the series of NACC, PfP, Europe Accords, etc., may therefore be expected. One step has been to subdivide Central European states into groups that will be allowed entry in various rounds; a second to enter 'bilateral' negotiations between NATO and Russia. Another form of delay is caused by the Intergovernmental Conference (IGC) of the EU, which started in March 1996. Only after the IGC – that is, not before at least June 1997 – does it make sense to reopen serious enlargement

---

21   Ole Wæver, 'The European Security Triangle', in de Wilde and Wiberg, *Organized Anarchy in Europe*, pp. 245-66.

negotiations. And even then, Central Europe has to wait for the EU's new Treaty to be ratified by the parliaments of the fifteen member states.

These tactical moves can be used to gain time, they further institutionalize the waiting room, but, most of all, they create time to make moves on a larger institutional chess board, where Russia shows fewer sensitivities. In the global context, institutional power politics is about the role of the Security Council, enlargement of the OECD and wider roles for the IMF, the World Bank and the World Trade Organization. The most likely stake for Russia at this level is to achieve fully recognized membership of the G-7 (sometimes mentioned as a potential economic security council). From that perspective, it would not be wise to frustrate the active integration of Central Europe in the institutions of the world economy. Russia has, indeed, never resisted initiatives by the OECD, IMF, EBRD, World Bank, WTO and EU's PHARE and TACIS in Central and Eastern Europe, including its own territory. Only when Russia has re-established its global position, or when it has decided to turn to East and South-East Asia for its economic recovery, can a new organizational borderline be drawn safely in Europe.[22]

Two Chess Boards

The existence of the IO theatre for power politics does not imply a complete replacement of the territorial theatre (even though in Western Europe this seems to be the case). Rather, the entire development can be compared with the impact of aviation on the role of the military in power politics: a new dimension has been added to the existing ones. Particularly with the arrival of satellites and ICBMs, the exploitation of this new dimension fundamentally altered the nature of strategic balances. But, as the success of Chechnya shows, the other dimensions of power politics retain their value. Again comparable to the development of air forces, the IO dimension of power politics has been developed over the years, passing various stages. The basic convention at its root is the principle of sovereignty and, therefore, IO power politics is a product of the Westphalian state system. Perhaps the *Ancien Régime*, with its sophisticated diplomatic rules for the conduct of war, should be analysed anew from an IO power politics perspective. In the Concert of Europe, The Hague Peace Conferences, as well as the first international public unions, all in the nineteenth century, the birth of IOs took place. They seemed ill-born in the League of Nations: the League meant for the development of international institutions what the zeppelin has been to the development of flying. Since

---

22 Vladisalv M. Zubok, 'Russia: Between Peace and Conflict', in Hans-Herik Holm and Georg Sørensen, eds, *Whose World Order? Uneven Globalization and the End of the Cold War* (Boulder, CO: Westview, 1995), pp. 103-18.

1945, however, the growth of international institutions has been enormous, both in quantitative and in qualitative terms. The UN system at the global level, the various regional organizations and, most sophisticated, the structure of interlocking institutions in Europe are proof of this.

One of the dominant questions is whether the IO dimension exists in spite of the other characteristics of the international system. How does IO power politics relate to the polarity in the system? But let me deal with a second question first, the question of how the IO dimension relates to the contemporary challenges of international stability that seem to come from 'below': civil wars, failed states, massive waves of refugees, spread of small arms, etc. Chechnya is but one of the contemporary examples of returning territorial battle grounds. The break-up of the Soviet Union, former Yugoslavia and Czechoslovakia, as well as the unification of Germany, emphasize the same principle: territorial borders still matter. The border disputes between Greece and Turkey, those on Cyprus, and the separatist move-ments in Scotland, the Basque Provinces, Catalonia, Corsica, northern Italy and Northern Ireland can also easily be analysed in traditional terms.

Some of these separatist battles are a direct effect of European integration: Madrid, London, Paris and Rome have to compete with Brussels; frustrated farmers have a hard time picking the proper location for their demonstrations – who is responsible?; Galician fishermen lose their battle with Canada in Brussels, while Madrid is caught in between; Scottish nationalists prefer to be European Scots than British citizens, etc. This means that IO power politics (including integration policies) may trigger new incentives for territorial ambitions.

IO power politics only boomed in Western Europe after 1945. Particularly because of America's hegemonic position and the solidarity required by the Cold War, West European countries were unable to translate their conflicts into territo-rial claims. The decolonization process, in which most of these states were entan-gled, did not encourage making such claims either. Stimulated by the 'never again (such a) war' attitudes and the conditions of the Marshall Plan, a new discourse was born.

The key word – the flag of the discourse – was no longer territorial sovereignty, but integration. Integration became a pivot in European power politics, similar to the principle of growth in economic policies: an end in itself. Also for those who oppose integration, integration is the subject of the debate. Speed, form and type of integration are structuring European relations and interests. Since the Cold War, all of Europe participates in this game. The ranking in hierarchy among European states is not determined by factual sovereignty and unilateral military and economic capabilities, but by location in the network of international institutions.

Nevertheless, it is important to note that, with the exception of the IO organs and the international civil servants involved in them, formal sovereignty remains a prerequisite to be allowed to participate in the IO games. Luxembourg is allowed a seat at the negotiation tables; Catalonia and Bavaria are not. This is an important link between the two realms of power politics, and it provides the traditional realm with current value. Estonia, Slovenia and Croatia have entered a first division, whereas northern Italy and Corsica remain regions only. The German Democratic Republic (although never fully independent and sovereign) lost all its power and identity in the international system due to its eagerness to integrate completely with the West.

These examples illustrate the complicated relationship between integration and disintegration, and underlines that for the foreseeable future it is unlikely that even European integration in the EU context will make the member states abandon their sovereignty rights. Keohane implicitly emphasizes the continued importance of sovereignty in institutional power politics:[23] in Europe, sovereignty functions as a bargaining chip, he argues. This power resource, however, is not renewable. If European integration results in a real union, another discourse has to come into force. The Schengen Treaty and EMU are pushing Europe in that direction, but the counter pressure is strong and the Maastricht Treaty was a victory for inter-governmentalism, featuring a future for sovereignty. In other words, the echoes of traditional power politics are still very strong in the post-modern IO games.

FRICTION

So far it has been argued that there are two theatres for power politics: one based on territorial sovereignty rights; the other based on membership of international organizations. The political functions of the military are still the bottom line of the sovereignty issues; the political role of the diplomats is the bottom line of the IO issues. Even though the two dimensions are related, the role of the military in the IO theatre has become entirely abstract and bureaucratic. The questions focus on whether the Western European Union (WEU) should be a European pillar within NATO and a defensive organization for the EU, the re-entry of France in NATO's military organization, and who is charge of all this? Nominations for Secretary-Generals are important indicators of the balance of power among the member states, but direct use of military forces to support moves in these struggles for power are unthinkable. Lobbying is the dominant tactic on the battlefield.

Also in a global context, warfare has become the symbol for the failure of state politics. Interstate wars have become rare, hegemonic wars have become self-destructive, and civil wars hardly add to the prestige of the challenged government. Paradoxically, this has turned warfare into an attractive emancipatory instrument for substate actors who want to conquer a seat at the negotiation tables. If violence lasts, is brutal and accompanied by diplomatic efforts abroad, the oppositional

---

23   Robert O. Keohane, 'Hobbes's Dilemma and Institutional Change in World Politics: Sovereignty in International Society', in Holm and Sørensen, *Whose World Order?*, pp. 165-86.

group will ultimately be recognized by members of the international system, not as an outlaw or a terrorist, but as a potential new government of the same or of a new state. The ANC and PLO are clear examples; the IRA has been close to success; the FIS will probably follow in their footsteps. As soon as they are accepted, however, they try to play the civilized (demilitarized) roles of the post-modern state (at least the ANC and PLO are trying), elections are organized, foreign investments invited and IO memberships applied for, or they will be marginalized as pariah states (like Iraq). Does this mean that lowering the criteria for independence should be the best advice to those who want to control substate violence? Why would states resist a sovereign Corsica, a sovereign Basque State, a sovereign Northern Ireland, etc., if they know that these newly born sovereigns have as their highest stakes to become faithful members of the 'international community of states'? In the former Soviet empire, allowing states to break away has worked fairly well.

These are not rhetorical questions. The *raison d'être* of states is to resist separatists and imperialists; it is not known what happens if they stop taking this role seriously – even though at the same time their own borders are arbitrary outcomes of historic circumstances. Friction rules.

GLOBAL STRUCTURE

Within the European subsystem the importance of IO power politics is evident, but what does it mean in a global context? 'Europe' is still searching for an identity that could make a difference. It is typical for IO power politics that the debate is about the future symbolic value of the Western European Union as an institutional bridge between transatlantic NATO and the so-called Second Pillar of the EU on a Common Foreign and Security Policy. This debate matters within Europe, but beyond its borders? Creating Combined Joint Task Forces in the context of NATO similarly points at the ability to overcome the problems of sovereignty in opera-tional terms, but how to formulate the required policy objectives for proper deployment remains to be seen. Obviously, in the face of clear threats that leave little space for interpretation, Europe is integrated at the IO level to such an extent that it can act. Optimists in this respect may argue that since the Cold War the threats to stability in Europe or world-wide have not been such that there has been a need to put aside national differences. The Gulf War was closest to a high political risk, and solidarity was overwhelming. The Balkans, Central Africa or the Cauca-sus, in that perception, were simply less urgent, and thus allowed for other institu-tional struggles for power to intervene; an example is the concurrence of the problems of recognizing Croatia and saving the 1990 Maastricht negotiations – France and Germany took time to find a trade-off. The problem in the longer run is, of course, that the open indecisiveness of EU member states reads as weakness, and thus prevents building up international prestige. Here the United States is still superior, also on the European continent, proved by not just the Dayton Treaty but also by keeping peace in the Aegean Sea.

The underlying question is how IO power politics affect the structure of the international system. Following Neo-realism, the international system can be analysed in terms of: a) its deep structure (anarchy versus hierarchy); b) its type of units; and c) the distribution of power among these units.[24] Where and how does IO power politics intervene in this scheme? Daniel Deudney has introduced the notion of a *negarchy* to describe structures that closely resemble what has been described here as interlocking institutions: situations characterized by competing competencies and overlapping authorities.[25] Within the European subsystem this seems to have affected the deep structure: neither the rules of anarchy nor those of hierarchy apply in power political analyses of European politics. Whether IO power politics affects the type of units in the (sub)system is more questionable. Even the most advanced of international organizations, the EU, is fully dependent on the willing compliance of the member states to sustain it.[26] On the other hand, the European Commission and the European Court of Justice have played crucial roles in European politics; and world-wide the situation is essentially different from the times when permanent secretariats, permanent national representatives and promising careers for international civil servants were non-existent.

IOs do affect the distribution of power, and more so the struggle for power. This dominant aspect of IO power politics is seldom discussed in Neo-realist literature. The struggle for power as such is taken as a constant, whereas it is a variable. In ancient times other qualities were required to win the struggle for power than in modern times. Skills on the battlefield have become less crucial, whereas managerial skills and media performance have become crucial. Similarly, much of politics is about bureaucratic skills, including the talents to manipulate international organizations. This discussion is still undecided. The present concentration of interstate relations on international institutions can be temporary, a fall-back to traditional geopolitics is a real option. Nevertheless it has already lasted since 1990, when the OSCE formed a face-saving forum to end the Cold War in Europe by signing the Treaty of Paris. It is often said that one cannot disinvent nuclear weapons – it is a question of parameter changes. Probably the same is true for international organizations.

---

24 Waltz, *Theory of International Politics*; Barry Buzan, Charles Jones and Richard Little, *The Logic of Anarchy: Neo-realism to Structural Realism* (New York: Columbia University Press, 1992).

25 Daniel H. Deudney, 'The Philadelphian System: Sovereignty, Arms Control, and Balance of Power in the American States-Union, circa 1787-1861', *International Organization*, Vol. 49, No. 2, 1995, pp. 191-228.

26 Hans Mouritzen, 'Twining Plants of International Cooperation Reflections on the Peculiarities of "Security" IGOs', in de Wilde and Wiberg, *Organized Anarchy in Europe*, pp. 65-84.

8 Strategy in a Post-Clausewitzian Setting

Jan Willem Honig

The eruption of so-called 'ethnic' and 'intra-state' conflict around the globe after the end of the Cold War is making many Western governments and militaries nervous. This type of conflict (together, perhaps, with terrorism emanating from 'rogue states') is generally seen as the major threat to Western security. Politicians overwhelmingly react to ethnic conflict with extreme caution. They claim that these conflicts are so intractable that anything short of massive military involvement will not work. At the same time, they insist that these conflicts are too far removed from vital national interests to merit serious involvement as a belligerent. The militaries share this assessment. They also oppose intervention, except a massive one – which they know finds little political support anyway. Underlying this attitude – no use of force except overwhelming force will work in the modern world – is a seriously flawed understanding of war and strategy. In effect, Western strategic thinking is facing a crisis, which has been long in the making, but whose true extent only the end of the Cold War is beginning to reveal.

In this chapter, the nature of the crisis in strategic thinking will be considered. Since Clausewitz stands at the root of these problems, the chapter's first part will focus on the great thinker's ideas. As will be argued, the crisis in strategic thinking is caused by the domination of a Clausewitzian strategic doctrine that is inappropriate to combatting or solving likely conflicts facing the West. Instead, what is needed – and this is the subject of the second section – is a concept, or even a doctrine, of limited war. The chapter will not provide a detailed concept or doctrine. Although it suggests some crucial parameters, its main objective is to make the case for such a doctrine.

Parts of the argument bear a close affinity to Martin van Creveld's views on future war[1] – though there are some significant differences. It does not, for example, share Van Creveld's key criticism of Clausewitz and his contemporary followers that they fail to recognize that conflict has moved beyond state-based, or

---

1   See chapter 2 by Martin van Creveld; see also his *The Transformation of War* (New York: Free Press, 1991), which was published in Britain by Brassey's under the title *On Future War*.

G.C. de Nooy (ed.), The Clausewitzian Dictum and the Future of Western Military Strategy, 109-121.
© 1997 *Kluwer Law International. Printed in the Netherlands.*

'trinitarian', warfare. The Clausewitzian idea of all military effort as being driven by an interaction between the trinity of government, military and people may have been based on the idea of the state, but it is easily adaptable to forms of warring social organizations that do not form states. Any community has its leaders, fighters and common people. It is unfortunate that Van Creveld's 'state-bashing' detracts from the immense value of his emphasis on the motivations and norms of the members of the state- or community-based trinity. He rightly claims that war is not simply fought for 'reasons of state', but that religious and legal factors can be equally, or more, important. Equally significant is his claim that all combatants adhere to certain conventions or 'laws of war'. As he succinctly put it during the conference in which this book was discussed: 'without laws of war, it is impossible to have war'. Motivation and norms are the key variables that need to be understood if we are to resolve the crisis in Western strategic thinking and the ways in which we might deal with the (supposedly) new threats facing us.

The Problem with Clausewitz

Clausewitz is more popular in the Western world than ever before. Most stunning is the success of his *magnum opus*, *On War*, in the Anglo-American world. The 1976 English translation by Michael Howard and Peter Paret[2] – in marked contrast to the earlier ones by J.J. Graham (1874; revised edition 1908) and O.J. Matthijs Jolles (1943)[3] – have enjoyed huge sales. On Sir Michael Howard's own admission, the royalties keep him 'in comfortable old age'. Even the supposedly less satisfactory Graham translation, which has been published by Penguin in an abridged edition, has sold some 250,000 copies since appearing in 1968. What accounts for the success? Obviously, it has a lot to do Clausewitz's approach to the subject of war and with the quality of his ideas. As Martin van Creveld suggests in his contribution to this volume, 'the constant juxtaposition of theory and historical reality' is a method congenial to modern academics and not too abhorrent to many practitioners of war. In terms of his ideas, two particular ones have been singled out time and again by Howard and Paret as particularly worthwhile and relevant: Clausewitz's contention that war is a political instrument and that two types of war exist, limited and total.

---

2   Carl von Clausewitz, *On War*, translated and edited by Michael Howard and Peter Paret (Princeton, NJ: Princeton University Press, 1976).

3   Carl von Clausewitz, *On War*, translated by J.J. Graham (London: N. Trübner, 1874), revised edition by F.N. Maude (London: Kegan and Paul, 1908); Clausewitz, *On War*, translated by O.J. Matthijs Jolles (New York: Random House, 1943). For some information on the relative commercial failure of these editions, see Christopher Bassford, *Clausewitz in English: The Reception of Clausewitz in Britain and America, 1815-1945* (New York: Oxford University Press, 1994), pp. 58, 183.

These two ideas were particularly striking to two academics whose formative years were dominated by the experience of the Second World War and whose professional years were spent under the shadow of the Cold War. Both Paret, as a refugee from Nazism, and Howard, as a Guards' officer, witnessed at first hand how political considerations in Germany succumbed to the military demands of the War and how the War became increasingly senseless as a result. On the British and American side, civilian democratic control over the war effort suffered great strain as well.

POLITICAL AIMS AND MILITARY STRATEGY

Re-establishing a clear link between rational political aims and military strategy lost none of its pertinence in the Cold War. Again the military demands posed by the conflict, when the United States and the United Kingdom created the largest peacetime military establishments in their history, posed a danger to the supremacy of political considerations. What is more, the destructive effect of nuclear weapons made the need to control war and keep the conflict limited more urgent than ever. It thus seemed fortunate that such a great military writer as Clausewitz had already made these concerns the cornerstones of his work.

A major problem with Howard and Paret, however, is that to a large extent they read these issues into Clausewitz.[4] Neither issue was central to Clausewitz in quite the way that they claim. For most of Clausewitz's life, the idea of war being a continuation of politics by other means was an obvious assumption. This idea he shared with most, if not all, European military thinkers of his time. Like them, Clausewitz could not conceive of war as being anything other than an instrument in the hands of the princes of Europe. Martin van Creveld has correctly emphasized that Clausewitz's theories are founded on the existence of an international system dominated by states.[5] His original aim in writing *On War* (note the title!) was not to explain how the interrelationship between war and politics worked. Rather, he wanted to analyse the inner workings of the phenomenon war. As one would expect, he was very much influenced by contemporary events in his analysis. The crushing

---

4   To give two quick examples of the extent to which Howard and Paret were influenced by modern conditions and concerns, they translate Clausewitz as writing 'the supreme, the most far-reaching act of judgement that the statesman and commander have to make is to establish ... the kind of war on which they are embarking ...'. The original sees the statesman and general as one and the same person: cf. Clausewitz, *On War*, p. 88 with Carl von Clausewitz, *Vom Kriege, Hinterlassenes Werk des Generals Carl von Clausewitz*, edited by Werner Hahlweg, 18th ed. (Bonn: Dümmler, 1972), p. 212. They also consistently translate 'Niederwerfung' with the far less decisive and blood-curdling 'defeat', for example in the title of Chapter 4 of Book VIII.

5   Van Creveld, chapter 2; and *The Transformation of War*. An important article by C.B.A. Behrens (reviewing Paret's biography of Clausewitz) also drew attention to this fact: 'Which Side Was Clausewitz On?', *The New York Review of Books*, 14 October 1976.

defeat of Prussia at the hands of Napoleon in 1806, which he witnessed as a young officer, was a seminal event in his life.[6] It demonstrated what became one of the fundamental elements of Clausewitz's thought, and which Azar Gat termed 'the imperative of destruction'.[7] Clausewitz believed that Napoleon had revealed the true nature of war: war was about the use of force, and its natural aim was to make the enemy defenceless.[8] The pre-eminent way of achieving this goal was through battles of annihilation.

Any war fought for limited operational aims was therefore to Clausewitz a historical anomaly. If an enemy aimed to make one defenceless by forcing a decisive battle – as Napoleon had done to the Prussians at Jena-Auerstedt in 1806 – then one had no choice but to aim to do the same to the enemy. In other words, Clausewitz concluded, escalation (or in his words, '*Steigerung zum Äußersten*') was inevitable as soon as one realized the existence of this fundamental principle. Clausewitz thus ended up with a very coherent and even practical theory of war. Quite independent of one's political aims, the sensible aim on an operational or strategic level had to be the destruction of the enemy's capacity to resist – which in Clausewitz's own day meant his armed forces. If one achieved this, one's political aim (whatever that might be) would automatically be achieved since the enemy had no choice but to concede.

It is well known that Clausewitz became increasingly troubled by the absence of great campaigns of annihilation from much of history. Late in his life he realized that the Napoleonic campaigns represented but one type of war and that, in reality, there must exist also a second type of war, more limited and politicized in nature. However, he died before he could adapt *On War* to reflect this growing realization. As a result, inconsistencies remained in the great work which confused many later readers and which led many, particularly German generals and editors, astray in their interpretation and even in their editing of the master text.[9] However, modern editors, starting with Werner Hahlweg who delivered the modern German edition in 1952 and, for the English-speaking world, Michael Howard and Peter Paret, have attempted to restore the original text with what they believed to be the appropriate exegetic emphasis on limited war and war as a political instrument.[10]

---

6   For example, *Vom Kriege*, Book VI, Chapter 28, especially pp. 820-2; Book VI, Chapter 8, pp. 658-9; Book VIII, Chapter 3A, p. 959. One of the very few writings which Clausewitz published during his lifetime was an account of the 1806 campaign: Clausewitz, *Historische Briefe über die großen Kriegsereignisse im Oktober 1806*, edited by Joachim Niemeyer (Bonn: Dümmler, 1977).

7   Azar Gat, *The Origins of Military Thought from the Enlightenment to Clausewitz* (Oxford: Clarendon Press, 1989), p. 200.

8   Note that Howard and Paret translate Clausewitz's consistent use of 'wehrlos' with the much less precise 'powerless'.

9   See Werner Hahlweg's introduction to Clausewitz, *Vom Kriege*, 18th ed., pp. 69-72.

10 But see note 4 above.

Unfortunately, Clausewitz never developed a theory of limited war. In his famous note dated 10 July 1827, which identified the dual nature of war, he juxtaposes what is a quite convincing fundamental law of war with an incidental observation:

> Diese doppelte art des Krieges ist nämlich diejenige, wo der Zweck das *Niederwerfen des Gegners* ist, sei es, daß man ihn politisch vernichten oder bloß wehrlos machen und also zu jenem beliebigen Frieden zwingen will, und diejenige, wo man *bloß an den Grenzen seines Reiches einige Eroberungen machen will*, sei es, um sie zu behalten, oder um sie als nützliches Tauschmittel beim Frieden geltend zu machen.[11]

The clarity of the operational aim in strategies of 'overthrow' contrasts sharply with those in wars of the second type. What aims in war are there other than the destruction of the enemy's armed forces? It is surely not in all cases the conquest of some territory? One looks in vain in Clausewitz's work for the development of a theory or a concept of what principle underlay this type of more limited operations.[12]

What is worse, his attempt to bring politics into war complicated rather than clarified the issue. To Clausewitz, the essence of the solution appeared to lie in the relationship between what in English can be distinguished conveniently as 'policy' and 'politics'. Limited war was not simply a possible result of sound policy by a statesman who strove to achieve limited political aims, but equally dependent on the nature of the political system in which he operated. In line with many of his more conservative-minded contemporaries, Clausewitz believed that the escalatory pressures on war also emanated from the participation of 'the people' in war (in addition to being inherent in war as well). To keep popular emotions under control required strong government. Only then could '*das bloße Verstand*' prevail over '*dem blinden Naturtrieb*' embodied by the people. Implicit in his argument is that governmental control could also somehow reign in the escalatory pressures inherent in the phenomenon of war. Clausewitz summed up this idea at the end of his celebrated first chapter of Book I in, what he called, the '*wunderliche Dreifältigkeit*':

> zusammengesetzt aus der ursprünglichen Gewaltsamkeit seines [that is, war] Elementes, dem Haß und der Feindschaft, die wie ein *blinder Naturtrieb* anzusehen sind, aus dem Spiel der Wahrscheinlichkeiten und des Zufalls, die ihn zu einer *freien Seelentätigkeit* machen, und aus der untergeordneten Natur eines politischen Werkzeuges, wodurch er dem bloßen *Verstande* anheimfällt.[13]

---

11 Clausewitz, *Vom Kriege*, 18th ed., p. 179 (italics in original).
12 There is not even much of a list of operational aims other than those aiming for decisive battle; cf. Clausewitz, *Vom Kriege*, Book VIII, Chapters 5, 7 and 8.
13 Clausewitz, *Vom Kriege*, Book I, Chapter 1, p. 213.

For many interpreters of Clausewitz since the Second World War, such as Raymond Aron in France and Gerhard Ritter in Germany, the trinity became a key concept in analysing the limitation of war – although the idea appears only once in the whole of *On War*.[14] Ritter's emphasis on statesmen with morals and Aron's on '*la raison*' betray not only a state-based structure as a precondition to control war, but even a particular kind of state.[15] Both Ritter and Aron were, not surprisingly, conservatives who cast a wary eye on the growing involvement of the people in politics and war.

Such ideas were clearly not wholly in tune with political developments in postwar Europe. The prevailing opinion regarding the relationship between politics and war came to be a fundamentally different, non-Clausewitzian, Anglo-Saxon liberal one: that the best hedge against total war was not a strong state, but democratic politics (though not, of course, against morally reprehensible authoritarian or dictatorial regimes). But whatever the validity of either one of these ideas, they still leave the question unanswered of how limited political aims translate into limited military aims. Both ideas implicitly assume that if the statesman or government keep control over political objectives, somehow the operational aims fall into place and the war as a whole remains limited.[16]

LIMITED POLITICAL OBJECTIVES

The relationship between politics and strategy continues to stump politicians, the military and scholars alike. On a political level, Western governments have come to accept, grudgingly perhaps, limited objectives. The Gulf War and Bosnia (like Korea and Vietnam in an earlier era) were limited wars in this sense. Governments may have felt under strong moral pressure from their domestic constituencies to force Saddam Hussein out of power in Iraq and to make the Serbs pay for their aggression in Bosnia, but the lack of vital interests at stake and worries about the

---

14 Gerhard Ritter, *Staatskunst und Kriegshandwerk: Das Problem des Militarismus in Deutschland*, Vol. I, *Die altpreussische Tradition (1740-1890)* (Munich: Oldenbourg, 1954); Raymond Aron, *Penser la guerre, Clausewitz*, Vol. I, *L'âge européen* (Paris: Gallimard, 1976). See also P.M.E. Volten, 'De wonderlijke Drievuldigheid', Rede uitgesproken bij de aanvaarding van het ambt van bijzonder hoogleraar in de krijgsgeschiedenis, in het bijzonder van de veiligheidsproblematiek, aan de Rijksuniversiteit te Utrecht, op 11 November 1985.

15 Ritter, *The Sword and the Sceptre: The Problem of Militarism in Germany*, Vol. I, *The Prussian Tradition, 1740-1890*, translated by Heinz Norden (Princeton Junction, NJ: The Scholar's Bookshelf, 1988), p. 325 (Afterword to the 2nd and 3rd editions); Aron, *Penser la guerre*, Vol. 2: *L'âge planétaire*, p. 174.

16 Although the term 'limited war' has become common, one of the striking conclusions of a detailed analysis of the development of concepts of war and strategy since Clausewitz is the absence of a concept of limited war. Contrary to conventional wisdom, there are only a handful of people who struggle with this idea and only since the Second World War and with little success. I am preparing a major article on this topic.

potential cost engendered in them a kind of willy-nilly realism that made the wars end in compromise.[17]

However, the translation of limited political aims into limited strategic aims has not fared too well. For the US military in particular, as a result of the Vietnam War, the word 'limited war' has become a byword for bad policy, bad strategy and defeat. In an October 1992 interview with the *New York Times*, the then Chairman of the Joint Chiefs of Staff, General Colin Powell, summed it up: 'As soon as they tell me it's limited, it means they do not care whether you achieve a result or not. As soon as they tell me it's "surgical", I head for the bunker'.[18]

The war against Iraq illustrates the difficulties that politicians and soldiers face in balancing political ends, operational goals and military means. The US administration and military described their respective objectives in terms that clearly reflected these difficulties. On the one hand, officials announced the use of 'overwhelming' force against Iraq with the aim of achieving an 'absolute, total victory'.[19] But on the other hand, they continually reiterated that the political objective of the war was limited to the liberation of Kuwait.[20] The type of victory sought thus did not correspond with the professed ultimate aim of the war.

What accounted for the contradiction? Part of the answer was undoubtedly political expediency. Threatening the 'destruction of the adversary' through the massive use of force (with the threat of overthrowing Saddam thrown in for good measure at various times) must have been thought a good strategy to scare Saddam into giving in before hostilities started in earnest. At the same time, it sought to convince US domestic public opinion that the conflict was serious and that the government would not accept defeat or even half-victory. But it also reflected a genuine confusion on the part of policy-makers about the meaning of words like 'absolute, total victory' and the relationship between political and strategic aims.

The US military took the threat made by their political leaders seriously. The Allied field commander General Norman Schwarzkopf planned a traditional,

---

17 The moral challenges caused by the tension between an unwillingness to compromise with unsavoury regimes and an unwillingness to pay the cost of using force can create serious problems in humanitarian interventions. See Jan Willem Honig and Norbert Both, *Srebrenica: Record of a War Crime* (Harmondsworth: Penguin, 1995).

18 Quoted in Colin Powell, *My American Journey* (New York: Ballantine Books, 1996), p. 544.

19 'The only acceptable outcome if hostilities begin is absolute, total victory' and 'I think he [Saddam Hussein] knows our response would be overwhelming'. Secretary of Defence Dick Cheney, in the *International Herald Tribune*, 22-23 December and 24-25 December 1990, respectively. 'Believe me, by being quick, massive and decisive, we will win'; Vice-President Dan Quayle in the *Washington Times*, 2 January 1991. See also the testimony by Colin Powell to the Senate Armed Services Committee, as quoted in the *New York Times*, 4 December 1990.

20 'Our objectives are clear. Saddam Hussein's forces will leave Kuwait, the legitimate Government of Kuwait will be restored to its rightful place and Kuwait will once again be free'; President Bush in the *New York Times*, 17 January 1991. See also Cheney's testimony to the Senate Armed Services Committee, as quoted in the *New York Times*, 4 December 1990.

Clausewitzian campaign, which drew its inspiration (just like General Schlieffen's notorious plan to defeat France in 1914) from one of the great battles of annihilation in history. Schwarzkopf later said that after the third day of the ground war, he believed that 'it was literally about to become a battle of Cannae, a battle of annihilation'. Schwarzkopf said that he had wanted to continue operations to achieve this aim, but was stopped by the President.[21] Despite the later disclaimers that Schwarzkopf's opinion did not mean that he disagreed with his President's decision to halt military operations, it is nevertheless clear that on an operational level the campaign plan had aimed not simply at liberating Kuwait, but at making Iraq defenceless.

The Schwarzkopf example illustrates that what was long feared as an issue – that war is a continuation of politics by other means – has not turned out to be a real problem. This principle that is ascribed to Clausewitz has become accepted. On the other hand, however, the other supposedly Clausewitzian idea of limited war has proved remarkably shallow. The military campaign was anything but a limited war. The talk about intervention scenarios in Bosnia also illustrates that Western militaries continue to think in terms of strategies of annihilation. The massive numbers of troops that were purported to be necessary for military intervention reflected this: if 120,000 was proposed as a minimum, the military generally preferred 400,000 to 500,000 troops.[22]

THE CLAUSEWITZ RENAISSANCE

The 'Clausewitz renaissance' has been a paradoxical one. As said, the publication of the 1976 Michael Howard and Peter Paret translation of Clausewitz's *On War* was clearly meant to provide a validation of the concept of limited war. Although *On War* was adopted as a textbook in the US naval, air and army war colleges in the late 1970s, limited war theory was resoundingly rejected by American armed forces. In fact, Clausewitz has ended up being used against limited war theory in two ways. US Army Colonel Harry Summers, who was in charge of a project in the late 1970s and early 1980s to provide an analysis that taught the US armed forces the Clausewitzian reasons for their failure in Vietnam and sought to prepare them properly for the next war, claims in his enormously popular *On Strategy: A Critical Analysis of the Vietnam War* that American policy-makers in the 1960s had failed

---

21 *New York Times*, 28 March 1991. The importance of the Cannae idea to Gulf War planning was confirmed by Schwarzkopf in a recent BBC documentary; on the importance of the 'Cannae Principle' in Schlieffen's thought, see Alfred von Schlieffen, *Cannae* (Berlin: E. S. Mittler, 1925).

22 James Gow, 'Nervous Bunnies: The International Community and the Yugoslav War of Dissolution', in Lawrence Freedman, ed., *Military Intervention in European Conflicts* (Oxford: Blackwell for *The Political Quarterly*, 1994), p. 26.

to 'invoke the national will' and mobilize the American people.[23] In other words, by concentrating on policy, they failed to perceive the importance of politics. Second, Summers argued that, on a strategic level, the graduated response practised by successive US administrations was bound to fail. It led to a piecemeal introduction of US forces into the conflict, which did not convey the intention to win the conflict. Only the use of overwhelming force and the single-minded pursuit of victory could have achieved that.[24] Ironically, perhaps, despite the distinct limited war slant of their translation, Howard and Paret have failed to veil the more authentic Clausewitz, the advocate of a strategy of overthrow.

One can sympathize with the attempt of the US military to bring battle back to the battlefield after the Cold War and demand clear operational concepts, but one wonders whether adopting a strategic doctrine that draws its inspiration from battles like Cannae is wise. For the earlier Cannae adept, German chief of staff General Count Schlieffen, the idea did not work too well. For one thing, the example of the First World War (and also the Second) shows that strategies of overthrow generate huge escalatory pressures. Because of the effort required to achieve victory, they easily lead to political goal inflation. The ends, after all, have to justify the means. The same problem was also apparent in the Gulf War. There was palpable disappointment in the United States when the massive military effort deployed in the Gulf succeeded only in liberating Kuwait and failed to topple the instigator of it all, Saddam Hussein. The doctrine of the strategy of overthrow may still have some validity (though an unsettling one) for traditional massive conventional inter-state conflicts, but one can ask whether it is at all useful for the much more likely types of conflicts that Western militaries face. Our military strategies are based on a capacity to escalate and destroy, whereas our political instincts demand restraint because of the dangers of escalation. If, as will be the case in most instances, a future threat is not serious enough to warrant giving the go-ahead for massive military action, the prevailing strategic doctrine is a recipe for paralysis. If the stakes do warrant it, they will be put under enormous pressure to be raised even further to justify the military effort. Either way, the doctrine of overwhelming force does not appear a very sensible one in the modern world.

---

23   Harry G. Summers Jr, *On Strategy: A Critical Analysis of the Vietnam War* (New York: Dell, 1984), p. 43. On the rediscovery of Clausewitz by the US armed forces and his introduction into the curriculum, see Summers, *On Strategy II: A Critical Analysis of the Gulf War* (New York: Dell, 1992), pp. 61-150.

24   Harry G. Summers Jr, *On Strategy*, pp. 83, 104-5, 116-7. See also Harry G. Summers, *On Strategy II*; and Christopher M. Gacek, *The Logic of Force: The Dilemma of Limited War in American Foreign Policy* (New York: Columbia University Press, 1994).

The Undeterrables

The types of conflict that exercise military minds the most since the end of the Cold War are ethnic conflicts. The aspect they find most worrying about these conflicts is the seemingly irrational motivations of the parties which originate in the murky, deepest depths of history. Describing Bosnia as 'an ethnic tangle with roots reaching back a thousand years' suggests that untangling the conflict is an almost hopeless task.[25] People motivated by ethnic hatreds easily appear unsusceptible to traditional forms of the use or threat of force. Classic concepts such as deterrence and coercion that are familiar from Cold War days seem unlikely to work – except, perhaps, if backed up by overwhelming force.

The same reasoning is applied to the other phenomenon worrying soldiers, that of 'rogue states', that is, states that refuse to adhere to common norms of international intercourse and wage undeclared wars of terrorism. The behaviour of states such as Libya and Iran is found puzzling, and this is reflected in muddled Western responses.

The option of overwhelming force against either of these types of warfare, however, is generally not practical. Quite apart from the problems inherent in the doctrine which were discussed above, interventions in rogue states appear too disproportionate a response to terrorist activity to be justifiable. Interventions in ethnic conflict are mostly driven by humanitarian impulses, not the defence of vital national interests. As a result, the political backing for massive use or even show of force is not usually forthcoming.

By default, Western actions concentrate on containment of these problems, rather than on their solution. Ethnic conflicts are fenced off in order to prevent much-feared spillover. Arms control treaties are proposed that seek to bind as many countries as possible to a regime that would prevent the most threatening weapon systems – such as nuclear, bacteriological and chemical weapons – from proliferating. Anti-ballistic missile defences are considered as a last-ditch defence against countries that refuse to submit themselves to arms control regimes and that might threaten the use of these weapons of terror.

In principle, one cannot fault such initiatives. But none of these measures will work against those that are not deterred by treaties and other defence measures. The West is, in effect, caught in an impasse: while containment is too defensive, current military doctrine is too offensive. The only alternative therefore is to ask whether ethnic conflict and terrorism can be managed or solved with the use of limited force. But can limited force have an effect on the supposedly 'undeterrable' nationalist and terrorist? Only if their motivations possess a rationality in the sense that they use force in order to attain a certain end and they accept that warfare is subject to

---

25   Powell, *An American Journey*, p. 544.

certain conventions, then it becomes possible to entertain the thought that counter-force can be targeted more precisely and that force can conceivably be limited.

LIMITATIONS TO WARFARE

Here we return to the two great ideas developed by Martin van Creveld in his *Transformation of War*: first, the suggestion that people at all times and all places accept certain limitations to warfare based on an understanding of certain conventions and laws of war; and, second, as the great Dutch historian Johan Huizinga argued more than half a century ago, that war can be more than a political instrument and possess culturally determined gamelike qualities.[26] An understanding of the role that warfare plays in different ways among different cultures must lie at the root of our thinking on limited war. Only when we understand the rules by which our enemies (and we ourselves) play, can we influence the outcome of the serious game of war.

But do irrational nationalists and terrorists play such games? Can they be influenced? Much of Van Creveld's argument suggests that this is extremely difficult: 'It is simply not true that war is solely a means to an end, nor do people fight in order to attain this objective or that. In fact, the opposite is true: people very often take up one objective or another precisely in order that they may fight.'[27] The suggestion clearly is that he who fights for the sake of fighting is not open to suggestions not to do it. Moreover, Van Creveld claims that the Western state system and defence organizations are singularly ill-equipped to withstand these forces of anarchy. He writes: 'Either modern states cope with low-intensity conflict, or else they will disappear; the suspicion grows, however, that they are damned if they do and damned if they don't.'[28]

There are two major problems with this argument. First, Van Creveld's emphasis on warfare as an activity ruled by conventions that human beings find difficult to break, implies that these conventions limit the use of force and provide opportunities for the settlement of a conflict under particular circumstances. These can be exploited through the use of force and diplomacy. It is, of course, possible that the conventions of two protagonists are so diametrically opposed that there is no common ground and no opportunity for a combination of force and diplomacy to work. But, in that case, provided one or the other party poses a sufficiently serious threat, the conflict will naturally escalate until a strategy of overthrow becomes

---

26   Johan Huizinga, *Homo ludens, Proeve eener bepaling van het spel-element der cultuur* (Haarlem: Tjeenk Willink, 1974).

27   Martin van Creveld, *The Transformation of War*, p. 226.

28   Martin van Creveld, *The Transformation of War*, pp. 224-5.

acceptable.[29] Second, Van Creveld's other claim that modern states and their armies find it impossible to cope with such conflicts is also difficult to accept. Although low-intensity wars are not fought *by* states, they are generally *about* states. The conflicts within Bosnia, Somalia and Israel are about state formation – just like the conflicts in Europe in the Middle Ages and early modern period. Western state and army formation are the pre-eminent examples of organizations that developed precisely because they were able to deal exceptionally well with sustained low-intensity conflict. If they coped so successfully in the past, why can they not be successful in the future? It appears better to assume that the state and its armed forces will adapt to the challenges it faces. And, given that these challenges may not be as fundamentally threatening as Van Creveld claims, this process need not be as hopeless as he suggests.

THEORY AND DOCTRINE OF LIMITED WAR

The Bosnian conflict demonstrated (and also Somalia and Rwanda) that the use of force was much better organized on the part of the ethnic groups than many in the West believed. Strategies were pursued. In Bosnia, it was possible to deal with the warring factions effectively by using limited force.[30] Indeed, there is still a close relationship with the level of political organization and scope and intensity of a conflict. The Bosnian conflict was so nasty precisely because the Serbian state, with all the powers at its disposal, used force as a means to an end.

This does not give us a ready-made doctrine of limited war. Our Western traditions do not provide us with one either. Conceptually, limited war is essentially a new problem. Europeans fought limited wars before Napoleon and Clausewitz, without the benefit of an elaborate body of theory and doctrine. Although the term 'limited war' entered common parlance in the 1950s, there still does not exist much in the way of a useful theory which could be the foundation for a doctrine.

A limited war theory was developed in the United States in the 1950s against the backdrop of possible nuclear war between the superpowers. This factor made it a very peculiar kind of limited war theory. As the United States and former Soviet Union were considered to have irreconcilable ideologies, the assumption was that the outcome of a conflict must involve the overthrow of one or other regime. But

---

29 One is reminded here of the famous 'realist' political scientist, Hans Morgenthau. He made the idea that common norms provided an opportunity for the settlement of international disputes the cornerstone of his early work. When he saw that this idea did not work in the conflict with Nazi Germany, he rejected it and instead became a realist who insisted on assuming the worst in one's potential enemies. Morgenthau, however, was too categorical in rejecting his earlier ideas: more often than not, there is common ground to solve a dispute. See Jan Willem Honig, 'Totalitarianism and Realism: Hans Morgenthau's German Years', *Security Studies*, Vol. 5, No. 2, winter 1995, pp. 283-313.
30 See Honig and Both, *Srebrenica*, chapters 4 and 7.

how could one avoid the problem of destroying both regimes in the process? Could one limit the use of unlimited means while trying to attain unlimited ends? The unlikelihood of this proposition made most limited war theorists ultimately counsel the avoidance of war with the former Soviet Union altogether.

For conflicts not directly involving the former Soviet Union and the danger of a nuclear exchange, a body of literature that theorized on deterrence and coercion emerged which might appear to provide a better starting point in identifying the common sensibilities and vulnerabilities that people, communities and states share *vis-à-vis* the threat or use of limited force. A major weakness with this approach, however, is that it ignores cultural factors that must be judged critical in finding vulnerabilities and opportunities for conflict resolution. Instead, it often assumes almost Pavlovian types of behaviour on the part of human beings. Rational actor modelling, where rationality is defined by one particular culture, leads almost inevitably to the conclusion that nationalists and terrorists from other cultures are irrational when they fail to exhibit the responses to stimuli predicted in the laboratories of American political science.

In conclusion, the emphasis on escalation and strategies of annihilation that pervades Clausewitz's work may no longer be a good idea (if it ever was), but his ideas (trite though they may be) on the instrumentality of force, on ends and means are still extremely useful. Wars are still fought between organized communities that pursue certain aims and that struggle with the peculiar characteristics inherent in the use of force (and that may even form a non-state-based trinity). Those aims may no longer centre on the defence of national interest (although for many ethnic groups it is), and the means may no longer be clearly identifiable armies, but force is still used to further particular, culturally defined aims. Knowing those aims and understanding how an enemy intends to go about achieving them, to what lengths he is willing to go, opens up the way to influencing him and forcing him to compromise. Herein lies the challenge for Western militaries: to devise an operational concept of limited war to deal with this cultural phenomenon.

9   Personnel in a Neo-Clausewitzian Setting

Kees Homan

The Armed Forces in a new Security Environment

TRINITARIAN WAR

One of Clausewitz's most famous insights is on what he called the 'remarkable trinity', now well known as 'trinitarian war'. 'As a total phenomenon', he wrote, 'its dominant tendencies always make war a remarkable trinity ... The first of these three aspects mainly concerns the people; the second the commander and his army; the third the government. The passions that are to be kindled in war must already be inherent in the people; the scope which the play of courage and talent will enjoy in the realm of probability and chance depends on the particular character of the commander and the army; but the political aims are the business of government alone'.[1]

This chapter will concentrate on the second element of this trinity, namely the armed forces and their future in a new security environment.

THE NEW SECURITY ENVIRONMENT

Looking at the present security environment, international relations between East and West have changed so dramatically that the possibility of a large-scale nuclear or conventional war has become, for the time being, fairly remote. But the changed situation since the fall of the Berlin Wall has lead to greater uncertainty as to where armed conflicts in and outside Europe may occur in the future, where military action will be required, under which circumstances and with which allies.

The international political developments of recent years also contributed to a fundamental redefinition of the concept of security, which also affects to a great extent the role of armed forces. Security, which had a mainly military character and

---

1   Carl von Clausewitz, *On War*, edited and translated by Michael Howard and Peter Paret (Princeton, NJ: Princeton University Press, 1976), p. 89.

G.C. de Nooy (ed.), The Clausewitzian Dictum and the Future of Western Military Strategy, 123-136.

was subject to a specific threat, is now multi-directional and multi-dimensional. It is unknown who will be the next enemy or the theatre in which armed forces will have to operate. And the military aspects of security now also need to be coordinated with the economic, political, psychological, administrative and humanitarian aspects, so that a coherent structure can be attained and a unity of command and policy maintained. In short: 'uncertainty', 'instability' and 'security risks' are the 'buzz-words' of the new security environment.

NEW TASKS IN A NEW CONFLICT ENVIRONMENT

It may be clear that as a consequence of these developments, the armed forces in many nations are facing a completely new future.

While armed forces can to a certain extent reduce their traditional defence efforts, at the same time conflicts in Somalia, Bosnia and Haiti have called for the definition of new tasks for the military, so that participation in UN (mandated) operations for peacekeeping and, if necessary, peace-enforcing purposes is now considered to be a normal part of the job for most military.

Although armed forces have to remain prepared for inter-state conventional combat, this is not sufficient.[2] Some observers even consider the Desert Storm model of conventional combat as largely irrelevant to the more likely security challenges in the post-Cold War world. They envisage an era of smaller, mainly unconventional and culturally motivated conflicts, waged for the most part inside rather than across established national boundaries. Based on the dominance of intra-state conflicts in recent years, it is highly probable that we are entering an era in which the predominant form of conflict will be smaller and less conventional wars, which will be waged mostly within recognized national borders. All 30 conflicts in 1995, in which more than 1000 persons died, were intra-state.[3] 'Failed states' in much of Africa, the collapse of the Soviet empire, the potential decomposition of Russia itself, and the likely spread of radical Islam, all portend a host of politically and militarily messy conflicts. They also forecast a continuation of strong pressures to participate in operations other than war, especially in peace, humanitarian relief, and nation-building operations.

MAKING DO WITH LESS

As a result, armed forces are undergoing tremendous changes in a period when domestic priorities and economic considerations have led to demands for what is

---

2   Jeffrey Record, *Ready for What and Modernized against Whom?*, (Carlisle Barracks, PA: Strategic Studies Institute, US Army War College, 10 April 1995).

3   Margareta Sollenberg and Peter Wallensteen, 'Major Armed Conflicts', in *SIPRI Yearbook 1996* (Oxford: Oxford University Press, 1996), p. 15.

called a peace dividend. In this respect, most armed forces nowadays cope with the problem that they have to move to smaller, more flexible and mobile forces, while in principle they try to hold on to the full range of capabilities to cover the whole conflict spectrum and do not take choices. Simply put, international and domestic realities have resulted in the paradox of declining military resources and increasing military missions.

The Armed Forces and Society

ALL-VOLUNTEER FORCES

Related to these developments is the march toward professionalism by the tendency to abolish conscription and to introduce All-Volunteer Forces (AVFs).[4] This decision was already taken quite some time ago by Western nations offshore from continental Europe, such as the United States and the United Kingdom. But conscription remained in mainland Europe so long as a continental war threatening national territories and constitutions was conceivable. However, the situation has also changed in mainland Europe and Belgium and the Netherlands have decided to abolish conscription. They will soon be followed by France and the Russian Federation, and probably also by Spain.

Countries that retain the draft have reduced the required time in uniform to as little as nine months, making meaningful training and specialization almost impossible.

Based on trends in the US Army since it became an AVF, it may be expected that introduction of AVFs will create opportunities to integrate more women and ethnic minorities in the armed forces. It is obvious that the armed forces will have to compete with civil organizations in the recruitment of personnel. This makes it of the utmost importance that no categories on the labour market be excluded from the military sector.

In the past, the armed forces had a social function as the 'school of the nation'. Military organizations could very well play the role of the nation's school once again. This applies especially to youngsters from ethnic minorities and other demographic newcomers, who may wish to seize new opportunities in the services for educating themselves and developing careers, both within and outside the military organization. In this respect it is relevant that in some countries, owing to changes

---

4   Joseph L. Soeters, 'Changing from Conscript to All-Volunteer Forces: The Dutch Experience', in Ernest Gilman and Detlef E. Herold, eds, *Democratic and Civil Control over Military Forces: Case Studies and Perspectives*, Monograph Series No. 3 (Rome: NATO Defence College, 1995).

in the demographic make up, some minorities will become majorities during the next century.

However, another major problem for the armed forces in modern times is how to retain the recruited personnel once they mature, get married, and raise families, on whose behalf they expect – or their wives expect – all the amenities and services with which they would be provided in civilian life.

REMILITARIZATION OR CIVILIANIZATION?

In this respect Michael Howard even wonders whether the armed forces have gone too far in accommodating themselves to the norms of the civilian community.[5] The question is about how much the military can reflect society and still be able to maintain combat effectiveness. It may be clear that in Western societies the military must certainly share the core values of the community and be dedicated to the principles of democracy, equity, justice, humanity and basic human rights. But this does not mean that it should be a representative cross-section, or accommodate all the alternative life-styles and norms that are tolerated in civilian life. The main requirement is that the armed forces, like other professions, should be efficient and 'representative' only to the extent that this contributes to its efficiency.

In this respect, one wonders whether the military has assimilated to the civilian community too much, especially in the field of management.[6] Can the armed forces really be run like a business? Can cost-benefit analysis effectively be applied to a body whose effectiveness must ultimately be judged by unquantifiable moral and psychological, rather than by quantifiable material criteria? How much can men be led by statistics when more fundamental values become predominate?

Armed forces have a unique character and role because of their connection with the means of legitimate violence. Thus they emphasize traditional institutional values of group solidarity; the importance of rank and command; physical robustness; the need to instil instincts – or a subculture – alien in civilian life in terms of dealing with fear of physical danger and acceptance of hardship; the importance of leadership; and so on.

The dilemma arises that, at the same time, all armed forces are dependent upon their host societies, from which they recruit and which they serve and from which they derive financial and moral support. It is the responsibility of the political leadership to ensure that a balance is struck between the need to retain the military qualities necessary for the effective performance of the armed forces in its various missions, and the need to ensure that supportive links between the armed forces and society are maintained.

---

5   Michael Howard, 'The Armed Forces and the Community', in *RUSI Journal*, August 1996, pp. 9-13.
6   Michael Howard, 'The Armed Forces and the Community', pp. 9-13.

Internationalization

MULTINATIONAL MILITARY FORCES

Another important development in the new security environment that affects the armed forces is the increase in the formation of multinational military forces.[7] For instance, NATO's 'London Declaration' of July 1990 prepared for a range of new multinational forces to be established. To obtain economies of scale and scope in a period of budgetary reductions and fear for the renationalization of defence structures, national military organizations were forced to form multinational units with the armed forces of other countries.

Different national attitudes, objectives and expectations have resulted in a range of new multinational formations in which there is no uniform structure: some are bi-national, tri-national or quadri-national; some are integrated at corps level and others at divisional level. However, they are all more the product of political considerations than of straightforward military desiderata.

Some interesting formations include:

* the Allied Command Europe Rapid Reaction Corps (ARRC) drawn from 13 different nations as the Supreme Allied Commander Europe's readiest crisis-management tool for both Article 5 and peace-support operations;
* the multinational Division (Central), a division of the ARRC, which is seeking to introduce the new operational concept of air mobility on a quadri-national basis;
* the Euro-Corps, which established the first European multinational force outside NATO's integrated military structure;
* the first combined German/Dutch Army Corps and the integration of the Dutch and Belgian Navies as examples of bi-national multinational forces.

PROBLEMS

Nevertheless, the structural multinational cooperation in the framework of an alliance or *ad hoc* in the framework of the United Nations poses several problems. The maintenance of cohesion in heterogeneous multinational coalitions often requires a considerable degree of tolerance for diversity. This results in lower military efficiency, as well as an understanding of the different cultures, interests and policies, which is substantially foreign to the traditional military logic and ethics.

---

7   Roger H. Palin, *Multinational Military Forces: Problems and Prospects*, Adelphi Paper 294 (London: International Institute for Strategic Studies, 1995).

Besides the logistical differences – because logistics are a national responsibility – there are significant differences in compensatory regulations for field training exercises, different financial compensation for extra, non-regular duties, and differing discipline for similar offences. Personnel serving in such units should be governed by some form of multinational regime. Otherwise, over time apparent inequity can undermine the sense of shared risk and common goodwill that binds a multinational force together.

CULTURAL ASPECTS

But cultural differences, in particular, can cause problems.[8] The intercultural aspects of international cooperation are most relevant in UN (mandated) operations, as both Western and non-Western nations participate in these operations. In the Gulf War, for example, the most celebrated concern was whether women should be allowed into the theatre of operations, and if so, in what roles. Women have been integrated into most Western forces and are employed in most roles, including combat roles such as air crew. But in Muslim states women are forbidden from such activity and there are strict rules governing their mode of living. Similarly, religious differences can cause unease – again in the Gulf War the import of Christian Bibles was banned. Such fundamental cultural nervousness can undermine the cohesion of a multinational force, and the need for tolerance and understanding must be emphasized.

Many countries also enter situations with special conditions attached because of domestic considerations. For example, Hindu troops sent in an Indian contingent to Somalia came with the proviso from their government that they might not engage Muslims – for the very understandable reason that such a development might incite difficulties at home.[9]

As many researchers have already indicated, the effectiveness of UN operations is related to their legitimacy, and the lower the legitimacy of a UN operation the less chance it will have of producing effective results. When only a limited degree of legitimacy exists, operational problems will develop because many, often smaller, Western and non-Western nations participate in these operations. Although many of the problems relate to the limited standardization of equipment and logistics, a number of managerial problems arise as a result of diverging national cultural backgrounds.

Another lesson is that the lower the intensity of the operations, the more demanding the maintenance of cohesion. In this case, in fact, the political factors

8   Roger H. Palin, *Multinational Military Forces.*
9   Anthony Zinni, 'Peacekeeping and Conflict Management', in *Allied Planning for Peacekeeping and Conflict Management: Tailoring Military Means to Political Ends* (Cambridge, MA: Institute for Foreign Policy Analysis, 1994), p. 81.

and non-military dimensions of the strategy prevail over the military components, and it is consequently more difficult to maintain cohesion within a multinational coalition. The unity of command during the Gulf War was certainly higher than that achieved in Somalia or Bosnia, irrespective of the will to collaborate and the discipline of the various national commanders. Inevitably, politics tends to divide, and only leadership and tolerance of an acceptable decrease in operational efficiency can maintain cohesion in a coalition. This latter aspect often represents the prerequisite for any possible political success; therefore it is more important than tactical success.

But Western multinational forces can also face cultural differences. A former commandant of the NATO multinational Division (Central) observed that in his four-nation division the four cultures were certainly more manifest and therefore recognizable in daily duties. In clarifying this by two words per nation, he said that the Germans are '*gründlich und pünktlich*', the Belgians 'loyal and hospitable', the British 'professional and traditional' and the Dutch 'flexible and computer-like'.[10]

Non-Traditional Missions

EXPANDED ROLE

As a result of the above-mentioned changes in the security environment, the role played by the military has diversified and expanded into fields not normally associated with the armed forces during the Cold War era. Nevertheless, while the possibility of a major regional conflict or a dramatic unforeseeable change in the geostrategic landscape can never be excluded, it is essential that credible and cohesive forces for the traditional defence of own or allied territory are maintained.

NON-TRADITIONAL MISSIONS

But given their superb logistical and organizational skills, their rigorous training and ability to operate in austere environments for extended periods, it is only natural that civilian policy-makers see the military as an ideal instrument for conducting so-called non-traditional operations.[11]

---

10   P. Huysman, 'Military Cultures', in T. de Kruijf, ed., *The Future Relationship between Germany and the Netherlands*, Report of the symposium held on the occasion of the 130th Anniversary of the Royal (Netherlands) Association for Military Science (Koninklijke Vereniging ter Beoefening van de Krijgswetenschap) (The Hague: 18 May 1995).

11   William Rosenau, 'Non-Traditional Missions and the Future of the US Military', in *The Fletcher Forum*, winter/spring 1994, pp. 31-49.

Additional reasons that might be mentioned are the advances in military technology, which have made massive airlift and sealift operations possible, and developments in communications technology, such as world-wide television news services like the Cable News Network (CNN) which can quickly mobilize international public opinion.

In the words of General Powell: 'Because we are able to fight and win the nation's wars, because we are warriors, we are also uniquely to do some of these other new missions that are coming along – peacekeeping, humanitarian relief, disaster relief – you name it, we can do it ... but we never want to do it in such a way that we lose sight of the focus of why you have armed forces – to fight and win the nation's wars'.[12] Speaking at Harvard University, Powell assured his audience that 'nothing gives your warriors greater satisfaction than to use their skills not to destroy life but to relieve human suffering'.[13]

Nevertheless, a number of critics consider these non-traditional missions as distractions which can better be left to non-military agencies and organizations. In their opinion they threaten to diminish combat effectiveness and thrust the military into dangerously political realms. In the words of an outspoken opponent of non-traditional missions, loading these novel responsibilities onto the back of the armed forces could have the perverse effect of diverting focus and resources from the military's central mission of combat training and warfighting. It could also inject the military into domestic politics to an unprecedented degree.[14]

Those critics base their concern on the consequences of the over-use and over-commitment of the armed forces in these roles. The arguments against non-traditional military missions can be grouped into three broad categories: (1) they will erode combat effectiveness; (2) they are better performed by civilian organizations; and (3) they will lead to a dangerous level of military involvement in civilian affairs.

Nevertheless, the military has been used world-wide throughout history in a large variety of highly political and demanding non-combat roles, both domestically and abroad. In that respect the term 'non-traditional' is a misnomer. The historical record also suggests that the distinction between purely warfighting and strictly civilian activities has been far fuzzier than the critics of non-traditional missions have admitted.

---

12 Quoted in 'Perspectives on Policy and Strategy', *Strategic Review*, autumn 1993, p. 70.

13 Quoted in William Rosenau, 'Non-Traditional Missions and the Future of the US Military', p. 36.

14 For critical remarks, see Samuel P. Huntington, 'Non-Traditional Roles for the US Military', in James R. Graham, ed., *Non-Combat Roles for the US Military in the Post-Cold War Era*, (Washington, DC: Institute for National Strategic Studies, National Defence University Press, Fort Lesley J. McNair, 1993). For a proponent of non-traditional operations, see Paul David Miller, *Both Swords and Plowshares: Military Roles in the 1990s* (Cambridge, MA: Institute for Foreign Policy Analysis, 1992).

Rather than continue to resist these missions, the armed forces should embrace them, albeit selectively. Of course, the military should not drop its commitment to preparing for war and reduce itself to an international relief agency. Applying combat power on the battlefield has been, and must remain, the primary responsibility of the armed forces. However, providing for common defence has never been limited solely to the battlefield.

So, in addition, armed forces have enhanced their capabilities to intervene militarily in areas ranging from humanitarian and traditional peacekeeping operations to crisis management, peacemaking and peacebuilding. These operations mostly do not involve vital interests, but they constitute a major challenge to armed forces, because of their high frequency and growing importance for the evolution of the international situation and the development of a world order.

GUARDIAN

Most nations are already actively facing and implementing this new and challenging role for their armed forces, especially in peace support operations. The figure of the military warrior is now being coupled with that of 'guardian' of public order, stability and international law, whose action is legitimated by the defence of international law and order rather than by direct national interests.[15]

In addition to the figure of 'general warrior', that of the general peacekeeper, administrator and erstwhile Samaritan is becoming widely known. Some people even talk about 'officer-diplomats', given that assigned tasks mostly do not require a military victory to achieve a favourable political situation. It is rather through negotiation, compromise and mediation between local warring factions that the desired political end will be achieved.

DIPLOMAT

In this respect, the officer should ideally have a talent for diplomacy, not only to accomplish the tasks assigned to him, but also to maintain cohesion within multinational coalitions.[16]

The armed forces, as mentioned before, are manned to work closely with a variety of national contingents, where it is necessary to overcome differences in culture, organization, training and equipment. They are also increasingly required

---

15 Gustav Daniker, *The Guardian Soldier: On the Nature and Use of the Armed Forces*, Research Paper No. 36 (Geneva: United Nations Institute for Disarmament Research, 1995).
16 Carlo Jean, *The Training of the Officer-Diplomat after the Cold War*, Paper presented to the XXVth Conference of Commandants, NATO Defence College, Rome, 21 March 1996.

to work alongside civilian international and non-governmental organizations, where working practices may at first appear strange.[17]

An essential element of the job will also be to maintain the confidence of local leaders, often in volatile situations, tainted with centuries of ethnic or religious rivalry and hostility.

Finally, every action may well be closely monitored by unprecedented national and international media attention. In this environment the officer-diplomat is expected to maintain the consent of local, national and international publics.

POLITICAL DIMENSION

In conventional warfare, the political and military dimensions of conflict could be readily identified as separate areas of concern.

In the future, the range of operational tasks is likely to have political implications at all levels of command. Thus, the military professionals of the future, including company-level officers and senior NCOs, are more likely to have to function as soldier-diplomats and soldier-statesmen than has been the case in the past.

It seems that the less traditional the operation, the less significant the military and technological dimensions and the more relevant the political, administrative and psychological aspects.

The doctrinal concepts of victory, centre of gravity, culminating point of victory and so on have radically changed in non-traditional operations. The politico-strategical, operational and tactical levels, which are quite distinct in traditional operations, are being compressed in this new context. Operations at the tactical level can now end up having a higher political and strategical impact than in traditional operations. In civil and ethnic strifes and conflicts of identity, the psychological aspects, which are strongly influenced by the mass media, play a major role; the media in turn, following their own logic, amplify marginal events, thereby giving them political and strategical importance. It is sufficient to think of the effects of the killing of the 18 American Rangers in Mogadishu.

In practice, military success and failure in the field are in themselves more prone to have tactical rather than strategical meaning. The strategic meaning seems to depend more and more on psychological factors and mass-media interpretation. This is why commanders, even at the lowest levels, should have a deep understanding of political and psychological issues at both the international and local levels. In peacekeeping operations, respect of the so-called 'Mogadishu line' – necessary to maintain at the minimum politico-strategical consent, and also to limit

---

17   Chris Seipe, *The US Military/NGO Relationship in Humanitarian Interventions* (Carlisle Barracks, PA: Peacekeeping Institute, Center for Strategic Leadership, US Army War College, 1996).

the use of force at the tactical level – requires political and psychological rather than technical-military evaluations.

This proves the truthfulness of Marshal Lyautey's statement: 'those who are only soldiers are bad soldiers'.[18] In a sense, the need for officers to acquire diplomatic professionalism greater than purely military professionalism has become as important as in the past.

INDIRECT STRATEGY

In this respect, the circumstances when direct strategy – in which victory had a greater strategic meaning – and military objectives were defined in relation to the political objectives has been replaced with a mainly indirect strategy. This entails very close coordination between military/humanitarian actions and peace-making/peacebuilding operations.

However, it sometimes looks as if the solution of the officer as a diplomat is a mere alibi for the politicians who, being unable to define both a political solution and the necessary military objectives to implement it, dispatch military units with unrealistic tasks under the impulse of CNN-driven politics and expect the military to find a solution on the field according to the circumstances.

Dilemmas for the Warrior

RISKS

However, two risks should be avoided with those new roles for the military. The first is that the military – with their military skills – and politicians – who are unable to identify political solutions – consider a military solution possible. Such a solution is inapplicable to those internal conflicts in which forces are called to intervene. In that respect, the assertion that a conflict is won at the military level and lost at the political level is meaningless. 'You know you never defeated us on the battlefield', the American colonel Summers said to a North Vietnamese colonel. The North Vietnamese colonel pondered this remark a moment. 'That may be so', he replied, 'but is also irrelevant'.[19]

Any victory has first and foremost a political rather than a military significance. The centre of gravity of the intervention forces' strategy is to be found in the link between the warring factions and civil society, rather than only in the former. The

---

18   Quoted in Carlo Jean, *The Training of the Officer-Diplomat after the Cold War*, p. 5.
19   Harry G. Summers Jr, *On Strategy: A Critical Analysis of the Vietnam War* (New York: Dell Publishing, 1984), p. 21.

culminating point of victory can more and more frequently be identified with the capability to retain the consent of local and international publics.

The second risk is the demilitarization of the military and the loss of the specific character and combat capability of the military profession. The risk exists that the armed forces become heavily armed police forces as a result of the assertion of values incompatible with those upheld by the military. Interventions become international policing operations. Political conditioning affects military efficiency. The taste for mediation and the search for consent at any price induce the military to become politicians and use the mass media for their national if not personal advantage. The unity of command of a multinational coalition is thus destroyed. There is a tendency to sacrifice military efficiency in the search for consent, popularity or media approval.

In short, even though soldiers must now, to a greater extent than in the past, accomplish tasks similar to those carried out by diplomats – which requires an adequate education – they must remain first of all soldiers. However, general culture and humanities should undoubtedly be given more room in the officers' education, but without prejudice to their military training and combat orientation. A soldier must remain a soldier even when he acts as a peacekeeper, an administrator and a diplomat. It must be avoided that in peacekeeping operations impartiality is turned into neutrality.

A maxim by Musashi Myamoto, Japan's Clausewitz, gives an excellent illustration of this view: 'Hold your sword tightly and hide behind a smile'.[20] The warring factions' awareness that the sword may drop on their heads unexpectedly is the key element in reaching the goals set by the political authorities. The latter are inclined to use a force proportional to the level of consent by the warring factions, to seek a level of stability of which all of them can take advantage and a sustainable peace that is acceptable not only to the belligerents but also to the allied countries taking part in the operation. It is also a prerequisite for not actually employing force and this, among other things, greatly improves the cost-effectiveness of each intervention. The best and less expensive military force is its potential utilization in roles of 'deterrence' and 'compellence'.

COMBAT RELUCTANCE

A fundamental problem now facing the political and military leadership is that because of the partial failures of the military operations in Somalia and Bosnia a growing and pervasive combat reluctance is afflicting Western democracies to

---

20   Quoted in Carlo Jean, *The Training of the Officer-Diplomat after the Cold War*, p. 10.

varying degrees.[21] Politicians cautiously assess the political climate before putting servicemen and women in harm's way.

The main problem in the post-Cold War world is the absence of any existent threat; hence the difficulty in defining where vital interests lie. And when force is to be committed for lesser 'national interests', it is much harder to determine exactly when, where and under what conditions this should be done.

The expectations and demands of a sometimes emotional public are of little assistance here. The pervasiveness of the media, and especially of international television coverage and instant commentary, hardly helps. Television is very good at covering the death of one soldier. But it is far less good at explaining, for instance, the many civilian deaths that may have been prevented in central Bosnia by UNPROFOR's deployment. Political leaders cannot simply court popularity.

The debate on the use of force in international affairs will continue. For those countries that are actually being asked to put their troops 'in harm's way', the dilemmas are all too real. Although not a solution, some countries have developed political and military criteria for the decision-making process for employing armed forces abroad.[22]

TECHNOLOGY AND WARFARE

In this respect some observers consider new technology to be a partial solution to the problem of combat reluctance. In 1991 Desert Storm created the expectation that military technology would make the traditional warrior unnecessary.[23] This conflict proved that the enemy, his military forces as well as the supporting society, could be destroyed at long distances from positions of (still) comparative safety. Knowledge came to rival both weapons and tactics in importance, giving credence to the notion that an enemy might be brought to its knees principally through destruction and disruption of the means for command and control. Some experts have even concluded that future wars will be a massive 'video game' and can be undertaken 'surgically'.

Whether in the air, on the ground or at sea, it was also increasingly felt that, in so far as close-quarter fighting was necessary, it should be left to small teams of specialists: Special Operations Forces and the Special Air Service.

---

21   'The Problem of Combat Reluctance', in *Strategic Survey 1995/96* (London: International Institute for Strategic Studies, 1996), pp. 48-57.

22   Charles A. Stevenson, 'The Evolving Clinton Doctrine on the Use of Force', in *Armed Forces and Society*, summer 1996, pp. 511-35.

23   Michael Howard, 'How Much can Technology Change Warfare?', in Michael Howard and John F. Guilmartin Jr, *Technology and Warfare* (Carlise Barracks, PA: Strategic Studies Institute, US Army War College, 20 July 1994), pp. 1-11.

However, a fundamental question remains. Notwithstanding all the modern technology, Somalia proved that the need still remains to engage in basic, primitive encounters of the agrarian age. And the Vietnam War taught that, if the capacity to do so appears, no amount of technology is going to help. In other words: soldiers must not only know how to kill, but must also be prepared if necessary to die. Death and destruction will remain the coins of war's realm. More important, the societies that commit soldiers to action must be prepared to see them die; and in those days of 'reality TV' quite literally so.

A readiness to engage in close combat in which there is a very high risk of mortality remains the basic requirement, not only of the specialists in violence, but of every man and woman in uniform. Future conflicts will not be so conveniently one-sided as was the Gulf War. Will future technology be able entirely to eliminate the need for the armed forces of Western societies to be placed in situations where they are required not only to kill, but accept the risk of being killed, perhaps in large numbers; and will our post-industrial societies find that acceptable? In short, can technology change what has until now been the essence of warfare?

Whatever changes have been brought about by social and technological transformation, warfare remains as Clausewitz defined it; just as the chameleon, whatever colour it adopts, still remains the same animal.[24]

---

24   Carl von Clausewitz, *On War*, p. 89.

10 Technology in a Neo-Clausewitzian Setting

Robert J. Bunker

This chapter evaluates the impact of technology on the requirements for the future use of military armed force(s) in the context of a Western security strategy. It does this by exploring the importance – or lack thereof – of the RMA (revolution in military affairs) *vis-à-vis* contingency-specific roles, missions, and tasks and the potential need for an alternative conceptual paradigm within which better to understand the significance of technology to these operations. A comparison of Clausewitzian and neo-Clausewitzian spatial interpretations of the battlefield is provided to contrast these competing perceptions of warfare and explain why traditional assumptions regarding the material means necessary for contingency missions must be fully reconceptualized. The chapter highlights the required material means for implementing future operational concepts and doctrines, taking into account the different battlespace environments and settings in which 'military' forces have to operate and the concomitant requirements for the material involved, including support and logistic considerations. Finally, the development of a European Joint Force and the components necessary to ensure the creation of a sensible and efficient composite element from which to structure the cooperation/integration of Western military forces for the demands of a neo-Clausewitzian security environment are discussed.

The Relevance of the RMA and Alternative Constructs

An increasing debate is surfacing over the relevance of what is known as the 'revolution in military affairs' (RMA) to the emergent neo-Clausewitzian security environment. The conceptual origins of the RMA are based on Soviet military writings from the late 1970s and early 1980s which talked about a 'military technical revolution' (MTR) taking place.[1] The technological aspect of this revo-

---

1   Jeffrey R. Cooper, *Another View of the Revolution in Military Affairs* (Carlisle Barracks, PA: Strategic Studies Institute, US Army War College, 15 July 1994), p. 27. These concepts were first introduced by Marshal N.V. Ogarkov and further developed by General-Major Vladimir I. Slipchenko.

G.C. de Nooy (ed.), The Clausewitzian Dictum and the Future of Western Military Strategy, 137-165.
© 1997 *Kluwer Law International. Printed in the Netherlands.*

lution was then broadened by American theorists to include such concerns as systems development, operational innovation, and organizational adaptation.[2]

Dominant Western military perceptions are that the current RMA is equivalent in magnitude to the technological and operational change which took place during the 1920s and 1930s leading up to armour, amphibious, carrier, and strategic bombing operations conducted during the Second World War. The 1991 Gulf War and future wars of that nature represent the archetype of this school of thought, one based on the enduring warmaking predominance of the nation-state. These perceptions are derived from flawed Russian (Soviet) modal warfare analysis, based on Sixth-Generation Warfare theory, and later American analysis of military revolutions set almost exclusively within the limited time-frame of the Clausewitzian paradigm.[3]

These conceptual limitations inherent in the RMA make it incompatible with the emergent neo-Clausewitzian battlefield, even as the advanced technologies traditionally associated with it – for example, precision munitions, real-time battlefield imagery, non-lethal weapons, and information warfare – are promoting that battlefield's development. As a result, a more encompassing 'revolution in political and military affairs' (RPMA) construct is needed to guide effectively the application of advanced technologies to increasing operations in 'failed states' and other so termed contingency-specific roles and missions.[4]

See Mary C. Fitzgerald, 'The Soviet Image of Future War: "Through the Prism of the Persian Gulf"', *Comparative Strategy*, 10, October-December 1991, pp. 393-435; Major General Vladimir I. Slipchenko, Ret., 'A Russian Analysis of Warfare Leading to the Sixth Generation', *Field Artillery*, October 1993, pp. 38-41; Mary C. Fitzgerald, 'The Russian Image of Future War', *Comparative Strategy*, 13, April-June 1994, pp. 167-180 and 'The Russian Military's Strategy for "Sixth Generation" Warfare', *Orbis*, 38, summer 1994, pp. 457-76.

2 Steven Metz and James Kievit, *Strategy and the Revolution in Military Affairs: From Theory to Policy* (Carlisle Barracks, PA: Strategic Studies Institute, US Army War College, 27 June 1995), p. 3. Leading theorists in this regard are Andrew W. Marshall and Andrew F. Krepinevich, (formerly) of the Office of the Secretary of Defense, Office of Net Assessment (OSD/ONA). See Andrew W. Marshall, 'Some Thoughts on Military Revolutions - Second Version', Memorandum for the Record, OSD/ONA, 23 August 1993; Andrew F. Krepinevich, 'Cavalry to Computer: The Pattern of Military Revolutions', *The National Interest*, 37, autumn 1994, pp. 30-42; and the many monographs published from the US Army War College Fifth Annual Strategy Conference, 'The Revolution in Military Affairs (RMA): Defining an Army for the Twenty-First Century', held 26-28 April 1994, with the assistance of OSD/ONA.

3 Few criticisms of these theories exist. For a recent synopsis and analysis of these two theories, see Dr Robert J. Bunker, 'Ricochets and Replies: RPMA Update', *Airpower Journal*, 10, summer 1996, pp. 3, 117.

4 The need for a RPMA conceptual model was first proposed in Robert J. Bunker, 'Rethinking OOTW', *Military Review*, 75, November-December 1995, p. 41; and Robert J. Bunker and T. Lindsay Moore, *Non-Lethal Technology and Fourth Epoch War: A New Paradigm of Politico-Military Force*, Land Warfare Papers, No. 23 (Arlington, VA: Institute of Land Warfare, Association United States Army, February 1996), p. 11.

The conceptual basis of a RPMA is that of an epochal shift in Western history when one energy-based civilization is replaced by another. The transitions between the classical and medieval world, A.D. 378 to 732, and medieval and modern world, A.D. 1346 to 1648, are representative of the earlier shifts from human to animal energy and animal to mechanical energy foundations of Western civilization. A third such transition, one from mechanical to post-mechanical forms of energy, is perceived to be currently taking place (See Figure 1).[5] This RPMA construct directly supports the theoretical insights developed by Martin van Creveld in *The Transformation of War*, because it promotes the contention that the transition from the modern to post-modern world is now under way.

Figure 1 *Epochal Shifts in Western Civilization*

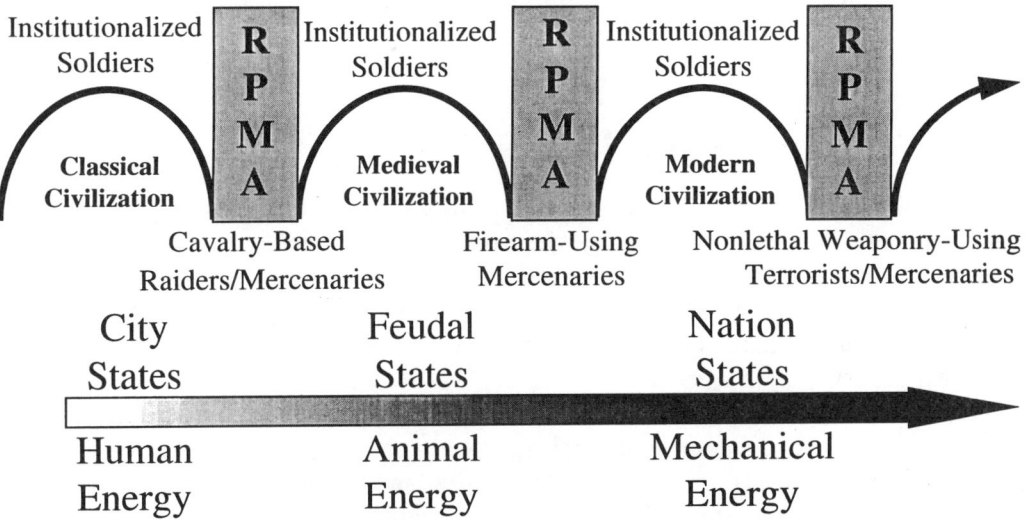

Based on the perceptions implicit in a RPMA, the impact of technology on the requirements for the future use of military armed force(s) in the context of a Western security strategy will be of critical importance because these forces will be required to operate on a more technologically advanced battlefield ultimately derived from post-mechanical energy sources. The magnitude of the dilemma that this battlefield poses for Western forces will be no different than that faced by the institution of medieval knighthood during the transition to the modern world. During that transition, the European knighthood was increasingly forced to operate within three-dimensional battlespace derived from mechanical energy as opposed to the two-dimensional battlespace derived from animal energy for which it had

5   For a basic outline of these epochal shifts, see Robert J. Bunker, 'The Transition to Fourth Epoch War', *Marine Corps Gazette*, 78, September 1994, pp. 20-32.

originally developed. Because the knighthood was unable to operate effectively within this more technologically advanced battlefield environment, military entrepreneurs (i.e. mercenaries), lacking the knight's institutional and ethical constraints and ultimately using firearms, were able to achieve a monopoly over the conduct of war.

The technological dilemma now faced by 'the military' element of the Clausewitzian trinity of the Westphalian nation-state will be very similar to that faced by the medieval European knighthood. It will be called upon to operate in a battlefield environment witnessing the increasing emergence of post-mechanically derived four-dimensional battlespace.[6] Many characteristics of this neo-Clausewitzian battlefield environment are currently under debate, but it is now possible to assemble a partial image of its ultimate form. Before doing so, however, a critical look at the Clausewitzian interpretation of the present and future battlefield environment is provided for the purpose of contrast.

Clausewitzian Interpretation of the Future Battlefield

As a point of departure, it can be stated with a great deal of confidence that the writings of Clausewitz accurately describe the phenomena of modern war as currently waged by the Westphalian nation-state. This form of war represents the successor to the pre-1648 mercenary-based dynastic struggles whose increasing technological sophistication resulted in the development of three-dimensional battlespace.

From a traditional military (i.e. Clausewitzian) perspective, the Gulf War is an excellent example of a conflict being waged within a battlespace defined as a three-dimensional box measured by its length, width, and height.[7] Within this scenario, the rapid advance of information and communication technology had a significant influence on the effective employment of military forces. Because Western Coalition forces possessed superior information and communication technology, they were able to dominate this box. This ability stemmed from the fact that Western Coalition forces could see opposing military forces, hit them, and then destroy or

---

6   For the conceptual basis of four-dimensional battlespace, see Robert J. Bunker, 'Advanced Battlespace and Cybermaneuver Concepts: Implications for Force XXI', *Parameters*, 26, autumn 1996, pp. 108-20.

7   Admiral William A. Owens, USN, former Vice Chairman of the Joint Chiefs, refers to a battle area as a 200-mile-by-200-mile box. This perception of the battlefield as a box continues and has found its way into *Joint Vision 2010*, 'Dominant maneuver will allow our forces to gain a decisive advantage by controlling the breadth, depth, and height of battlespace', p. 20. This conceptualization of the battlefield was apparently never questioned and thus represented a universal truth accepted by modern military officers. Office of the Chairman of the Joint Chiefs of Staff, *Joint Vision 2010* (Washington, DC: The Pentagon, Joint Staff Publication, July 1996).

neutralize them as an outcome of the opening air campaign. As a by-product of this campaign, the problem of placing 'steel on the target' is viewed as being solved by superior technology. With the premier problems solved, it is of little wonder that many proponents of the RMA, looking through the lens of the traditional Clause-witzian paradigm, now view Western domination of the battlefield as complete.[8]

Advances in information and communication technologies have, however, turned out to be a double-edged sword. With the advent of the Cable News Network (CNN) and competing real-time media organizations, 'the people' now regularly see unedited film clips of the battlefield.[9] Images once reserved only for soldiers are now shown back home to the public, including family members. This has an undermining effect on foreign operations, because casualties taken by either side in a conflict may shift public opinion, potentially resulting in the termination of operations.[10] Indeed, the 'highway of death' had a great impact on the Gulf War's termination.

Analysts coming from the Clausewitzian perspective have used the case of the Gulf War to draw lessons for the employment of forces in future battlefield environments. Based on successes in that instance, it is advocated that, when engaging opposing forces belonging to a belligerent non-Western state either in a general war or punitive action, maximum use should be made of stand-off precision-guided munitions so that Western forces can physically stay off of the battlefield and limit their potential risk of taking casualties.[11] In these circum-stances, the opponent is essentially in our battlespace box and we are outside of his. This is seen to take full advantage of the West's domination of the three-dimen-sional battlefield. It is believed that collateral damage, casualties, and environmen-tal degradation and the negative effects on public perceptions that they generate can be minimized through both the use of these precision-guided munitions and,

---

8   The basis of American sway over the battlefield is derived from dominant battlespace knowledge, advanced C4I, and precision force. Admiral William A. Owens, USN, 'Introduction', in Stuart E. Johnson and Martin C. Libicki, eds, *Dominant Battlespace Knowledge*, revised edition (Washington, DC: Center for Advanced Concepts and Technology, National Defense University, April 1996), pp. 1-14.

9   See Chuck de Caro, *Sats, Lies and Video-Rape: The Soft War Handbook* (Washington, DC: Aerobureau Corporation, 1994); Frank J. Stech, 'Winning CNN Wars', *Parameters*, 24, autumn 1994, pp. 37-56; Richard H. Sinnreich, 'The Changing Face of Battlefield Reporting', *Army*, 44, November 1994, pp. 30-4; and Lt.Col. Terrance M. Fox, USAF, Ret., 'Closing the Media-Military Technology Gap', *Military Review*, 75, November-December 1995, pp. 10-16.

10 For how this affects Western governments, see Edward N. Luttwak, 'Where are the Great Powers? At Home With the Kids', *Foreign Affairs*, 73, July-August 1994, pp. 23-8; 'Toward Post-Heroic Warfare', *Foreign Affairs*, 74, May-June 1995, pp. 109-22; and 'A Post-Heroic Military Policy', *Foreign Affairs*, 75, July-August 1996, pp. 33-44.

11 Stealth platforms are also being advocated because of their ability to remain undetected by opposing forces. More discussion of this capability takes place later in this chapter.

potentially, through the use of a new class of weapons, designated 'non-lethal', now being considered as an adjunct to lethal force.[12]

In a just-war scenario, such as the Gulf War, real-time media coverage, or the 'CNN effect', while a concern, does not represent as significant a problem as it is in peacekeeping/enforcement operations or in punitive raids against a belligerent state, where the rationale behind the use of force is not as obvious to observers. Furthermore, the envisioned battlefield dominance gained by the West as an outcome of the Gulf War, while readily apparent against non-Western states, breaks down in those peacekeeping/enforcement and humanitarian operations in 'failed-states' where the problem of figuring out just 'what is a target' represents the primary consideration.

From the orientation of a Clausewitzian three-dimensional battlefield, this is a critical development, because the premier problems concerning the destruction of a target have been in determining 'where it is' and 'how to hit it'. The problem of recognizing just 'what is a target' has not been a concern, because our conventions of war ensure that soldiers wear uniforms and their war machines bear insignia designating them as an opposing force. It is here that the mistake commonly made by military analysts of projecting the future battlefield environment by means of a three-dimensional Clausewitzian lens rather than by a four-dimensional neo-Clausewitzian one becomes critical.[13]

In peacekeeping/enforcement and humanitarian operations, recent observations provide little guidance given the former viewpoint. Since these 'other than war operations' exist outside of the Clausewitzian paradigm, this is not surprising. In these operations, real-time information is being denied to our forces because we cannot identify the targets, the global news media has been manipulated to work against us, non-state groups reject accepted Western laws of war, and stand-off precision-guided munitions have low utility given the context within which these operations take place. Because of the nature of these conflicts, we are being forced to engage in manpower-intensive operations rather than our preferred tech-

---

12   These weapons are defined in US Department of Defense, 'Policy for Non-lethal Weapons', No. 3003.3, 9 July 1996, as 'Weapons that are explicitly designed and primarily employed so as to incapacitate personnel or material, while minimizing fatalities, permanent injury to personnel, and undesired damage to property and the environment. Unlike conventional lethal weapons that destroy their targets principally through blast, penetration and fragmentation, non-lethal weapons employ means other than gross physical destruction to prevent the target from functioning. Non-lethal weapons are intended to have one, or both, of the following characteristics: a. they have relatively reversible effects on personnel or material; b. they affect objects differently within their area of influence.'

13   Two well-known analysts who utilize such a Clausewitzian lens are Joseph S. Nye Jr, and Admiral William A. Owens, Ret.; see 'America's Information Edge', *Foreign Affairs*, 75, March-April 1996, pp. 20-36.

nologically-intensive ones. As an outcome, these operations represent no-win situations for Western security forces.[14]

Based on the Clausewitzian perspective, the most reasonable advice would be for the military not to become involved with peacekeeping/enforcement operations. Since these conflicts are not 'war', a nation's military forces need not become involved in them.[15] For some nation-states this may well become the preferred course of action as they turn a blind-eye to the 'failed state' phenomena. Most Western states, however, because of strategic interests and humanitarian considerations, currently have no option other than to become involved in these operations. These states currently have two methods by which to undertake such involvement. Based on the Bosnian experience, one method of operation is to provide overwhelming artillery, air, and armour support when soldiers travel and to confine them to fortified bases while off duty to minimize the potential for unnecessary casualties or for a 'media event' to take place.[16] Other states, however, as a result of public and media pressure or governmental policy, will seek a different method of supporting these operations without directly committing their armed forces. These states will either provide limited support in terms of ferrying food and medical supplies to safe staging areas or by economically supporting groups such as third-party states, private corporations or a form of permanent mercenary-based United Nations reactionary force.[17] This latter method of contracting out missions to private security corporations is of particular concern. One such corporation, Military Professional Resources Inc. (MPRI), is beginning to resemble the twenty-first century equivalent of an early modern European mercenary company.[18] Such firms possess economic, operational, and political advantages over 'the military',

---

14 Robert J. Bunker, 'Rethinking OOTW', pp. 38-9. The US Army has recognized its past inability successfully to operate in these environments and is now actively attempting to address them. See Lt.Col. John B. Hunt, USA, Ret., 'OOTW: A Concept in Flux', *Military Review*, 76, September-October 1996, pp. 3-9; and FM 100-20, *Stability and Support Operations*, Final Draft (Fort Leavenworth, KS: US Army Command and General Staff College (USACGSC), April 1996).

15 Essentially the argument found in Harry G. Summers Jr, *The New World Strategy: A Military Policy for America's Future* (New York, NY: Simon & Schuster, 1995).

16 Harvey M. Sapolsky, 'Director's Statement', *Defense and Arms Control Studies Program Annual Report 1995-1996* (Cambridge, MA: Massachusetts Institute of Technology, 1996), p. 7.

17 Calls for 'Peace Mercenaries' in the popular press can be found in Alvin and Heidi Toffler, *War and Anti-War: Survival at the Dawn of the Twenty-First Century* (Boston, MA: Little, Brown and Company, 1993); and Jonah Blank, 'Want Peacekeepers with Spine? Hire the World's Fiercest Mercenaries', *US News and World Report*, 121, 30 December 1996 - 6 January 1997, pp. 42-3.

18 Mark Thompson, 'Generals for Hire', *Time*, 148, 15 January 1996, pp. 34-6; Peter Slevin, 'Ex-US Army Brass Confident of Shaping Up Bosnia's Forces', *Philadelphia Inquirer*, 20 July 1996, p. 5; and John Pomfret, 'First American Arms Shipment Arrives in Bosnia', *Washington Post*, 30 August 1996, p. 28.

and we are consequently seeing their role increasing in peacekeeping/enforcement operations.[19]

The large-scale return of mercenaries to the battlefield, however, would be a catastrophic development for the Westphalian nation-state. Not only would it threaten to destroy internally 'the military' element of the Clausewitzian trinity but it would endanger the future survival of the middle class which arose concurrently with late eighteenth-/early nineteenth-century industrialization. That social class, which represents the basis of the modern nation-state, obtained many of its political rights because of its utility in providing military personnel. It could just as easily lose those rights and decline if its direct military value as a social class ceases.

If these trends are not enough cause for concern, successful involvement in 'other-than-war operations' takes on an even greater imperative due to the proximity of potential 'failed states' to Western nations. With regard to the European nations, the potential spread of the Bosnian conflict throughout the Balkan region is disturbing. For the United States, the potential for a failed Mexican state to emerge on its southern border is a growing security concern. Ultimately, if 'the military' is to begin to operate effectively in the new battlefield environment that these conflicts represent, and not be eventually eclipsed by mercenary forces, its interpretation of how technology will influence future war must be fundamentally reinterpreted.[20]

Neo-Clausewitzian Interpretation of the Future Battlefield

While the Clausewitzian paradigm may still be applicable to traditional nation-state versus nation-state conflicts, we can see that it offers little utility in responding to contingency-specific roles, missions, and tasks. We will proceed here under the premise that Clausewitzian projections of future warfighting are obsolete, and therefore that interpretations drawn from the Gulf War and applied to peacekeeping/enforcement and humanitarian operations on this basis are inaccurate.

---

19   'They serve under competitive contracts stipulating how much money they will be paid, their forces are not required to follow strict rules of engagement (ROEs) which inhibit their operational effectiveness, and, when casualties are taken by their "employees", no public outcry is generated back home. That intra-state operations are not recognized as war only helps to further rationalize such a policy.' Robert J. Bunker, 'Epochal Change: War Over Social and Political Organization', *Parameters*, 27, summer 1997.

20   The perception that mercenaries may reappear as significant military components because of their superior skill levels can be found in Chapter 9, 'Computer Science, Artificial Intelligence, and Robotics: Impacts on Future Wars', Science and Technology Subcommittee of the Committee on Strategic Technologies for the Army, National Research Council, *STAR 21: Technology Forecast Assessments*, Export Restriction (Washington, DC: National Academy Press, 1993), p. 121.

The West, rather than approaching these operations as victors and continuing to do what has worked so well in the past, and in the process fail, must in these instances now come from the perspective of the vanquished. The vanquished, in this instance, will be said to be those who do not subscribe to the Westphalian nation-state, or its regional successor in Europe, as the world's dominant form of human social and political organization.

The reference here is to peoples who have no hope of competing with the West in the three-dimensional battlespace box. While this has been the case since 1500 when the West began to establish its global dominance during the last great historical transition between the medieval and modern world, it is only now with the advent of another RPMA that the West's monopoly on warfare is being eroded. Post-mechanical forms of energy are now promoting the emergence of a technologically advanced form of battlespace based on four-dimensions rather than on three.[21]

This new battlespace paradigm is defined by two spatial regions. The first, termed humanspace, represents the Western-dominated three-dimensional battlespace box. As the Gulf War has proven, this box represents the killing ground of future war. The second region, termed cyberspace, exists outside of the box in the non-human sensing dimension. This advanced dimension consists of what would be considered traditional cyberspace, as found in the electromagnetic spectrum (e.g. the internet) as well as those places immune from physical harm where stealth-masked forces reside.

Humanspace and cyberspace, which can both exist in the same volume of battlespace, will be said to be separated by a 'human-sensing dimensional barrier' which keeps these two regions apart (See Figure 2). This barrier can be said to be informational in nature. Stealth allows a military force to leave humanspace and enter cyberspace by dimensionally shifting out of it. To bring a stealth-masked force back into humanspace, data fusion, or the application of adaptive information processes to stealth-masked forces, is employed to fix it in time and space and bring it back into the killing ground.

Four-dimensional battlespace is rapidly developing as an outcome of two processes, one technology-generated and the other idea-generated. The technology-generated process is driven by the West and principally takes place in the electromagnetic domain of cyberspace. It is the driving force behind concepts like the internet, information warfare, and shared battlespace awareness. Human beings are incapable of perceiving this form of cyberspace without 'sensors' represented by their information machines. One of the most significant capabilities provided by electromagnetic-based cyberspace is the ability to get around the physical limita-

---

21 This spatial interpretation of four-dimensional battlespace is an extension of the concepts developed in Robert J. Bunker, 'Advanced Battlespace and Cybermaneuver Concepts: Implications for Force XXI', pp. 108-20.

tions of three-dimensional space. For example, a soldier who is wounded in the field can get expert medical attention by doctors thousands of kilometres from the battlefield via a telemedicine uplink. The life-saving outcome is equivalent to the wounded soldier and the doctors essentially being within the same field hospital.

Figure 2   *Spatial Premises of Advanced Battlespace*[22]

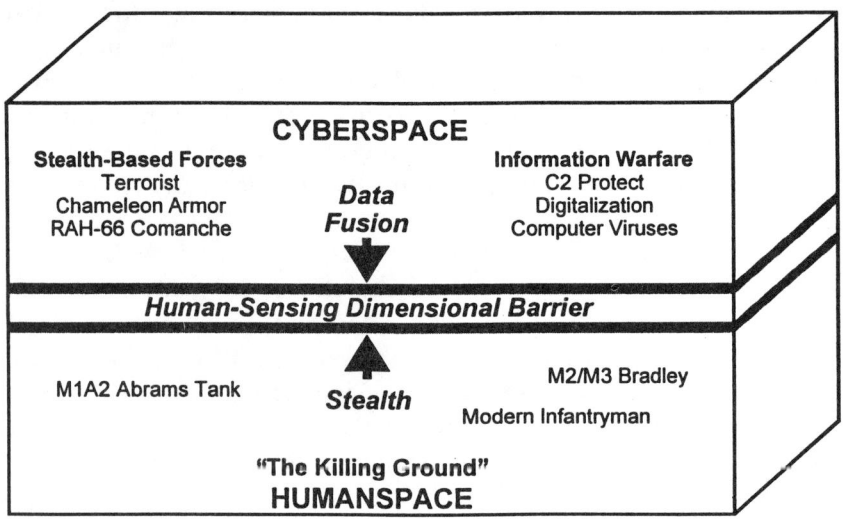

That domain of cyberspace where military forces are immune from physical harm stems from both idea- and technology-generated processes. The technology-generated process can also once again be seen to be taking place with the advent of the stealth fighter. It similarly provides advanced military forces with defensive advantages, but is based on that aspect of stealth-masking a target that is derived from the 'where it is' consideration.

The non-Western idea-generated process is more ominous because it is gained by means of a cheat.[23] Rather than relying upon advanced technology, it is obtained by rejecting the agreed upon 'what is a target' convention in Western war. In the Somali operation, because Western forces could not determine who were the combatants and who were the non-combatants, opposing forces effectively exited

---

22   *Source:* Robert J. Bunker, 'Advanced Battlespace and Cybermaneuver Concepts: Implications for Force XXI', *Parameters*, 26, autumn 1996, p. 113.

23   This breakdown of the rules of Western war is blurring the distinction between soldier and criminal and war and crime. During a RPMA, when war is waged as a struggle over future social and political organization, this blurring is a natural by-product of the transition between civilization forms. It should be noted that 'non-Western ideas' can also be held by disenfranchised segments of the Westphalian nation-state such as street gang members, militia members, and right-wing extremists.

from the three-dimensional battlespace box. This is of great significance because it means that:

> ... a terrorist in civilian garb who is standing five metres from a US soldier and whom the US soldier views as a non-combatant is at a much greater battlefield range from that soldier than a hostile tank that is visible 1000 metres away – and yet is potentially far more dangerous to the soldier than is the tank.[24]

Thus, once again, the use of cyberspace allows the ability to get around the physical limitations of three-dimensional space. This time, however, it works in reverse. Instead of bringing humans together from thousands of kilometres apart, the use of cyberspace here takes humans a few metres apart and separates them as if they were thousands of kilometres away from each other. As with electromagnetic-based cyberspace, human beings, specifically Western soldiers, are incapable of perceiving this form of cyberspace without 'sensors', because combatants and non-combatants all look alike when military uniforms are removed and weapons are hidden.

The warfighting implications stemming from these two simultaneous processes are dramatically apparent. The three-dimensional battlespace box dominated by the West will become increasingly insufficient.[25] Traditional operational opportunities such as exploiting gaps or weak points between military forces, driving deep behind enemy lines for purposes of encirclement, and devastating columns of military vehicles by precision-munitions are meaningless in a fourth-dimensional battle-space environment. On a more ominous note, our modern concepts of sovereignty – a three-dimensional construct – breakdown in such a battlespace environment. The warping of humanspace by cyberspace will thus increasingly help to undermine the political legitimacy of the Wesphalian nation-state.

From a neo-Clausewitzian interpretation, much of 'the military's' inability to operate successfully in contingency missions can thus be understood. In a 'failed-state' scenario where Western forces are up against non-national groups, those groups are successfully utilizing fourth-dimensional battlespace against them. For defensive purposes, they are using idea-generated cyberspace so as not to be acquired and killed or neutralized. The process of distancing their forces from the physical battlefield is in effect. For offensive purposes, they are using technology-generated cyberspace against the West. Via real-time media broadcasts and, more

---

24 Robert J. Bunker, 'Advanced Battlespace and Cybermaneuver Concepts: Implications for Force XXI', pp. 116-7.

25 This insufficiency does not imply that a three-dimensional presence will not be required, only that, by themselves, physical dimension-dominating Western forces have no hope of contending with cyberspace-residing non-national forces. For a related debate on this issue, see Colin S. Gray, 'The Continued Primacy of Geography', and 'A Rejoinder', *Orbis*, 40, spring 1996, pp. 247-60 and 274-6; and Martin Libicki, 'The Emerging Primacy of Information', *Orbis*, 40, spring 1996, pp. 261-73.

recently, websites, they are allowed to bring 'the people' of the Westphalian nation-state to the physical battlefield so that they can be subjected to its horrors.[26] Rather than employ an offensive strategy which seeks, as Western forces do, to destroy things residing in physical space, these groups rely upon an alternative target set focused upon breaking the bonds/relationships which hold 'the people', 'the government', and 'the military' of the Westphalian nation-state together. The primary means of attacking this target set is by those criminal activities which we in the West term 'acts of terrorism'.

Non-national forces are required to utilize these warfighting methods because they do not stand a chance of effectively taking on the Western security forces which dominate three-dimensional battlespace. While many of these groups currently lag far behind Western forces in their use of technology, the future warfighting concepts that they employ are, however, highly advanced from the perspective of a neo-Clausewitzian lens.[27]

Required Material Means for Implementing Future Operational Concepts and Doctrines

Advanced Western operational concepts and doctrines, currently under development, are required to counter the 'failed-state' phenomenon and those non-national groups which effectively employ fourth-dimensional battlespace. These new military missions will include such 'other than war operations' as peace support/building operations, unconventional warfare, humanitarian support, counter-terrorism, and urban riot suppression.

For Western forces to conduct successfully these contingency missions in the new conflict environment that has emerged, they will be required to retain their dominance of the three-dimensional battlefield while at the same time actively expanding their capabilities into fourth-dimensional battlespace. As the transition into the post-modern age progresses and the barriers between three-dimensional and fourth-dimensional space further blur, the overall battlespace environment (i.e. both cyberspace and humanspace) will likely require the same material means. In the interim, however, it may be best to associate conceptually the required material means with the spatial environment in which they will be employed.

---

26 Technology-generated cyberspace is also being used for communications between non-national groups. E-mail messages effectively get lost in the growing message traffic of the internet and for that reason are secure as a result of the stealthing effect all of the 'noise' provides.

27 For an example of this non-Western approach to warfighting, see Charles J. Dunlap Jr, 'How We Lost the High-Tech War of 2007: A Warning from the Future', *The Weekly Standard*, 29 January 1996, pp. 22-8.

Before exploring these material requirements, the dangers associated with overreliance upon technology to the exclusion of other attributes of the West's warmaking capacity should be mentioned. Furthermore, the misapplication of technology from allowing it to drive our concepts of operation and ethical values, instead of the other way around, has the potential to become part of the security dilemma now facing the Westphalian nation-state.

The creation of a successful security strategy requires both the emergent threat environment and Western trinitarian capabilities and limitations to be placed in their broader context. The application of technology must be subordinated to such a security strategy. The required material means must additionally never be allowed to have adverse financial implications on the fielding of Western armed forces. Rather, those means must allow Western armed forces to attempt to do more with fewer resources in an increasingly hostile world.

Furthermore, the technological developments highlighted in this chapter will result in massive change over the course of the next two decades. Soldiers and civilians will die (or suffer) in new and unexpected ways, machine soldiers will be built, unique life-forms engineered, humans cloned, and cyborgs potentially created. Unexpected technological interactions will produce new opportunities and dilemmas for Western security planners. It no longer seems outside the realm of possibility that by 2015 A.D., mercenary corporations could be deploying genetically re-enhanced soldiers armed with second-generation acoustic and laser weaponry and protected by stealth-masked body armour. This RPMA may thus represent the beginning of the next renaissance, dark age, or a combination of the two.

Ultimately, in the new world that is emerging we must not forget that personnel loyal to the principles upon which the Western nation-state is built are our most important military asset. Technology will not replace soldiers on the ground in a neo-Clausewitzian setting. However, if those soldiers are not properly trained and equipped for four-dimensional battlespace operations, they stand little chance when deployed against non-state, criminal forces which increasingly are.

The Material Requirements of Humanspace

Humanspace material requirements will centre on taking and holding three-dimensional space, the bringing of stealth-masked forces into humanspace, the destruction or neutralization of opposing forces via precision-strikes, and the physical defence of advanced forces whose stealth capability has been compromised or less advanced forces which do not possess organic stealth. These operations can be expected to be increasingly conducted in the world's growing urban

centres and sprawling slums as an outcome of changing global demographics.[28] The
required material means for humanspace operations will include:[29]

NON-LETHAL WEAPONS

These weapons have existed throughout history, but were given new emphasis
during the Vietnam War era as a means to counter domestic civil unrest in America
and in European countries such as Northern Ireland. Now that similar types of
conflict have increasingly broken out in Western urban centres and in 'failed-
states', such weapons are taking on increasing importance.

   More than anything else, these weapons provide new politico-military force
options which did not exist earlier. Non-lethal weapons thus specifically provide a
1-99 per cent force capability between the use of no force (0 per cent) and lethal
force (100 per cent) inherent in Clausewitzian era weapons.[30] They can be applied
against personnel, material, and infrastructure targets. The deployment of these
weapons by the United States against personnel is currently focusing on 'Non-
lethal Weapon Capability Sets' under the executive agency lead of the Marine
Corps (See Table 1).

   Because of their advanced nature, many of these weapons – such as those which
are acoustic, electromagnetic, and optical-based – require post-mechanical energy
sources for proper functioning. Others, however, such as those which are barrier,
entangler, marker, obscurant, and projectile-based, represent less-advanced technologies.[31] Unlike traditional weapons whose battlefield potential has been fully
exploited, non-lethal weapons offer the promise of yet unexplored military capabilities.

---

28 'Military Operations Other Than War', *The Arroyo Center Annual Report*, AR-5921-A (Santa
    Monica, CA: The RAND Corporation, March 1994), p. 22.
29 Technology/requirement listings can be found in General Carl Stiner, US Army (Ret.), Chairman,
    Report of the Senior Working Group on Military Operations Other Than War (OOTW), Contract
    No. MDA972-93-C-0016 (Arlington, VA: Advanced Research Projects Agency, May 1994); and
    Decision Brief for Approval of Military Operations on Urban Terrain (MOUT) ACTD (Fort
    Benning, GA: US Army Dismounted Battlespace Battlelab (DBBL), April 1996).
30 What 1-99% force looks like is not currently understood. These weapons are recognized as providing
    short-term disablement and long-term disablement but even those concepts are amorphous. Primitive
    continuums of force and force matrices exist which attempt to categorize force thresholds. Two of
    these methods can be found in Robert J. Bunker and T. Lindsay Moore, *Non-lethal Technology and
    Fourth Epoch War: A New Paradigm of Politico-Military Force*, p. 4; and Col Frederick M. Lorenz,
    '"Less-Lethal" Force in Operation UNITED SHIELD', *Marine Corps Gazette*, 79, September 1995,
    p. 73.
31 For an overview of these weapons, see Robert J. Bunker, ed., *Non-lethal Weapons Guidebook: Terms
    and Reference*, INSS Occasional Paper 13 (US Air Force Academy, CO: Institute for National
    Security Studies, forthcoming).

Table 1 *Non-lethal Weapon Capability Sets*[32]

Fiscal Year 1996 Non-lethal Weapons Procurement

The Commandant of the Marine Corps was assigned the joint executive agent for non-lethal weapons and the Corps was directed to plan for the reprogramming of $2.1 million in Marine procurement dollars for the purchase of non-lethal weapons and equipment last March. The Marine Combat Development Process is purchasing 14 'Non-lethal Weapon Capability Sets' designed for use by a battalion landing team. The estimated cost per set is $148,000, making for a total buy of just under $2.1 million. Each set includes:

200	riot face shields	40	full length riot shields
200	31-inch riot batons	2	riot baton training suits
12	training batons	9	rifleman's combat optics
13	10-watt bullhorns	3	handheld spot lights
5,000	caltrops	200	flexicuff packs (10 per)
45	squad pepper spray (OC)	18	squad OC training canisters
92	fireteam OC dispensers	120	fireteam OC training canisters
891	individual OC dispensers	400	individual OC training canisters
81	shotgun ammo pouches	27	12-gauge shotguns (redistributed)
236	shotgun training rounds	741	shotgun bean bag rounds
27	shotgun gas grenade launchers	348	blank/shotgun launching cartridges
4,050	buckshot cartridges	798	fin-stabilized rubber shotgun rounds
702	40mm rubber rounds	702	40mm wooden rounds
1,512	40mm stinger cartridges	162	40mm non-lethal ammo carrying pouches
162	stingball/flashbang pouches	72	stingball training grenades
729	stingball grenades	729	Mk 141 flashbangs

ANTI-LETHAL WEAPONS

These weapons conceptually represent a subset of non-lethal weapons. However, owing to the differing capabilities that they provide, they warrant separate discussion.[33] Rather than being strictly applied against personnel, material, and infrastructure targets, these weapons are used to negate the lethal effects of other weapons. While similar in nature to precursor systems, such as point-defence systems on warships which destroy incoming missiles, new forms of anti-lethal weapons and related technologies greatly expand these capabilities.

---

32 *Source:* CWO5 Charles 'Sid' Heal, USMCR, 'Non-lethal Technology and the Way We Think of "Force"', *Marine Corps Gazette*, 81, January 1997, p. 26.

33 Chris and Janet Morris and Thomas Baines, 'Weapons of Mass Protection: Non-lethality, Information Warfare, and Airpower in the Age of Chaos', *Airpower Journal*, 9, spring 1995, p. 24.

One of the best examples of this type of weapon are electronic sniper-locating systems based on acoustic, shock-wave or infra-red measuring technologies. Such systems provide the location of a hostile sniper to a sniper team or to an automated counter-sniper system which can fire either a kinetic round or low-energy laser at the hostile sniper.[34] Other anti-lethals include those devices based on electronic field generators, which prematurely detonate mortar and artillery shells by signalling to them that they have reached their target, and radio-signal coded personalized guns which are unable to fire when they are not in the hands of their transponder-wearing owner.[35]

DATA FUSION

These technologies represent the application of adaptive information processes to stealth-masked forces for target detection, identification, and location.[36] They are based on advanced 'sensors' which fuse data gathered in the electromagnetic spectrum, thus allowing humans to peer into fourth-dimensional space and bring threat forces into humanspace where they can be dealt with. One example would be ground-penetrating radar: a sensor that can detect non-geologic objects and human engineered structures beneath the ground by analysing the return of electromagnetic waves travelling through geologic structures. Detection of buried mines and discovery/mapping of underground bunkers represent practical, non-lethal applications.[37]

Man-portable non-imaging radar units, in turn, can be used to detect motion through non-metallic walls and floors in built-up areas.[38] Another example of data fusion is based on 'retro-reflectivity' which provides the logic behind an electro-optical sensing mode that can be used to find opposing electro-optics employed at

---

34   Col. Rex Applegate, *Riot Control Materiel and Techniques* (Boulder, CO: Paladin Press, 1981), pp. 300-1; Scott R. Gourley, 'The Sniper's Latest Nightmare', *International Defense Review*, 28, April 1995, p. 66; and John G. Roos, 'Nowhere to Hide: High-Tech Counter-Sniper Systems Unmask Urban Terrorists', *Armed Forces Journal International*, 123, July 1996, p. 18.

35   Pat Cooper and Jeff Erlich, 'US Troops to Field Shortstop Against Shells in Bosnia', *Defense News*, 11, 5-11 February 1996, p. 22; D.R. Weiss, D.J. Brandt and K.D. Tweet, *Smart Gun Technology Requirements Preliminary Report*, Contract IAA-94-IJ-R-021 (Albuquerque, NM: Sandia National Laboratories, n.d.); and Gordon Witkin, 'Can "Smart" Guns Save Many Lives?', *US News and World Report*, 121, 2 December 1996, pp. 37-8.

36   Robert J. Bunker, 'Advanced Battlespace and Cybermaneuver Concepts: Implications for Force XXI', p. 111.

37   Description provided by Lt.Col. Matthew Begert, USMC, Military Assistant to the Director, Precision Guided Weapons Countermeasures Test and Evaluation Directorate, an Office of the Secretary of Defense field activity, November 1996. For additional information see *Defense News*, 'Countermine Technologies Flow from Increased Threat', 8-14 July 1996, p. 10.

38   Sid Heal and Paul Evancoe, 'Non-lethal Disabling Technology: A Future Reality', *Police and Security News*, September-October 1996, pp. 3-16.

night.[39] Facial recognition technology, on the other hand, promises to provide the capability to identify terrorists, guerrillas, and narco-traffickers in large crowds and airport terminals.[40]

ROBOTIC SYSTEMS

Robotic units, both teleoperated and autonomous, offer much potential to Western forces engaged in military operations.[41] They can go where humans cannot and minimize the risk faced by combat troops.[42] During the Gulf War in 1991, at the village of Az Zawr, the first instance of a human surrendering to a robot (in this instance an unarmed remotely piloted vehicle or RPV) took place.[43] Both static and mobile systems exist and they can be configured as data fusion sensors, serve as weapons platforms, and as logistical vehicles.

The EOD robot (explosive ordnance disposal robot), which is a commercial off-the-shelf item, could already be used for contingency operations. It is fitted with a .12 gauge shotgun, black-and-white video camera, claw tipped arm, and fibre-optic and radio control systems.[44] While not meant for such tasks, it could just as easily be used for perimeter duty or to clear a room. With minor modifications, an infra-red viewing system and upgraded lethal, non-lethal, or anti-lethal armaments could be added to increase its effectiveness. Other systems which exist include biomorphic robots, also known as insectoids, and minuscule devices known as

---

39 Description provided by Lt.Col. Matthew Begert, USMC, November 1996.

40 For background information, see Patrick J. Rauss, P. Jonathon Phillips, Mark K. Hamilton and A. Trent DePersia, 'FERET (Face-Recognition Technology) Recognition Algorithms' (Ft Belvoir, VA: US Army Research Laboratory/Arlington, VA: Defense Advanced Research Projects Agency). Appears in 'Proceedings of the Fifth Automatic Target Recognizer System and Technology Symposium', sponsored by the Automatic Target Recognizer Working Group, 23-25 July 1996.

41 For background on this subject, see Mack Mattingly and Robert Finkelstein, 'Combat Robotics: From Kaiser to the New World Order', in *Defence Yearbook 1992* (London: Brassey's (UK) Ltd, 1992), pp. 235-60; Major Thomas J. Kelly, US Army, 'The Robots are Here!', *Military Review*, 70, November 1990, pp. 57-63; and Colonel Jose Carlos Albano do Amarante, Brazilian Army, 'The Automated Battle: A Feasible Dream?', *Military Review*, 74, May 1994, pp. 58-61.

42 Pat Cooper, 'US Mulls Lethal Robots: DoD Takes Second Look at Unmanned Weaponry', *Defense News*, 11, 17-23 July 1995, pp. 3, 29; and 'US Readies UAVs for New Battlefield Roles', *Defense News*, 12, 13-19 January 1996, pp. 4, 26; and Mark Hewish, 'Robots on the March', *IDR Extra*, 1, August 1996, pp. 1-7.

43 Ernest Blazar, 'From Guns to Robots: A History', *Navy Times*, Marine Corps Edition, 30 January 1995, p. 18.

44 Per unit cost in 1989 is estimated to be in the neighbourhood of $45,000 each for a production run of 72. This included an explosive detector, a 'sniffer', for each unit. Jay Schaff, 'Explosive Ordnance Disposal Robot', *Military Police*, December 1990, p. 33.

microelectromechanical systems (MEMS).[45] Both could have wide applications in treacherous urban environments containing partially demolished buildings and underground sewer systems.

BATTLE-SUIT SYSTEMS

These systems represent outer coverings and technological devices worn by soldiers, which protect them from combat environmental dangers and provide them with advanced capabilities. These suits will be required to provide both fragmentation/small arms and nuclear, biological, and chemical (NBC) protection.[46] An antiseptic bio-sheathing on the inside of this garment, which coats the soldier's body and closes over wounds, cuts, and abrasions, may also be warranted.[47]

The basic unit should be lightweight and modular in design with the capability of affording additional protection via armour sections for increased threat environments. These suits will be required to come with visors which provide protection against low-energy lasers and shell fragments, air filtration systems and radio and satellite data links. Each suit will come with a computer, retinal eye or visor display, and data-fusion sensing. Additional capabilities which could be provided by such a system include an identification friend-or-foe (IFF) system, internal global positioning system (GPS), emergency medical monitor/administrator, a distress beacon, and language translator.[48]

---

45 Arthur Knoth, 'March of the Insectoids', *International Defense Review*, 27, April 1994, pp. 55-8; Pat Cooper, 'Send in the Marines? Ok, But First Send in the Crabs', *Navy Times*, Marine Corps Edition, 12 June 1995, p. 27; and Lisa Burgess and Neil Munro, 'Tiny Terrors: Microscopic Weapons may Reshape War', *Navy Times*, 7 March 1994, p. 34.

46 Such systems are emerging on both sides of the Atlantic. They developed out of the Soldier Modernization Plan (SMP) promoted by the US Army in the late 1980s. Many articles referring to the US system can be found in *Army RD&A Bulletin* between 1990 and 1995. As of May 1996, the American Land Warrior system weighed 75 pounds and cost $35,000 per unit. For an overview, see Mark Hewish and Rupert Pengelley, 'New Age Soldiering', *International Defense Review*, 27, January 1994, pp. 26-33; and 'Marching into the New Millennium: Soldier-System Developments for the Twenty-First Century', *International Defense Review*, 29, May 1996, pp. 30-8; and Richard J. Sterk, *Tailoring the Techno-Warrior*, Landpower Essay No. 96-5 (Arlington, VA: Association United States Army, Institute of Land Warfare, June 1996).

47 Ralph Peters, 'Our Soldiers, Their Cities', *Parameters*, 26, spring 1996, pp. 45-6.

48 Some of these characteristics can be found in Chapter 9, 'Computer Science, Artificial Intelligence, and Robotics: Impacts on Future Wars', Science and Technology Subcommittee of the Committee on Strategic Technologies for the Army, National Research Council, *STAR 21: Technology Forecast Assessments*, pp. 116-8. See also Mark Hewish, 'Wearable Information Tailored to Battlefield', *IDR Extra*, 1, November 1996, pp. 1-7.

POST-MECHANICAL ENERGY

For advanced forms of humanspace-based weapons and technologies to function efficiently, post-mechanical energy sources are required.[49] One of the current restraints on battle-suit system initiatives has been power restrictions. Current battery technology is simply not advanced enough to meet the power requirements of such systems. Furthermore, at ± 170 batteries per company per day, new logistical burdens are being created.[50]

While hand-held low-energy lasers have been fielded, high-energy ones have not, as more advanced power sources do not currently exist. Acoustic generation devices also require large amounts of energy. Main battle tanks are unable to utilize rail guns because they can require twice the power generation of their main engines.[51] This recognized need for post-mechanical energy sources is now beginning to influence Army After Next (AAN) planners. They '... are beginning to hypothesize that new sources of battlefield energy – for vehicles, as propellants in weapons, and for communications and other uses – will be the next major leap ahead for military forces ...'.[52] Such a revolution is foreseen as taking place in the post-2020 time-frame as a follow-on to the information revolution.

The Material Requirements of Cyberspace

Because fourth-dimensional battlespace is a relatively new phenomena, a basic lack of understanding still exists with regard to the material needs of Western forces while operating within Cyberspace. With this in mind, projected material requirements for cyberspace operations will be said to based on the four broad areas of stealth technologies and processes, informational related needs and concerns, psychological technology, and biotechnical developments:[53]

---

49 For an overview of current research, see 'Part VII: Propulsion, Power, and High-Power Directed Energy', *STAR 21: Technology Forecast Assessments*, pp. 477-609.

50 Keith Dugas, Selma Nawrocki and Eleanor Raskovich, 'A Parameteric Model for Soldier Individual Power', *Army RD&A Bulletin*, July-August 1993, pp. 8-11; and correspondence with Capt. James T. Anibal, US Army concerning the Dismounted Soldier System, December 1996.

51 Richard M. Ogorkiewicz, 'Novel Tank Guns?', *Armor*, September-October 1986, p. 19.

52 Col. Bob Killebrew, USA, 'The Army After Next: TRADOC's Crystal Ball eyes the Service's Shape Beyond Force XXI', *Armed Forces Journal International*, 134, October 1996, pp. 44-5.

53 Psychological technology and biotechnology were noted for their potential to provide critically needed capabilities in conflict short of war. Steven Metz and James Kievit, *The Revolution in Military Affairs and Conflict Short of War* (Carlisle, PA: Strategic Studies Institute, US Army War College, 25 July 1994), pp. 31-2.

STEALTH

Two forms of camouflage show great promise for allowing Western ground forces to begin to gain the defensive advantages that fourth-dimensional battlespace provides. 'Active' or 'chameleon' camouflage is:

> Created by dynamically matching the object to be camouflaged to its background colours and light levels rendering it virtually invisible to the eye ... This is accomplished through a sophisticated colour and light sensor array which detects an object's background colour and brightness. This data is then computer matched and reproduced on a pixel array covering the viewing surface of the object to be camouflaged ...[54]

'Metamorphic' camouflage utilizes chemicals which change colours based on light and heat conditions. They can be applied as paints on vehicles or impregnated into uniforms. Such camouflage would be extremely useful for night and day operations and those taking place in urban environments.[55]

Other methods of stealth masking include anti-noise technology, which can be used to negate the noise of a vehicle's engine by means of sound waves, reduce the radar cross-section (RCS) of advanced aircraft via radar-absorbent materials and reduce sharp angles in airframe configurations.[56] One initiative is currently seeking to make the proposed arsenal ship electronically invisible so that it would be impossible to lock onto.[57] Similar technology may provide such a capability for ground and air forces.

---

54   Pixels can be based on light emitting diodes (LED) or liquid crystal diodes (LCD). Based on descriptions provided in Paul Evancoe, 'Non-lethal Alternatives Weighed by Law Officers', *National Defense*, 73, May-June 1994, pp. 28-30; and Sid Heal and Paul Evancoe, 'Non-lethal Disabling Technology: A Future Reality', *Police and Security News*, September-October 1996, p. 3.

55   Paul Evancoe, 'Non-lethal Alternatives Weighed by Law Officers'; and Paul Evancoe, 'Non-lethal Disabling Technology'.

56   For articles regarding stealth's surface naval and air applications, see Capt. John W. McGillvray Jr, US Navy, 'Stealth Technology in Surface Warships', *Naval War College Review*, 47, winter 1994, pp. 28-38; Robert P. Haffa Jr and James H. Patton Jr, 'Analogues of Stealth: Submarines and Aircraft', *Comparative Strategy*, 10, 1991, pp. 257-71; and Capt. James H. Patton Jr, USN (Ret.), 'Stealth is a Zero-Sum Game: A Submariner's View of the Advanced Tactical Fighter', *Airpower Journal*, 5, spring 1991, pp. 4-17; and 'Stealth, Sea Control, and Air Superiority', *Airpower Journal*, 7, spring 1993, pp. 52-62.

57   *National Defense*, 'Project Will Electronically Cloak New Navy Attacker – Arsenal Ship', 81, October 1996, p. 9.

INFORMATION TECHNOLOGY

Concepts of offensive and defensive information warfare need to be integrated into contingency operations.[58] Furthermore, expansion of Western C4I battlespace dominance into cyberspace and increased reliance on expert systems to assist in the decision-making process is required. These capabilities will be based upon information technology such as computer hardware and software, fibre optics, communication devices, and networking.[59] At the individual soldier level, hardware needs to be miniaturized so that it can be worn, and emergent voice recognition capabilities, to free soldier's hands, must be capitalized upon.[60]

Because computing power is dramatically increasing while per unit cost is steadily decreasing, commercial products with their 'shorter acquisition cycles' are now out-performing military systems. This is a dangerous trend, because it means that potential non-national opponents can gain competitive or even superior capabilities over Western forces by purchasing off-the-shelf commercial products.[61] This will require a re-evaluation of military product specifications and the security trade-offs inherent in employing commercial information technology for warfighting purposes. Rather than allow hackers to attack Western governmental websites or seize control of its military platforms, a defensive capability must be established while, at the same time, non-national cyberspace assets are targeted.[62]

PSYCHOLOGICAL TECHNOLOGY

As mentioned earlier in this chapter, Western forces focus on destroying and/or neutralizing things. Solely influencing such a target set will be insufficient for dominating the future battlefield environment. To expand Western military capabilities, the alternative target set utilized by non-Western forces will need to be

---

58 See David S. Alberts, *The Unintended Consequences of Information Age Technologies* (Washington, DC: Center for Advanced Concepts and Technology (ACT), Institute for National Security Studies, National Defense University, April 1996); and *Defensive Information Warfare* (Washington, DC: Center for Advanced Concepts and Technology (ACT), Institute for National Security Studies, National Defense University, August 1996).

59 See Brian Nichiporuk and Carl H. Builder, *Information Technologies and the Future of Land Warfare*, Arroyo Center, MR-560-A (Santa Monica, CA: RAND), pp. 7-19.

60 In the +2004 time-frame, speech recognition will have developed because of microprocessors being created which have reached the hundred million transistor level. James Flanigan, 'Intel is Betting All of its Chips on the Future', *Los Angeles Times*, Sunday 19 January 1997, p. D1.

61 Brian Nichiporuk and Carl H. Builder, *Information Technologies and the Future of Land Warfare*, p. 22.

62 Pat Cooper and Frank Oliveri, 'Hacker Exposes US Vulnerability', *Defense News*, 10, 9-15 October 1995, pp. 1, 37; and Associated Press, 'Hackers Deface Web Site of US Justice Department', *Los Angeles Times*, Sunday 18 August 1996, p. A20. Some computer programs may be thought of as another form of non-lethal weapons, ones which exist only in cyberspace.

redirected back against them. This target set, based on the breaking of bonds/re-
lationships, would be focused upon '... the manipulation of images, beliefs,
attitudes, and perceptions' of our non-national opponents.[63] Research will be
required to determine whether such groups possess their own Clausewitzian-like
trinity which can be undermined.[64]

At the same time, the bonds/relationships of the Westphalian nation-state, and
its regional successor, need to be protected from attack. Propaganda, media
management, and psychological operations which influence the perceptions of
'people', all represent elements of a required offensive and defensive capability.
Applying principles of 'soft war' and determining its technical needs should be
further explored and developed.[65] The same logic holds true for 'Netwar' theory,
which offers great potential for helping to determine future psychological technology requirements against non-hierarchically based adversaries.[66]

BIOTECHNOLOGY

Advances in biotechnology, potentially more profound than those in information
systems, have generally gone unnoticed because of all the attention that the more
mature information revolution has received from RMA scholars.[67] One aspect of
this research concerns genetically engineered organisms. Mammalian organisms,
such as rodents with a 'wetware' computer implant, could be utilized for military
purposes. Less sinister applications of this technology would focus on lower-level
organisms which would monitor chemicals and bio-toxins on the battlefield or
represent living neural computer networks.[68]

Biotechnology also has non-lethal weapons applications. Biodegrading microbes could be used to attack an opposing force's infrastructure and/or material,
calmatives released to put terrorists to sleep, pheromones utilized to influence a

---

63   Steven Metz and James Kievit, *The Revolution in Military Affairs and Conflict Short of War*, p. 31.
64   This insight was gained from discussions with Mark T. Clark, Director, National Security Studies
      programme, California State University, San Bernardino.
65   Chuck de Caro, *Sats, Lies, and Video-Rape: The Soft War Handbook* (McLean, VA: Aerobureau
      Corporation, 1994).
66   John Arquilla and David Ronfeldt, *Cyberwar is Coming!*, P-7791 (Santa Monica, CA: The RAND
      Corporation, 1992); and John Arquilla and David Rondfeldt, *The Advent of Net War* (Santa Monica,
      CA: The RAND Corporation, 1996).
67   Metz and Kievit suggest that two simultaneous RMAs are taking place, an electronic one and a
      biotechnical one. I argue that they are both attributes of the greater RPMA within the post-mechanical
      transition underway. See Steven Metz and James Kievit, *The Revolution in Military Affairs and
      Conflict Short of War*, p. 32.
68   Pat Cooper, 'Naval Research Lab Attempts to Meld Neurons and Chips: Studies May Produce Army
      of "Zombies"', *Defense News*, 10, 20-26 March 1995, pp. 1, 50; and William Matthews, 'Library in a
      Cube: New Computers may Inherit Genes for Super Memory', *Naval Times*, 7 November 1994,
      p. 48.

mob's behaviour, or cultural-specific malodorous agents employed as a perimeter defence around a detention centre.[69] Other areas of military significance may include gene technologies, biomolecular engineering, bioproduction technology, targeted delivery systems, biocoupling, and bionics.[70]

Other Material Considerations

The afore-mentioned humanspace and cyberspace material will not exist in solitude. Rather, they will dramatically impact on future support and logistical considerations and, as a result, require the development of advanced forms of combat services support. 'Mountains of iron' will become a thing of the past because they are manpower and resource intensive, inefficient for resupplying the warfighter, and pose tempting targets for destruction and/or seizure by indigenous non-state forces. The problems faced by peacekeeping troops at the Mogadishu port facility in Somalia present a case in point.

Two new forms of logistics will need to develop. The first form will be primarily directed towards humanspace requirements and based upon a more focused form of logistical support.[71] It would be applicable to both military operations or as a stand-alone capability in support of humanitarian missions.[72] Military forces would transmit information concerning depleted supplies and ordnance to support elements so that efficient resupply can take place. This method has been successfully employed by major retailers and allows them to keep the minimum required stockpiles on hand at their outlets.

Due to security concerns, these support elements will need to be positioned off-shore or based in friendly host nations. Supplies could then be routed, via specialized software, so that this support function becomes more efficient. Locations of items will be known at all times by means of radio frequency tags and laser cards,

---

69   Stuart Howard and William D. Hitt, *Intercultural Differences in Olfaction*, ARPA-Project AGILE Report (Columbus, OH: Battelle Memorial Institute, 2 May 1966); David C. Morrison, 'Alternatives to Bashing', *National Journal*, 24, 6 June 1992, pp. 1358-60; Arthur Knoth, 'Disabling Technologies: A Critical Assessment', *International Defense Review*, 27, July 1994, pp. 33-9; and Major Joseph W. Cook, III, USAF, Major David Fiely, USAF, and Major Maura T. McGowan, USAF, 'Non-lethal Weapons: Technologies, Legalities, and Potential Policies', *Airpower Journal*, 9, Special Edition 1995, p. 83.

70   Board on Army Science and Technology, Commission on Engineering and Technical Systems, National Research Council, *STAR 21: Strategic Technologies for the Army of the Twenty-First Century* (Washington, DC: National Academy Press, 1992), pp. 11-12.

71   TRADOC Pamphlet 525-5, *Force XXI Operations: A Concept for the Evolution of Full-Dimensional Operations for the Strategic Army of the Early Twenty-First Century* (Fort Monroe, VA: Army Training and Doctrine Command, 1 August 1994), pp. 3-13 to 3-15.

72   United States Army, 'Focused Logistics', *Army Vision 2010*, location: [http://www.army.mil.:80/2010/focused_ logistics.htm.].

which will allow for computer system uplinks to satellites so that supplies can be tracked through the distribution system.[73] For more specialized needs, such as computers, a built-to-order product supply sub-system could also be established.[74]

Cyberspace logistics will exist in near real-time and will become the preferred means of operational support because of the capacity to get around the spatial limitations of humanspace. Bulky technical manuals will be replaced by digital versions which can be accessed as required. Telemaintenance will utilize interactive technology and step-by-step video segments which will provide repair instructions, diagnostic tools, and expert systems, allowing for shortened repair and maintenance times.[75]

Software programs and data, such as newer versions of anti-viral packages and mapping information, will be downloaded by military forces via the cybersupply net, thus eliminating the physical movement of tonnes of materials. The survivability of Western force personnel will also be enhanced by new capabilities such as 'internet triage' and 'telemedicine', the latter of which was battle-tested in Somalia.[76]

European Joint Force

The emergence of the RPMA based on a neo-Clausewitzian viewpoint will dramatically impact on future Western force structure requirements. These force structure requirements, in turn, will be implemented within the context of the larger European integration process. Unlike the United States, which is attempting to move from a handful of individual services to a unified joint force within its own intra-state environment, the European states face a far greater challenge.[77] They will be attempting to create a joint force across an inter-state, or regional, environment, out

---

73   Based on concepts of Total Asset Visibility (TAV) and In-Transit Visibility. See 'Synchronization Matrix Details: Logistics', and CWO4 Daniel C. Parker and Jim Caldwell, 'Battlefield Distribution for Force XXI', *Army Logistician Magazine*, July 1995, reprint, *Force XXI Personnel, Logistics & RDA Homepage*, location: [http://204.7.227.67/infonet/per-log/per-log.html#logistics]; Mark Hewish and Rupert Pengelley, 'From Fort to Port to Foxhole', *IDR Extra*, 1, April 1996, pp. 1-7.

74   Dan McGraw, 'The Kid Bytes Back: Michael Dell, a Generation X Success Story, Revives his Computer Company', *US News and World Report*, 12 December 1994, p. 71.

75   'Synchronization Matrix Details: Logistics', *Force XXI Personnel, Logistics and RDA Homepage*.

76   United States Army, 'Focused Logistics', *Army Vision 2010*; and Steve Salerno, 'The Cutting Edge of Combat Medicine', *The American Legion*, 138, March 1995, p. 20. For more information, see Maryann Karinch, *Telemedicine: What the Future Holds When You're Ill* (Far Hills, NJ: New Horizon Press, 1994).

77   This initiative in the United States can be seen with the growing importance of the journal *Joint Force Quarterly* and the proliferation of joint publications.

of dozens of discrete military services formerly belonging to individual European Union members.

Governmental and financial factors are generally perceived to be the dominant mechanisms behind the development of a European Joint Force. For integration to take place, national militaries, like monetary policies, will need to be merged into a larger regional system. At the same time, many nations are suffering from an increasing lack of financial means to support their own national military component. The creation of a unified European force is thus looked upon favourably by many nations for the 'integration dividend' it will provide.

The battlefield requirements of the future use of military force(s) also make a European Joint Force an increasingly critical necessity. As mentioned earlier in this chapter under the Clausewitzian paradigm, three-dimensional boundaries and relationships (that is, humanspace) presented physical weak points which could be exploited by opposing forces. In the emergent neo-Clausewitzian era, concepts of vulnerability have shifted to fourth-dimensional boundaries (that is, cyberspace), presenting informational weak points such as the communication, sensing, command, and control flows and seams, both within 'the military' and between it and 'the government' and 'the people' which it defends.

Based upon these future warfighting requirements, separate national military components for each individual state within a larger European Union would lead to disaster. Numerous informational weak points would exist, such as non-conforming digital interoperability protocols, differing real-time logistical reporting systems, and incompatible software operating environments, which would either indirectly degrade the exchange of information or provide direct opportunities which could be exploited by opposing forces.

Given these considerations, a dominant requirement of a European Joint Force is to determine the most sensible and efficient composite element (or building block) for the structuring of cooperation/integration of Western military forces within the various operational concepts now under development. This component element will need to differ from the traditional Clausewitzian articulation based upon a divisional structure. That structure reflected mature mechanical concepts, such as 'interchangeable parts' and 'division of labour', which represented an approach to warfighting based on the application of superior masses of men and material against an opposing force. Furthermore, the command and control mechanism utilized by that structure is becoming increasingly inefficient because of the limitations and vulnerabilities inherent in its restricted hierarchical information flows. This restriction can be viewed against the more efficient information-flows of a non-hierarchical structure (Figure 3).

Figure 3 *Command Information Structures*[78]

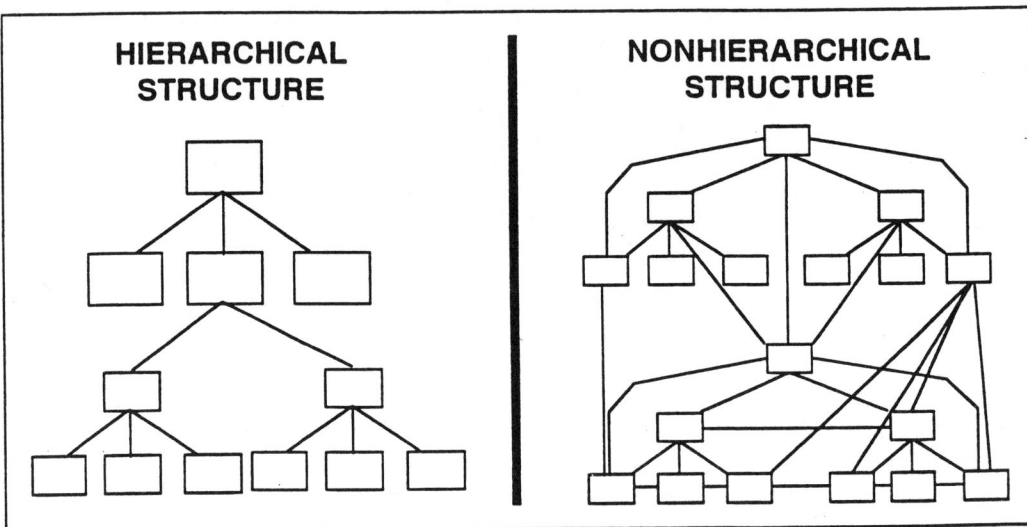

The dominance of post-mechanical technologies in future operations dictate that a new form of building block will be required to provide the basis of European Joint Force structuring. Post-mechanical concepts, such as 'tailored production' and 'environmental security', would provide much of the logic behind its development. While many characteristics of these neo-Clausewitzian era technologies are still speculative in nature, those listed below suggest the organic components that an element should strive to possess.

CONNECTIVITY

This composite element should have all of its components networked. Furthermore, it should be able seamlessly to attach to and detach from other military forces and support elements with relative ease. Once an element is so connected, it should be able rapidly to exchange information and network awareness data with other forces. Sub-component connectivity, at the individual soldier level, should be composed at a minimum of a wearable computer, weaponry datalink, and virtual retinal display (VRD) which would turn each soldier into a weapons system and sensor.

---

78   *Source:* TRADOC Pamphlet 525-5, *Force XXI Operations: A Concept for the Evolution of Full-Dimensional Operations for the Strategic Army of the Early Twenty-First Century* (Fort Monroe, VA: Army Training and Doctrine Command, 1 August 1994), pp. 2-9.

NETWORK AWARENESS

Each composite element should be able to generate its own 'intranet' which its military forces can access.[79] This will allow for a networked approach to warfighting, thus providing many benefits, including real-time logistical updates, redundant C^2 flows, the creation of shared battlespace awareness, and opposing force mission projections. For more specific needs, an 'internet' would be accessed for which virtually any mission-specific query could be either searched or bulletin board posted.

DUAL-DIMENSIONALITY

The capability to operate in both three-dimensional and four-dimensional space is required. This would mean a mixture of humanspace forces such as battle-suited infantry, their vehicles, and armed robotic systems which would provide a visible presence on the ground, while snipers, informants, static and mobile data fusion arrays, and tele-information warfare specialists would provide a cyberspace capability. Operations conducted simultaneously in both dimensions against opposing forces would likely benefit from a synergistic effect.

TAILORED RESPONSE

A tailored response capability in contingency operations is vital because it would allow for the precise application of politico-military force. Clausewitzian concepts of force, based solely on killing or destroying opposing personnel and material, are in variance with the development of non-lethal and anti-lethal weapons and informational and psychological technologies. These weapons and technologies, when combined with advances in lethal weapons such as tubular projectiles, allow for the means to dominate the force continuum because they provide options which can be tailored to meet specific circumstances or threats in both humanspace and cyberspace. Furthermore, they offer a means to attack the bonds/relationships of opposing non-national entities which represent a new target set for Western forces to exploit.

79　Conceptually similar to an 'information carousel' but would differentiate between an 'intranet' and 'internet'. See Brian Nichiporuk and Carl H. Builder, *Information Technologies and the Future of Land Warfare*, pp. 68-71.

RESOURCE CONSERVATION

The ability to utilize resources efficiently and eliminate unnecessary waste would be another organic component. Personnel and material represent valued resources which must be conserved. For this reason, modular system designs for easy upgrades and the recycling of equipment, including the creation of organ and tissue banks derived from deceased soldiers, must be explored. Furthermore, the elimination of shell casings, garbage dumps, worn tires, and other material via advanced means (for example, caseless ammunition and biodegrading microbes) would deny opposing groups resources that could be used against Western security forces.[80]

SUSTAINABILITY

Each element must be operationally independent and defensively robust once deployed to the field. It should be able to sustain itself logistically in an operation and fulfil its own security and informational needs. It should possess a very low signature and, of necessity, a small logistical footprint. In intra-state conflicts where decisive victory may not be achievable, strategy may have to be refocused on not losing rather than on winning. Hence, like the medieval Byzantine cavalry turma, this building block should be hard to defeat and, if required, possess the stamina to outlast opposing forces.

With the development of a European Joint Force, the rationale for a continued functional separation of Western ground, air, naval, marine, and military police forces must be questioned. A persuasive reason for continuing functional separation, both from a warfighting and socio-political perspective, may be that of the threat of 'institutional shock' to Western military forces. National militaries would become integrated while at the same time losing their distinct service identities. This may represent too much change all at once for them to handle.

On the other hand, no pressing reason to support such a rationale can be found from a neo-Clausewitzian perspective on technology. Rather, the opposite is true. Only a joint force would possess the necessary mandate and clout to issue and enforce an 'information solidarity' directive on Western security forces. Furthermore, by promoting such large-scale change, institutional barriers to the creation of a European Joint Force would be less likely to compromise its development.

Each proposed element, then, should be composed of formerly discrete service components within a unified European military service structure.[81] Specialities fo-

---

80 This would include personalized guns, which, if captured, would be unable to fire and thus would be rendered useless to their new owners.

81 This service structure needs to be flatter and configured as an entrepreneurial organization. For concepts relating to developing organizational structures, see General Gordon R. Sullivan and Colonel

cused on information, special forces, military police, air/space, ground, and naval operations and their sub-specialties and hybrid-specialties, information-special forces, could delineate this service's career tracks. While it would represent a departure from past military logic, the establishment of such a military structure would better promote the material means that are needed for advanced operational concepts and doctrines to succeed. This, in turn, would allow for more efficient application of the future use of military force in the context of a Western security strategy.

James M. Dubik, *War in the Information Age* (Carlisle Barracks, PA: Strategic Studies Institute, US Army War College, 6 June 1994).

11 Workshop Proceedings: Topical Highlights and Tentative Conclusions

Gert de Nooy and Rienk Terpstra

This chapter attempts to highlight the arguments of the individual contributions and to single out the relevant points emerging from the workshop debate. What then can be construed from the preceding pages and debate? Four queries in particular have been addressed.

First, the fundamental question arose of whether the Clausewitzian theory of war is still applicable for present-day wars and conflicts, and, if that is no longer the case, whether it is being replaced by a new theory on the convention of war? Second, attention was focused on the trends and developments within the elements of the Clausewitzian trinity supporting the nation-state: society, government, and armed forces. Third, the impact that these trends and paradigm shifts might have on the West European nation-state was discussed. Finally, the debate evolved around the effect that these changes and trends might have on the role, size, and composition of Western armed forces. The arguments and responses relevant to these queries are laid out below, and the structure of this chapter therefore reflects that of the book itself.

The Clausewitzian Theory and its Applicability

The main issues of the workshop debate under this heading focused on the possible causes of the demise of Clausewitzian thinking, the applicability of his theory to unconventional warfare (such as counter-insurgency and low-intensity warfare), the disappearance of the nation-state as a foundation for trinitarian concepts, and the lack of a new, balanced theory of war replacing the former, trinitarian one.

Where it concerns the possible causes of the demise of Clausewitzian theory, several lines of thought were developed. First, it was suggested that the steady erosion of the monopoly on armed force through state institutions contributes to the demise of trinitarian thinking, in particular because this monopoly is the corner-stone of both the nation-state and the Clausewitzian theory of war. Parallels were drawn with the European situation before the emergence of the Westphalian nation-

G.C. de Nooy (ed.), The Clausewitzian Dictum and the Future of Western Military Strategy, 167-175.
© 1997 *Kluwer Law International. Printed in the Netherlands.*

state, and it was argued that the medieval analogy held true in many ways. Second, it was argued that the introduction of nuclear weapons was the main cause of 'the death of Clausewitzian theory'. It was proposed that Bernard Brodie was right when he stated in 1948 that conventional wars would no longer be fought between the possessors of nuclear weapons. Along these lines and reflecting the historical record of wars and conflicts since the Second World War, it was observed that conventional wars only occurred between or against states that did not possess nuclear weapons. Moreover, it was pointed out that for this reason states regularly involved in conventional conflicts either strived to possess their own nuclear weapon or relied on one of the nuclear weapon states to provide a nuclear umbrella. Finally, the economization of international relations, as put forward by Luttwak, was proposed as another cause of the demise of Clausewitzian theory. As economic interdependence and social and individual mobility are ever increasing, the likelihood of conventional trinitarian wars occurring between economically linked states and their volatile inhabitants is almost becoming an unimaginable feature of postmodern society. The Netherlands was highlighted as an example. It was argued that it is not conceivable for the Netherlands to wage another war against either its neighbours or states further afield. What would be plausible, however, is an increase in domestic unrest, societal disobedience, and low-intensity urban conflict – all forms of so-called unconventional warfare which were thought not to be ruled by trinitarian or Clausewitzian theory.

The issue of whether Clausewitzian theory is applicable to unconventional war centred around the suggestion that although Clausewitz had written a brilliant chapter on popular war, his arguments ran along non-trinitarian lines and so foresaw the present-day situation where 'the regular soldiers are against guerillas what robots are to men'. In other words, the record of failure in unconventional warfare by the armed forces of coalitions or individual states can be explained by the fact that the Clausewitzian-inspired approach by the intervening military ultimately never paid off. A whole range of examples was cited: from the British expeditionary force in East Asia, the Americans in Vietnam, and, more recently, the coalition forces in Somalia.

Moreover, it was argued that although much has been written about how to conduct unconventional warfare – Mao Zedong was one of the writers quoted – the literature on how to handle or combat unconventional warfare is sparse if not nonexistent. It seems that there is no interest by the armed forces of Western states to involve themselves with a non-trinitarian approach. This 'hot potato' strategy might be explained by the reluctance of regular armed forces to leave the beaten and conventional path of warfare, with all the consequences that this might have for their position within the nation-state. It was therefore argued that failures in unconventional warfare will continue to be the norm unless drastic and strategic changes within the military of Western states take place, based on a revision of the convention of war and of the definition of 'just who is allowed to kill whom, for what ends, under what circumstances, and by what means'.

The disappearance of the state as the corner-stone of trinitarian theory might lead to new forms of political entities, each with their own constituent elements which almost certainly will not resemble the elements of the Clausewitzian trinity of society, government, and armed forces. It was suggested that the present-day nation-state is slowly being 'crushed' between two opposite forces, leading to the leakage or dissolution of state sovereignty in many ways. Both the forces of integration and fragmentation have this effect.

It was argued that the fall of the nation-state would lead to two possible alternatives which are not mutually exclusive. The first alternative for the nation-state would be larger political entities such as the European Union, within which state sovereignty would be dissolved and in which new constituent elements, other than those forming the present nation-state, would set the stage. As an example, the eagerness with which newly independent states in Central and (South) Eastern Europe were ready to give up their sovereignty to become members of a larger political collective such as the European Union was cited, even when that state sovereignty had been forcefully fought for or had not even matured or come about.

Trends and Developments within Society

Central to this was the question of how Western democratic governments, now and in the future, are going to motivate society to provide them with armed forces that are ready and willing to die and fight for national or collective interests, whatever they may be. Linked to this question was the global trend for state- and non-state actors increasingly to contract mercenaries or para-military firms to do a military job. The emergence of mercenaries and private military-security firms shows a distinct parallel with medieval times when the state as such was not yet fully developed.

On the topic of motivation, two lines of thought were developed: the first had a definite political science character, while the second reflected the sociologist's viewpoint. In the political science model, it was argued that the motivation of military personnel could be different in different phases of career: during the first phase, the recruitment phase, motivation was said to be a reflection of the close social and economic environment of the person rather than the more general call for the defence of collective values. In other words, the opinion of family members or team-mates from the sports club will override any other opinions such as those of the government or the media. Furthermore, sense of adventure plays an important role in the decision to become a professional military man. Not surprisingly, recruiting for the armed forces emphasizes the 'job' aspect, the material and financial benefits and the adventurous character of life in the military: no reference is made to 'the willingness to die' or the preparedness to kill; nor are the international legal order or collective humanitarian values used as a motivating factor.

During the second phase, the fighting phase, it was argued that small-group solidarity and coping, risking, and searching for vital solutions were the key motivations for the military to keep going even in the most adverse and pointless fighting conditions. It was pointed out that the will to fight – and kill – only comes about when there is an unconditioned willingness to die. Moreover, Western democracies and their people, it was argued, no longer possess this willingness to die, which leads to the conclusion that armed forces no longer have the capability to wage wars or manage conflicts between parties that do possess this quality.

Motivation during the last phase, the post-fighting phase, hinges on the reconciliation of the soldier with his acts during the fighting phase. It was assumed that in this phase collective values, Western democratic norms, etc., could finally come into play as motivational factors, albeit factors of a more symbolic and retrospective nature.

The sociologist's line of argument upheld the theory that the motivational question was a single and personal one and did not agree with the different phases. Moreover, it argued that collective norms and values, including culturally determined parameters, influenced motivation and hence the willingness of a person to fight and die for their country: 'the recruit is not a dumbo signing a contract without knowing what is in store for him/her'. The big question here remains whether the future military is prepared to engage itself in new forms of warfare, such as protracted operations in either low-intensity conflict (such as the Israeli situation) or unconventional and counter-insurgency warfare.

On this question of the 'mouldability' of society to produce well-motivated and capable soldiers, it seems that Western governments are having more and more problems in linking state interests and objectives to 'the willingness to die' or the motivation to wage war or conduct combat operations in an effective manner. This leads to two developments. The first is described above and could be termed the professionalization and privatization of the armed forces. This trend involves a decoupling of armed forces and society, the demise of conscript and reserve forces and an increase in private companies and firms catering for soldiers of fortune and 'dogs of – peace and – war'. Whether this trend is conducive for the survival of the nation-state, and hence of the international legal order, is questionable.

The second trend is best described by the following military dilemma, resulting from the fact that Western democratically orientated governments are increasingly hesitant to put their armed forces at risk for interests that are not deemed vital (that is, the survival of the state itself). On the one hand, armed forces risk becoming irrelevant as there is no longer a requirement for armed forces to defend the 'territory' of the state in view of the absence of any threat of occupation. It will either result in the military instrument becoming a very expensive ornament of state, or governments having to reinstate conscription and reserve mechanisms to fill a possible *Reichswehr* model. It is feared that in both cases societal support for the armed forces will rapidly dwindle. On the other hand, armed forces risk being restructured because of international requirements to cope with less than vital interests such as far-away conflicts and humanitarian relief operations. In this case, however, armed forces might be restructured towards special (police) forces, leading to them also becoming irrelevant as the political will is lacking to form expeditionary forces.

Trends and Developments within the Government

The debate on the role of government within the state trinity focused on the relationship between state formation and sustainment, political and socio-economic integration, and the functions and institutions of state. It was emphasized that an important distinction exists between formative factors and sustainment factors. The point was raised that although state formation in general terms comes about in reaction to a commonly perceived external threat or danger of war, state sustainment is almost solely influenced by how effectively it performs its socio-economic functions such as decision- and rule-making, taxation, and providing social security (education, health care, jobs, etc.). Moreover, it was pointed out that when discussing global security it is important to note that the process of state formation is in different stages of development and has reached various levels of success in different regions of the world. In Western societies the development of a highly intrusive and functional state system is almost complete. In the Pacific region state formation is at a stage comparable to the Western stage during the Interbellum; the chances of inter-state war are high as state formation is still in progress. In the 'Third World', especially Africa, one could say that state formation only began after the decolonization process and does not seem to be successful at all. It is not surprising to see that the majority, if not all, of the failed states are located within this region of budding state formation.

In the same vein it was remarked that the state as such is changing rapidly, in particular where its institutions are concerned. It was argued that for a state to function effectively, as it does nowadays, the state institutions responsible for rule-making, taxation, and the distribution of collective social benefits and economic welfare have changed dramatically. They hardly resemble the original institutions of the classical state. This trend has affected the sovereignty of the European state in an irrevocable manner. The leakage of sovereignty towards integrated European institutions which now carry out state functions is also affecting the state function of physical protection of the state's citizens: where *de jure* the sovereignty over armed forces still resides with the individual governments, *de facto* and practically sovereignty has leaked away towards all kinds of bilateral or multilateral alliances, arrangements and non-state actors.

This in turn strengthens the development of a growing divergence between the employment of armed forces by the government and the requirements of society for its physical protection. The split between societal requirements and government policy on the use of its military instrument is illustrated, on the one hand, by the continued use of nuclear weapons as state tools and military instruments, and the emergence of so-called 'gated' communities (30,000 in the United States) which provide for their own physical security through private security firms, on the other. In the United States, private security officers outnumber civilian police officers by two to one.

It was argued that if the relationship and harmony between society, governments and armed forces was to be restored, it would result in major upheavals within Western armed forces, as they would have to transform into a security and protection institution dealing with transnational and badly defined threats and risks to the common interests of European society at large (organized crime, environmental hazards, drug smuggling, nuclear blackmail). Moreover, it implies a thorough reorganization and restructuring of present-day armed forces to face tasks which resemble more those of police or constabulary forces adapted to fight against a volatile, high-tech and well-motivated opponent. It becomes clear that within this concept there is no space for either the possession of nuclear weapons or the sovereign employment of instruments for inter-state 'classical' war. Finally, restoration of the relationship mentioned above is essential if governments of Western democratic states are to function just as well in the realm of physical protection of society as they do in the other fields of security.

The Future Military: Strategy, Role and Composition

The exchange of ideas and arguments under this heading dealt most intensively with Clausewitz's core business: those who wage war or alternatively – try to – keep the peace, the military.

Due to the overall reduction of the conventional threat perception by societies of stable democratic nation-states, their armed forces are experiencing increasing difficulty in maintaining present levels of defence spending and in recruiting high-quality personnel. It is no longer *en vogue* voluntarily to spend a considerable amount of tax revenue on the armed forces, to sacrifice one or more of the best years of one's life as a conscript, or even to embark on a professional military career. For these reasons many states have drastically cut the size of their armed forces, their defence budgets in general, have abolished conscription and introduced a fully professional military.

STRATEGY

On the topic of future military strategy, it was stated that the strategic doctrine of Clausewitz – that is, his thinking of warfare as a means of overthrow – does not fit present-day conflicts. The discussion mainly centred around two intertwining questions: does Clausewitz really exclude limited war from his thinking?; and the definition of limited warfare. The overall conclusion was that Clausewitz does not mention limited conflict as such. Nowadays, however, crisis management in intra-state conflicts can be performed through the use of more robust military power than was thought possible several years ago. The peacekeeping operations in Bosnia, for instance, can be seen as a form of limited war played by unwittingly fine-tuned rules of some Western powers.

Modern-day intra-state conflict has forced Western strategic thinking into a crisis. It was argued by some that Clausewitz is to blame for this, because he promises success and has proved to deliver in conventional warfare. To the Prussian strategist, war is escalatory by nature. Also because of the uneasy relationship between the German text and its contemporary English adaptation, this notion prevents the military from envisioning the translation of limited political goals into limited operational objectives. According to some, the famous Clausewitzian trinity is merely a way of concealing this irregularity. To Anglo-Saxon interpreters, the trinity became a makeshift recipe for limited warfare.

Although propagated in theory, the Western military does not practise limited warfare. In both intra-state conflicts and against rogue states, Cannae-like strategies of annihilation are proposed. This is not necessary. Even 'irrational' nationalists and terrorists play by certain rules. Modern Western states and armies can learn to adopt to these principles. However, if states are not able to cope with this new reality, they could find themselves in a vulnerable position when they are suddenly involved in something that might be termed a Low-Intensity Conflict (LIC), and which resembles guerilla warfare or sustained terrorism. This could be as a party to the conflict or through the deployment of peace support troops.

However, Western armed forces tend to respond to LICs with technologically superior arms in order to limit casualties. This high-tech approach towards low-tech conflicts has been made possible by the fact that the West and its armed forces in particular are unwittingly currently experiencing a monumental military, political and technological transformation (RPMA). It was argued that in military-strategic terms this RPMA adds another dimension to the three-dimensional 'battlespace box', which has existed since the birth of the Westphalian nation-state and is the traditional object of Clausewitzian military thought. It was pointed out that at present this battlespace (or humanspace as it was labelled) is under absolute Western domination, as the military outcome of the Gulf War has proven.

Moreover, it was argued that the necessity of adding another element to traditional warfare is caused by the high risk run by an intervening military force when the conflicting parties do not 'play' according to Western rules and conventions. By adding a fourth dimension (labelled cyberspace) to the traditional battlespace, future military should be able either to get the enemy out of battlespace into cyberspace and neutralize him there or – if forced into humanspace – ensure survival through domination while still keeping control of the electromagnetic part of cyberspace.

The counter argument in the RPMA debate – although seen as a revolutionary vision – ran as follows. Although post-modern warfighting methods are indeed required, the non-traditional solution for this specific military-strategic problem had a traditional character, in the sense that it relies heavily on a technology advantage and is basically nothing but a continuation of the well-known arms race. But, more importantly, it might have an adverse impact on the role and composition of future armed forces.

Belief in and reliance on technology makes Western democracies even more susceptible to the actions of those non-state actors which choose to wage a low-intensity operation either against the state or against another non-state actor. In this case, Western forces will also be opposed by more primitive warriors. However, as Western democracies are, on the one hand, increasingly unwilling to bear the human cost of warfare, they are, on the other hand, less inclined to bear the financial costs for high-tech weaponry which is expensive.

ROLE

Providing physical security for society has transformed the military into a multidimensional issue. The nature and role of the armed forces have changed likewise. Nevertheless, the modern All-Volunteer Forces (AVFs) are, and must remain, distinctly different from the civil society in values and tasks. In contrast to the Cold War epoch and in the spirit of peace support operations, today's soldier must be tolerant towards other cultures, have diplomatic skills and must consider himself a guardian of the international legal order. Two risks should be avoided: military deployment cannot be an excuse for political inability to solve problems; and the military should not be demilitarized as peacekeepers but retain their core business as warriors. Neither can technology offer a definite solution in this respect.

However, in today's peace support operations, the importance of 'showing the flag' by deploying considerable numbers of troops on the ground is increasing. Because these conflicts pose no direct physical threat, societies are inclined to see the soldiers involved in these operations more as individual members of the community in a particular hazardous situation than as military professionals doing their job. Notably, the outcome of these modern conflicts is determined by the balance of political stakes rather than by the balance of military capabilities.

The debate on the profile of the future soldier focused on questions pertaining to the relationship between peace support and traditional military operations.

Indeed, focusing too much on the first will hamper an effective performance of the latter, but can one soldier be trained to do both tasks? Peacekeeping can be seen as reversed training for real war. Moreover, can Western young people who apply for the military be expected to be 20-year-old supermen? Besides, soldiers who have only experienced peace support operations tend to regard them as actual warfare while they are not. This may lead to armed forces whose readiness for genuine conflict is inadequate. In short, the lack of a conventional security threat has led to the increasing political and military importance of peace support operations, which in turn could lead to personnel who are less competent in combat.

ORGANISATION

The paradox, therefore, is that states governed by the people are ill-equipped to provide security for the people. A practical solution to this problem, which could at least limit the harm done to the security of Western democracies, would be the establishment of backbone armed forces, also known as the *Reichswehr* model. It entails a sharp reduction in personnel, leaving a small corps of highly qualified professional soldiers who are capable of serving both in peace support and combat operations, sufficient investment in technology and the possibility to enlist large numbers of reserves in times of crisis. Because size is limited, an international division of labour – that is, burden-sharing by democratic states in a deepened collective security system – becomes a necessity.

The backbone armed forces' model was regarded as interesting but not practical in the West European case. It was thought to be politically unlikely that conscription will ever be reinstituted, thus crippling expansion capabilities. A different approach was proposed in the form of an age policy: young soldiers will perform battle duties, while older military are designed for more police-type functions such as peacekeeping. Furthermore, can the disarmament trend be regarded as a general phenomenon or one that is only realized by Western democracies? This development points to an analogy between the 1920s and the present time. Finally, it was noted that since the stakes of the intervening party are minor, yet the stakes of the party being intervened are exigent, this must have repercussions on the motivation of the respective soldiers on the battlefield.

About the Authors

Robert Bunker is Adjunct Professor of the National Security Studies Program at the California State University in San Bernardino and Professor of Unconventional Warfare at the American Military University in Virginia.

Martin van Creveld is Professor at the History Department of the Hebrew University in Jerusalem.

Kees Homan is Director of the Netherlands Defence College.

Jan Willem Honig is Lecturer in War Studies at King's College in London.

Koen Koch is Senior Lecturer in International Relations at the Department of Political Science at Leiden University and holds the Jean Monnet Chair in Political-Administrative Studies of European Integration.

Zeev Maoz is Head of the Jaffee Center for Strategic Studies and the Department of Political Science at Tel Aviv University in Israel.

Jan van der Meulen is Director of the Netherlands Foundation for Society and Armed Forces.

Gert de Nooy, Commander, Royal Netherlands Navy, is the military research fellow at the Netherlands Institute of International Relations 'Clingendael'.

Jan Geert Siccama is Director of Studies of the Netherlands Institute of International Relations 'Clingendael' and Honorary Professor in International Security at the University of Utrecht.

Rienk Terpstra is Defence Analist at The Netherlands Defence Staff.

Jaap de Wilde is Research Fellow and Lecturer in International Relations at the Faculty of Public Administration and Public Policy of the University of Twente in the Netherlands.

Clingendael Publications

Books

The Role of European Ground and Air Forces after the Cold War, Gert de Nooy (ed.), Kluwer Law International, 1997, 227 p. Price: Dfl 95,00
ISBN 90 411 0397 X

The United Nations and NATO in Former Yugoslavia, 1991-1996: limits to diplomacy and force, door D.A. Leurdijk, Den Haag: Atlantische Commissie en Instituut Clingendael, 1997, 152 p. Price: Dfl 34,95 ISBN 90 73329 07 8

Cooperative Security, the OCSE, and its Code of Conduct, Gert de Nooy (ed.), Kluwer Law International: The Hague, 1996, 158 p. Price: Dfl 95,-
ISBN 90 411 0316 3

Selective Engagement. American foreign policy at the turn of the century, Marianne van Leeuwen, Auke Venema, (eds.), Gelderland offset: Nijmegen, 1996, 137 p. Price: Dfl 29,75 ISBN 90 73329 06 x

Between Development and Destruction. An Enquiry into the Causes of Conflict in Post-Colonial States, Luc van de Goor, Kumar Rupesinghe, Paul Sciarone (eds.), MacMillan Press Ltd: Hampshire, 1996, 376 p. Price: Dfl 50,65
ISBN 0 333 65038 7

The Role of European Naval Forces after the Cold War, Gert de Nooy (ed.), Kluwer Law International: The Hague, 1996, 204 p. Price: Dfl 95,-
ISBN 90 411 0227 2

A UN Rapid Deployment Brigade; strengthening the capacity for quick response, Dick A. Leurdijk (ed.), 1995, 95 p. Price: Dfl 25,- ISBN 90 5031 045 1

The Future of the International Nuclear Non-Proliferation Regime, Marianne van Leeuwen (ed.), Martinus Nijhoff Publishers: Dordrecht, 1995, 326 p.
Price: Dfl 140,- ISBN 0 7923 3433 7

Restructuring Armed Forces in East and West, Jan G. Siccama & Theo van den Doel (eds.), Westview Press: Boulder, 1994, 141 p. Price: Dfl 40,-
ISBN 0 8133 2476 9

Central Europe: The New Allies? The Road from Visegrad to Brussels, door Theo van den Doel, Westview Press: Boulder, 1993, 126 p. Price: Dfl 40,-
ISBN 0 8133 8844 9

Americans and the Palestinian Question; The US public debate on Palestinian nationhood, 1973-1988, door M. van Leeuwen, Rodopi: Amsterdam, 1993, 545 p. Price: Dfl 165,- ISBN 90 5183 533 7 (CIP)

The Disintegration of Yugoslavia, Yearbook of European Studies 5, M. van den Heuvel and J.G. Siccama (eds.), Rodopi: Amsterdam, 1992, 218 p. Price: Dfl 35,-
ISBN 90 5183 353 9 (paper)

Anerkannt als Minderheit. Vergangenheit und Zukunft der Deutschen in Polen, Hans van der Meulen (Hrsg.), Nomos Verlagsgesellschaft: Baden-Baden 1994, 256 p. Price: Dfl 77,50 ISBN 3 7890 3634 X

Deutschland im Superwahljahr 1994; Beobachtungen aus deutscher, niederländischer und französischer Sicht, Friso Wielenga, Harald Fühner (Hrsg.), Van Gorcum: Assen, augustus 1994, 70 p. Price: Dfl 20,- ISBN 90 5031 039 7

Im historischen Würgegriff. Die Beziehungen zwischen Ungarn und der Slowakei in der Vergangenheit, Gegenwart und Zukunft, Robert Aspeslagh, Hans Renner, Hans van der Meulen (Hrsg.), Nomos Verlagsgesellschaft: Baden-Baden, 1994, 180 p. Price: Dfl 45,- ISBN 3 7890 3290 5

Bekannt und unbeliebt. Das Bild von Deutschland und Deutschen unter Jugendlichen von fünfzehn bis neunzehn Jahren, door Lútzen B. Jansen, Maart 1993, 100 p. Price: 8,-

Clingendael Papers

Political-military Cooperation in an Enlarging Europe, door G.C. de Nooy, A. van Staden, M. Wohlfeld, mei 1997, 43 p. Price: Dfl 10,- ISBN 90 5031 059 1

The WEU's Role in Crisis Prevention and Management, door Wlodzimierz Aniol, januari 1997, 37 p. Price: Dfl 10,- ISBN 90 5031 056 7

Mapping Central Europe, door Elena Zamfirescu, mei 1996, 76 p. Price: Dfl 10,-
ISBN 90 5031 050 8

Towards a Military Core Group in Europe?, door G.C. de Nooy, maart 1995,
31 p. Price: Dfl 10,- ISBN 90 5031 043 5

*Adversaries All Around? (Re)Nationalization of Security and Defence Policies in
Central and Eastern Europe*, door Pál Dunay, januari 1994, 69 p. Price: Dfl 10,-
ISBN 90 5031 037 0 (Research Paper)

Through the backdoor; PLO-US contacts, 1974-1988, door Marianne van
Leeuwen, augustus 1992, 40 p. Price: Dfl 10,- ISBN 90 5031 028 1
(Research Paper)

The political debate over a bill of rights for South Africa, door Henk Botha,
augustus 1992, 54 p. Price: Dfl 10,- ISBN 90 5031 029 (Policy Paper)

Nationalism and political change in post-communist Europe, door André W.M.
Gerrits, april 1992, 44 p. Price: Dfl 10,- (Research Paper)

Changing Hearts? The Bush administration, American public opinion, and the
Arab-Israeli conflict, door Marianne van Leeuwen, november 1991, 40 p.
Price: Dfl 10,- (Research Paper)

Occasional Papers

*Revision of Maastricht: Implementation and Proposals for Reform. A Survey of
National Views*, Sixth Edition, July-December 1996, 51 p. Price: Dfl 10,-

The Netherlands' Presidency of the European Union, Clingendael/ISEI/TEPSA
Conference, The Hague, 15/16 November 1996, Editor Hans H.J. Labohm, 74 p.
Price: Dfl 10,-

*Revision of Maastricht: Implementation and Proposals for Reform. A Survey of
National Views*, Fifth Edition, January-June 1996, 59 p. Price: Dfl 10,-

*Conflict Prevention and Early Warning in the Political Practice of International
Organizations*, samenstelling: K. van Walraven en J. van der Vlugt, april 1996,
91 p. Price: Dfl 17,50

*Revision of Maastricht: Implementation and Proposals for Reform. A Survey of
National Views*, Fourth Edition, Summer-Autumn 1995, 56 p. Price: Dfl 10,-

Report of the Third Indonesia-Netherlands Conference, The Hague 1 and 2 September 1995, H.H.J. Labohm (ed.), 53 p. Price: Dfl 10,-

Revision of Maastricht: Implementation and Proposals for Reform. A Survey of National Views, Third Edition 1995, 55 p. Price: Dfl 10,-

Report of the Conference Enlargement of the European Union with Central European Countries; Challenges and Constraints, H.H.J. Labohm (red.), 17-18 March 1995, ± 80 p. Price: Dfl 10,-

Revision of Maastricht, Implementation and Proposals for Reform; A Survey of National Views, Second Edition, februari 1995, 37 p. Price: Dfl 10,-

Report of the Conference Challenges to the New World Trade Organization, The Hague, January 13, 1995, Pitou van Dijck and Gerrit Faber (eds), 75 p.
Price: Dfl 10,-

The Czech Republic: From Visegrad to Brussels, door Vlastimil Fiala, januari 1995, 97 p. Price: Dfl 10,-

Report of the Round Table The World Bank, The First Fifty Years and Beyond, H.H.J. Labohm, 30 november 1994, p. Price: Dfl 10,-

Report of the Round Table on the Transatlantic Relationships in the Field of Security and Economics, The Hague, September 15-16, 1994, H.H.J. Labohm (editor), 1994, 65 p. Price: Dfl 10,-

Redefining the Security Interests of Russia in the post-Soviet Era, Conference Report of the International Seminar February 17-19, 1994, 24 p. Price: Dfl 7,50

Case-Studies in Second Generation United Nations Peacekeeping, januari 1994, 65 p. Price: Dfl 10,-

Developing Romania's Energy Resources: The Prospects for Cooperation between the European Community and Romania, door I. Daduianu-Vasilescu, 1993, 56 p. Price: Dfl 10,-

G-7 Economic Summits: A View from the Lowlands, door Hans H.J. Labohm, februari 1993, 40 p. Price: Dfl 10,-

Around NATO's new strategy, Report of a seminar for experts in the field of defence strategy, september 17-18, 1992, December 1992, 87 p. Price: Dfl 10,-

Continuity and change in post-communist Europe, door Jadwiga Staniszkis, juni 1992, 37 p. Price: Dfl 10,-

A short guide to Diplomatic Training, door P.W. Meerts, augustus 1991, 32 p. Price: Dfl 10,-

Clingendael Publications can be ordered at:
The Netherlands Institute of International Relations 'Clingendael'
Research Department
Clingendael 7
P.O. Box 93080
2509 AB The Hague
Telephone 31-70-3245384 ext. 353, 360
Telefax 31-70-3282002
E-mail: research@Clingendael.nl
Website: http://www.clingendael.nl